EDEXCEL INTERNATIONAL GCSE (9–1)
ENGLISH AS A SECOND LANGUAGE

Teacher's Book

Nicky Winder
Laurence Gardner

Published by Pearson Education Limited, 80 Strand, London, WC2R 0RL.

www.pearsonglobalschools.com

Copies of official specifications for all Pearson qualifications may be found on the website: https://qualifications.pearson.com

Text © Pearson Education Limited 2017

Edited by Andy Pozzoni and Catherine Zgouras

Development edited by Anna Cowper

Designed by Pearson Education Limited

Typeset by Tech-Set Ltd, Gateshead, UK

Cover design by Pearson Education Limited

Cover photo © Getty Images: Laurie Campbell/Nature Picture Library

Inside front cover photo: Shutterstock.com: Dmitry Lobanov

The rights of Nicky Winder and Laurence Gardner to be identified as authors of this work have been asserted by them in accordance with the Copyright, Designs and Patents Act 1988.

First published 2017

20 19 18

IMP 10 9 8 7 6 5 4 3 2

British Library Cataloguing in Publication Data

A catalogue record for this book is available from the British Library

ISBN 978 0 435 18895 5

Copyright notice

All rights reserved. No part of this publication may be reproduced in any form or by any means (including photocopying or storing it in any medium by electronic means and whether or not transiently or incidentally to some other use of this publication) without the written permission of the copyright owner, except in accordance with the provisions of the Copyright, Designs and Patents Act 1988 or under the terms of a licence issued by the Copyright Licensing Agency, Barnard's Inn, 86 Fetter Lane, London EC4A 1EN (www.cla.co.uk). Applications for the copyright owner's written permission should be addressed to the publisher.

Printed in the UK by Ashford Press Ltd

COURSE STRUCTURE	**IV**
ABOUT THIS BOOK	**VI**
INTRODUCTION TO THE COURSE	**VIII**
EXAM OVERVIEW	**X**
COURSE PLANNERS	**XI**
01 READING PREPARATION	**2**
02 WRITING PREPARATION	**24**
03 LISTENING PREPARATION	**44**
04 SPEAKING PREPARATION	**72**
05 READING PRACTICE	**81**
06 WRITING PRACTICE	**105**
07 LISTENING PRACTICE	**128**
08 SPEAKING PRACTICE	**164**
GLOSSARY	**173**

COURSE STRUCTURE

UNIT	FOCUS	THEME	AOs	GRAMMAR
Reading Preparation	Reading Part 1 (p. 2)	Places to visit	1A	Countable and uncountable nouns Articles *some* and *any*
	Reading Part 2 (p. 10)	Celebrities, fame and entertainment	1B, 1C, 1D	Present simple Present continuous Present simple and present continuous
	Reading Part 3 (p. 17)	History and time	1B, 1C, 1D	Adjectives Comparative and superlative adjectives
Writing Preparation	Writing Part 4 (p. 24)	Food and drink	2A, 2B, 2C	Present perfect
	Writing Part 5 (p. 31)	Colours	2A, 2B, 2C	Past simple Past simple and present perfect
	Writing Part 6 (p. 38)	Speech and communication	2A, 2B, 2C, 2D	Past continuous Past continuous and past simple *would* and *used to*
Listening Preparation	Listening Part 1 (p. 44)	The world of work	3A, 3B	*Wh-* questions and question tags Inversion
	Listening Part 2 (p. 52)	Pets	3B, 3D	Prepositions of time Prepositions of place and movement
	Listening Part 3 (p. 58)	Games	3C, 3D	Adverbs of frequency Intensifiers
	Listening Part 4 (p. 66)	Shopping	3B, 3D	Phrasal verbs (separable and non-separable) Passive Passive: all tenses
Speaking Preparation	Speaking (p. 72)	Fashion	4A, 4B, 4C	Past perfect Past tenses
Reading Practice	Reading Part 1 (p. 81)	Travel and hospitality	1A	Modal verbs (obligation, advice and permission)
	Reading Part 2 (p. 88)	Technology and the future	1B, 1C, 1D	*will* or *going to* Future simple and future continuous Future perfect Other ways to talk about the future
	Reading Part 3 (p. 97)	Buildings	1B, 1C, 1D	Conditionals (zero, first, second, third)
Writing Practice	Writing Part 4 (p. 105)	Work and jobs	2A, 2B, 2C	Perfect continuous tenses
	Writing Part 5 (p. 113)	Transport	2A, 2B, 2C	Possessives
	Writing Part 6 (p. 120)	Mind and body	2A, 2B, 2C, 2D	Linking words and phrases Discourse markers
Listening Practice	Listening Part 1 (p. 128)	Sport and fitness	3A, 3B	Modals in the past tense Modals of speculation and deduction
	Listening Part 2 (p. 137)	Science	3B, 3D	Gerunds and infinitives
	Listening Part 3 (p. 145)	People and language	3C, 3D	Relative pronouns and relative clauses Defining and non-defining relative clauses Reported speech
	Listening Part 4 (p. 155)	The environment	3B, 3D	*make* and *do*
Speaking Practice	Speaking (p. 164)	The home	4A, 4B, 4C	Tense review

COURSE STRUCTURE

VOCABULARY	EXAM SKILLS	PRACTICE TIME
Adjectives	Skimming and scanning Lexical words Sorting information	Tourist leaflet: 'Honeycomb Hives: the ultimate bee experience!'
Nouns (celebrities and fame)	Selection Identifying synonyms	Newspaper article: 'The shadow side of celebrity'
Phrasal verbs	Verifying information (true, false or not given) Identifying facts, ideas and opinions	Newspaper article: 'Amazing discovery of the Biggest Dinosaur Ever'
Collocations (food and drink)	Understanding register Relevance and word limit	Informal email: cooking a birthday meal
Idioms (colours)	Considering context and purpose Considering audience	Formal letter: school sports day
Verbs (communication)	Finding equivalent expressions Paraphrasing and summarising	Summary (Scientific journal: 'How babies talk')
Nouns (the world of work)	Listening for the overall message Listening for detail	Extracts: restaurants
Collocations (health and training)	Identifying detail Identifying viewpoints (stated and implied)	Dog-training advice
Adjectives and adverbs	Considering statements and implications Identifying facts and opinions	Interview with a writer
Verbs and expressions (shopping)	Identifying important information and details	Changes in shopping patterns
Adjectives (fashion)	Speaking skills Pronunciation skills Intonation and stress	Fashion
Compound adjectives	Reflect and evaluate: Reading exam skills	Tourist brochure: 'London with Lonsdale Tours' Holiday leaflet: 'Halliday's Holidays'
Phrasal verbs	Reflect and evaluate: Reading exam skills	Newspaper articles: 'Driverless cars are going to save the world'; 'The Teaching Assistants of the Future?'
Nouns and verbs (buildings)	Reflect and evaluate: Reading exam skills	Website: 'Pyramids' Magazine article: 'Learning about the Leaning Tower!'
Phrasal verbs (work)	Reflect and evaluate: Writing exam skills	Informal emails: part-time jobs
Idioms and expressions (travel)	Reflect and evaluate: Writing exam skills	Report: transport Article: 'My favourite journey'
Collocations (mind and body)	Reflect and evaluate: Writing exam skills	Summaries (Journals: 'Adolescence – a time of challenges'; 'Maintaining emotional health')
Phrasal verbs (sport and fitness)	Reflect and evaluate: Listening exam skills	Extracts: sports venues Extracts: extreme sports
Phrasal verbs (separable and non-separable)	Reflect and evaluate: Listening exam skills	Lecture: moles Class talk: gemstones
Suffixes	Reflect and evaluate: Listening exam skills	Interview with a linguist Dialogue between teachers
Prefixes	Reflect and evaluate: Listening exam skills	Podcast: the wandering albatross School talk: the deep sea
Adjectives (the home)	Reflect and evaluate: Speaking exam skills	The home

ABOUT THIS BOOK

This course is written for students following the Pearson Edexcel International GCSE (9–1) English as a Second Language specification. It can be used for a two-year course, and can also be used flexibly to suit different classroom requirements. This Teacher's Book is designed to support the Student Book.

English as a Second Language is a course which supports teachers and learners through cumulative language acquisition and practice, and encourages inter- and intra-personal as well as cognitive skills. The course promotes learner autonomy, for example, through the Writing and Grammar Reference materials included in the Student Book.

Overview
This provides a guide to the main learning and practice points of the chapter, and summarises the information found in the course structure (pages iv and v of this book). The 'Additional Resources' section should help you to prepare your lessons.

Extension
Suggested extra activities range from short additional practice to longer project-style work. These include various activity formats such as group work, pair work or self study.

Key
Answers to all activities are provided. Suggested answers or key structures are provided for open answers.

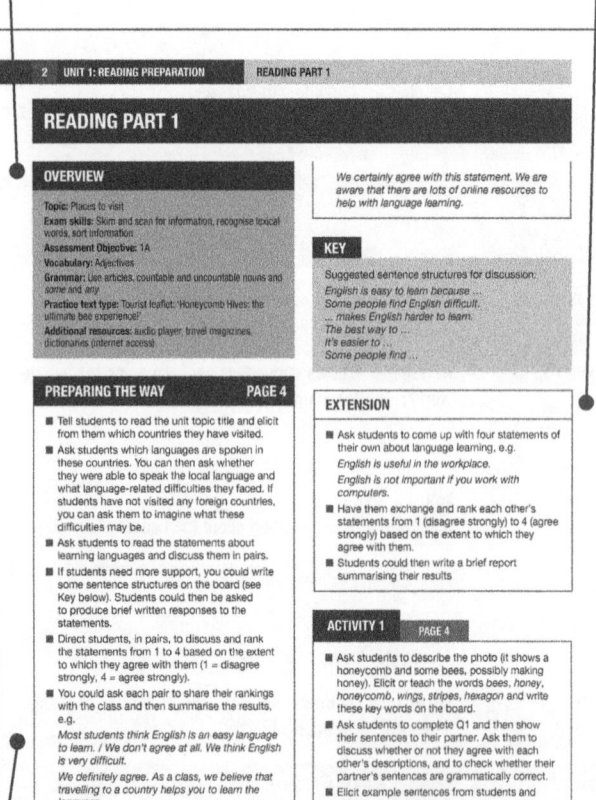

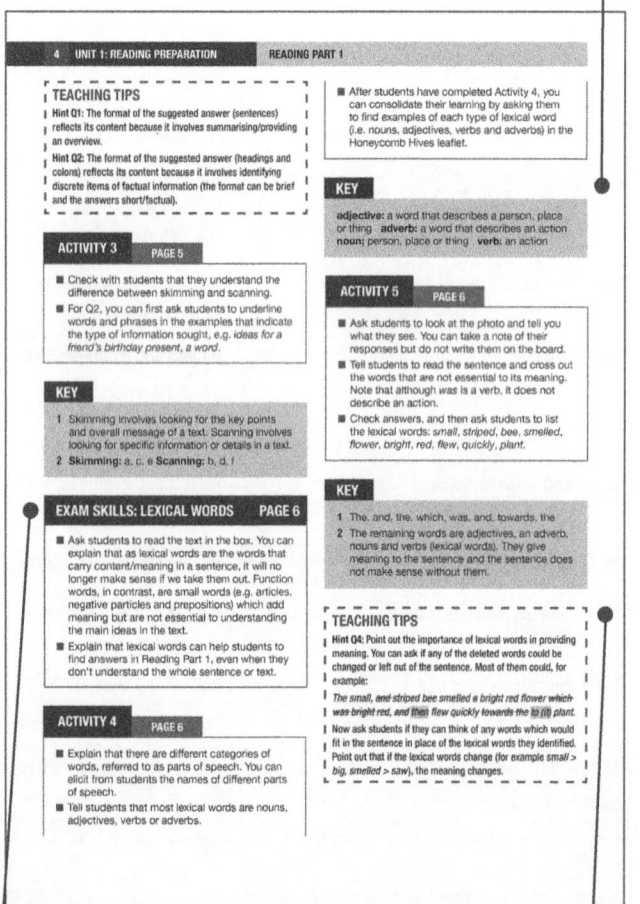

Teaching notes
Step by step suggestions are provided for every activity.
Background information sections give extra context about the themes and images in the book where helpful.

Exam skills and self evaluation
Extra notes help you to make sure that students can focus on and monitor their learning.

Teaching Tips
Extra language notes help you guide students away from common errors. Further explanations about how to find the answers (for example in the Practice Time tests) are also included.

ABOUT THIS BOOK

The course is structured around the different parts of the examination. Each chapter is built around practice of one specific part of the examination paper. The course is divided into units: Reading, Writing, Listening and Speaking. The sections in one unit cover all the parts included in the exam, i.e. three parts each for Reading and Writing and four parts for Listening. The Speaking units have one section only.

The course is divided into two 'cycles': preparation and practice. In the first cycle, emphasis is placed on familiarising students with exam requirements and exam skills learning and practice. In the second cycle, extra guided exam practice is provided and students are given tips on monitoring and improving their performance.

Audio recordings and extra audioscripts are provided online and in the Teacher Resource Pack. The Student Book free ActiveLearn eBook contains links to the recordings which are included at the back of the Student Book. Other recordings (such as the Practice Time tests) are available for teachers only.

Sample answers
Sample answers to writing activities are provided.

Exam skills and self-evaluation
Extra notes help you to make sure that students can focus on and monitor their learning.

Audioscripts
All audioscripts are provided in the Teacher's Book. These include those not provided at the back of the Student Book, for example the Practice Time scripts, and scripts which are extracts from a previous recording. Annotations help to locate answers, or find clues to the answers.

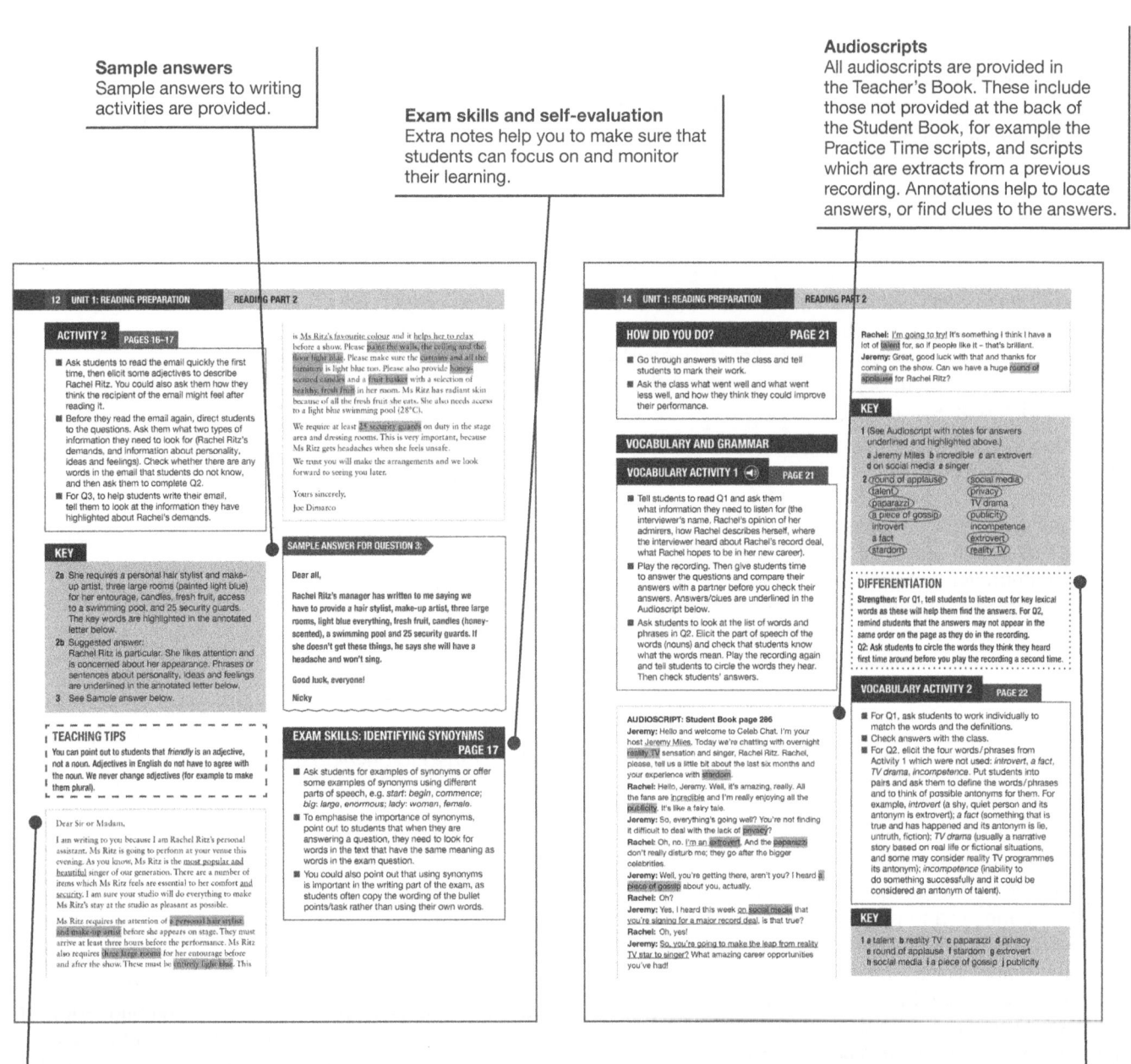

Student Book Extracts
Annotations help to locate answers.

Differentiation
Activity ideas for strengthening or challenging students' ability give you extra flexibility in the classroom.

INTRODUCTION TO THE COURSE

TEACHING APPROACHES

PRESENTATION
The Pearson Edexcel International (9–1) GCSE English as a Second Language (ESL) Student Book offers skills-based development and practice for intermediate to upper-intermediate level students through a range of engaging topics. These topics have been carefully chosen to generate discussion and provide students with opportunities for expressing their own thoughts.

New language is always contextualised, usually through a reading or listening activity. This gives the students a clear understanding of how the language is actually used, and provides example sentences that really mean something to the students.

EXAM PREPARATION
There is a theme-based focus on each section of the exam. Two structures for this are employed: in the first part of the book students are guided through the requirements of each exam section, and are provided with a range of strategies and exam hints to help them, as well as an exam practice paper. Exam skills needed to meet the assessment objectives are presented, taught and practised.

In the second half of the book these exam sections are all revisited. This time students have two practice papers to work through, and there are plentiful opportunities for peer, self and teacher assessment, as well as evaluation and self-reflection on performance and on potential areas for improvement. Sample responses are provided throughout, together with commentaries, and students have the opportunity to explore successful and less successful responses, sharpening their awareness of the exam requirements.

GRAMMAR
Pearson Edexcel International GCSE (9–1) ESL covers all the main language areas expected at intermediate to upper intermediate level, and also indicated in the examination specification.

The structure of the grammar course (see the course structure pages iv and v) allows students to revisit and recycle previous knowledge constructively. The main grammar points in each section have been carefully selected to be a suitable match for the themes and skills practised. There are extra dedicated grammar practice activities at the end of each section. Students can also refer to the Grammar Reference at the back of the Student Book for clarification and revision.

VOCABULARY
New vocabulary is introduced in topic-related sets, which will help learners to discuss and write about the topic of the chapter. Additionally, learners will develop an understanding of key areas where grammar and vocabulary cross over, looking at discourse markers and linking words, prepositions, multi-part verbs and collocation. Plenty of controlled practice is provided and the students are also provided with opportunities to use their newly acquired language in speaking and writing tasks.

MEANINGFUL PRACTICE
Once students are clear about the meaning and form of the language, they are given plenty of opportunity to practise it. Form-based activities to help them gain confidence in manipulating the language. These are followed by more communicative, personalised work, often leading into skills-based speaking or writing activities.

REFERENCE MATERIAL
Students can be referred to the Grammar Reference and Writing Reference at the back of the Student Book whenever they need extra detail or further examples.

SKILLS
The course is made up of chapters which focus on one exam paper, for example Reading Part 1 or Listening Part 4. However, all four skills are practised within each section so that every lesson can be as varied or balanced as you choose.

READING
A range of text types are covered, including those found in the Pearson Edexcel International GCSE (9–1) English as a Second Language (ESL) exam. Students are encouraged to develop the appropriate reading skills for different questions and text types in the hints positioned near the relevant task.

WRITING
A wide variety of genres are included with task types, which are representative of those found in the exam. Students learn about the features and typical language for each type. There are short focused writing tasks to be done in class, where the teacher can offer support, as well as more extended tasks to be completed at home. There is also work on the mechanical skills of writing: punctuation, spelling and paragraphing.

There is also a Writing Reference that gives concise information about the requirements for each Writing question, and guidance about the genres in which students may be required to write.

LISTENING

Each unit contains several listening activities to give students plenty of confidence-building practice. These range from short dialogues to longer radio-style interviews which offer practice in the kind of task types found in the Pearson Edexcel International GCSE (9–1) ESL exam. As with the reading texts, the topics have been chosen for their appeal and interest.

The recorded material features a variety of different accents, including some non-native speakers. Different subskills are focused on, such as helping students to pick out key pieces of information or to understand a speaker's attitude or opinion. Tasks are supported with tips in hint boxes.

SPEAKING

Pearson Edexcel International GCSE (9–1) ESL offers students topics they want to talk about and plenty of ideas to get them started. The speaking activities are well supported, carefully staged and include regular focus on useful or functional language to help them develop their ability to carry out a variety of speaking tasks and practise for the exam. This language often comes from a previous listening task, helping them to make the connection between receptive and productive use of English.

Practice in Pearson Edexcel International GCSE (9–1) ESL exam tasks is provided, including all parts of the exam. Advice and guidance are provided within the first chapter focusing on Speaking.

PRONUNCIATION

Students learn about word and sentence stress, intonation and sounds, and weak forms, helping to make their spoken English sound more natural.

Pronunciation practice is included in the Speaking units and also in some of the grammar and vocabulary activities, especially in the Listening units.

EXAM OVERVIEW

The aim of the Pearson Edexcel International GCSE (9–1) in English as a Second Language (ESL) is to test students' English language ability through realistic tasks.

Two separate examination papers test their reading, writing and listening skills, and they will be awarded a grade from 9 to 1 for their performance in these two papers. Each of these three skills contributes $33\frac{1}{3}$ per cent to a student's total score. In addition, your students have the option of taking a speaking test for which they will receive a separate grade. Students are not allowed to use a dictionary for any of the papers, so they will need to make sure they have learned lots of vocabulary throughout your course!

PAPER 1: READING AND WRITING

This paper is worth $66\frac{2}{3}$ per cent of the total marks for International GCSE (9–1) ESL and assesses students' reading and writing skills in separate exercises. They will take a 2-hour examination paper which has been set by Edexcel and which will be marked by Edexcel examiners. The total number of marks available is 100: there are 50 marks for reading and 50 marks for writing.

READING

In this section, students will find three reading passages of increasing length and difficulty. The passages are taken from a range of sources, including newspapers, websites and fiction, and may include factual information, explanations, opinions and biographical writing. A variety of tasks will be used to check their understanding of these reading texts. These tasks include multiple choice questions, note completion and sentence completion. For tasks where students have to write words, correct spelling in their answers is very important. There will be 10 marks available for the first reading passage, 15 marks for the second and 20 for the third. (An additional 5 marks are available in the final part of the Writing paper.)

WRITING

There are also three parts to the writing section and students are free to choose the order in which they attempt them. The tasks are different in each of the three parts. Usually, a context and target reader are identified in order to give a purpose for students' writing, and they will need to take these into consideration in producing their answers. It is also important that students make sure they write in a style and register which is suitable for the particular task and lay their answer out correctly to match the genre required. The word limit for each task is between 75 and 100 or 100 and 150 words and it is very important that they stick to this limit.

PAPER 2: LISTENING

This skill is assessed through a 50-minute examination paper, set and marked by Edexcel. The total number of marks available is 40, and this represents $33\frac{1}{3}$ per cent of the total International GCSE marks. Students will be expected to understand standard spoken English in a range of different situations. The recorded texts may be in the form of monologues, dialogues and occasionally there may be three speakers involved. A variety of tasks will be used to check student understanding of the recorded texts. If they have spelled a word incorrectly, but it is clear which word it is, they will not lose marks. This paper consists of four parts, each based around a single recorded text. Students will be given time to read the questions before each part of the recording begins, and they should answer the questions as they listen. They will hear each recorded text twice.

PAPER 3: SPEAKING

This paper is optional and is separately endorsed. Students' communication skills are assessed via a recorded interview between them and an interlocutor, based on supplied task cards. The task cards invite student to express themselves fluently, spontaneously and appropriately in a range of speaking contexts. The interlocutor is selected by the centre, and is normally a teacher from the centre and the interviews will be recorded for marking.

The total number of marks available is 40. The test lasts approximately 10–12 minutes and is divided into three parts:

- Part 1 is a short introductory interview between the student and the interlocutor, lasting two to three minutes.
- In Part 2, the student has one minute to prepare a talk in response to a task card plus one to two minutes to give their talk.
- In Part 3, the student is expected to engage in an extended discussion with the interlocutor for a maximum of five minutes.

HOW TO USE YOUR PLANNERS

PLANNERS

The planners on pages xii and xiii are designed to guide teachers through the course and lesson planning processes.

Completing the forms will help teachers to plan effectively and anticipate which materials and equipment they will need – and to avoid potential problems. The completed forms provide a useful aide memoire for future planning, handover notes to the next teacher, or simply a record of work done.

If necessary, the forms can be enlarged to A3 size on a photocopier.

COURSE PLANNER

The form on page xii includes space for administrative information, for example, location and time of lessons, date of the exam, as well as space for a summary of lesson-by-lesson plans. There is room to make notes about which parts of Pearson Edexcel International GCSE (9–1) ESL you will be using, additional materials you may need to gather together before the lesson and ideas for homework tasks.

The course planner is designed as a pre-course tool but you will probably want to revisit it as you adapt your teaching to the needs of your students.

LESSON PLANNER

The form on page xiii is designed to help you plan effective lessons. The form guides you through thinking about the balance of input in the lesson, the purpose of each stage and the type of interaction – plus any materials that are necessary. A line at the bottom of the sheet for you to jot down anything you want to remember for the following lesson.

With classes that you know well, you may choose to plan your lessons in advance and to make minor adjustments as you go along. Alternatively, with new classes, you can plan on a week-by-week basis as you get to know your students' strengths and weaknesses.

Couse planner

(For notes on how to complete planner, see page xi.)

Class _____   Location _____

Hours _____   Mock date _____

Time _____   Exam date _____

Week/Lesson	Date	Objective/s	ESL materials	Additional materials	Homework

Lesson planner

(For notes on how to complete planner, see page xi.)

Lesson _____

Objectives: 1 Language _____

2 Skills _____

3 Exam training _____

4 Other _____

Stage	Teaching/learning point	Interaction	Timing	Materials
1				
2				
3				
4				

Homework _____

Notes for next lesson _____

UNIT 1: READING PREPARATION

READING PART 1

OVERVIEW

Topic: Places to visit
Exam skills: Skim and scan for information, recognise lexical words, sort information
Assessment Objective: 1A
Vocabulary: Adjectives
Grammar: Use articles, countable and uncountable nouns and *some* and *any*
Practice text type: Tourist leaflet: 'Honeycomb Hives: the ultimate bee experience!'
Additional resources: audio player, travel magazines, dictionaries, coloured marker pens (internet access)

PREPARING THE WAY — PAGE 4

- Tell students to read the chapter topic title and elicit from them which countries they have visited.
- Ask students which languages are spoken in these countries. You can then ask whether they were able to speak the local language and what language-related difficulties they faced. If students have not visited any foreign countries, you can ask them to imagine what these difficulties may be.
- Ask students to read the statements about learning languages and discuss them in pairs.
- If students need more support, you could write some sentence structures on the board (see Key below). Students could then be asked to produce brief written responses to the statements.
- Direct students, in pairs, to discuss and rank the statements from 1 to 4 based on the extent to which they agree with them (1 = disagree strongly, 4 = agree strongly).
- You could ask each pair to share their rankings with the class and then summarise the results, e.g.
  Most students think English is an easy language to learn. / We don't agree at all. We think English is very difficult.
  We definitely agree. As a class, we believe that travelling to a country helps you to learn the language.
  We ranked this sentence with a 3. We think it is easier to speak English than to read or write English.
  We certainly agree with this statement. We are aware that there are lots of online resources to help with language learning.

KEY

Suggested sentence structures for discussion:
English is easy to learn because …
Some people find English difficult.
… makes English harder to learn.
The best way to …
It's easier to …
Some people find …

EXTENSION

- Ask students to come up with four statements of their own about language learning, e.g.
  English is useful in the workplace.
  English is not important if you work with computers.
- Have them exchange and rank each other's statements from 1 (disagree strongly) to 4 (agree strongly) based on the extent to which they agree with them.
- Students could then write a brief report summarising their results.

ACTIVITY 1 — PAGE 4

- Ask students to describe the photo (it shows a honeycomb and some bees, possibly making honey). Elicit or teach the words *bees, honey, honeycomb, wings, stripes, hexagon* and write these key words on the board.
- Ask students to complete Q1 and then show their sentences to their partner. Ask them to discuss whether or not they agree with each other's descriptions, and to check whether their partner's sentences are grammatically correct.
- Elicit example sentences from students and write them on the board.
- For Q2, ask students to write sentences in pairs. Then ask them to to read their answers out in class.

READING PART 1 — UNIT 1: READING PREPARATION

KEY

1 Students' own answers. Suggested answers:
There are about ten bees in the picture.
The spaces/holes in the honeycomb have six sides.
The bees have two wings.
The bees have four/five yellow/black stripes.

2 Students' own answers. Suggested answers:
The bees are black and yellow.
The honeycomb is yellow.
The honeycomb is made of hexagons.
The bees have black legs/eyes.
The bees have round heads/eyes.

FOCUSING ON THE EXAM — PAGE 4

- Ask students to read the text in the box and tell you what they think they will find challenging about this part of the exam.
- The Reading Part 1 Assessment Objective is:
  Assessment Objective 1A: Understand the overall message of a text.
  Students need to identify the key themes and content.
- Explain that Reading Part 1 carries 10 marks and includes a range of short texts, e.g. adverts, timetables, leaflets.
- Go through the task in Reading Part 1: multiple matching of information with descriptions. Make sure students understand what this task involves.
- Tell students that in this chapter they will learn about and practise two important exam skills: skimming and scanning. These skills will help them meet Assessment Objective 1A.

EXAM SKILLS: SKIMMING AND SCANNING — PAGE 5

- Check that students know what skimming and scanning are. You could refer them to the definitions in the Glossary on page 244.
  scan to read something quickly
  skim to read something quickly to find the main facts or ideas in it
- Explain that we skim a text to get the overall gist or meaning, whereas we scan a text in order to identify specific information. Tell students that they will need to do both in Reading Part 1, and that they will practise these skills in this chapter.

- Tell students that in Reading Part 1 they will need to use skimming skills to get an overall sense of the passage (e.g. in Activity 2), and of each paragraph. To get high marks, they will need to work out which of two similar paragraphs is the best match for multiple-choice items in the question. This may also involve scanning for specific details.
- Warn students that candidates often lose marks because they do not follow instructions properly, for example by filling in two boxes instead of one. They may also miss boxes out. Emphasise that students should spend time reading through the questions carefully before they begin. Also encourage them to answer every question, even if they are not sure of the answer.

ACTIVITY 2 — PAGE 5

- Ask students to read the questions. Clarify that Q1 involves the skill of skimming, while Q2 involves the skill of scanning.
- To answer Q1, tell students to first skim the leaflet. Make sure they understand that this involves reading quickly through the whole text in order to get the general idea. Then elicit from students what they think the passage is about.
- Ask students if there are any words in the leaflet that they don't know and then tell them to scan the text for the specific information they need to answer Q2. When checking answers, ask students what they noticed about the information they had to scan for, e.g. it was easier to spot/involved numbers.

KEY

1 The leaflet is about a specialist bee centre called Honeycomb Hives. It is a popular attraction. Other details include what visitors think about the centre and brief comments from two members of staff.

2 **People** Tour guide: Dave Chandler, Manager: Scott Sterling, Visitors so far: 10,000+
   Date Opened: 1 June
   Times Opening time: 10 a.m.,
   Closing time: 5 p.m.

UNIT 1: READING PREPARATION — READING PART 1

> **TEACHING TIPS**
>
> **Hint Q1:** The format of the suggested answer (sentences) reflects its content because it involves summarising/providing an overview.
>
> **Hint Q2:** The format of the suggested answer (headings and colons) reflects its content because it involves identifying discrete items of factual information (the format can be brief and the answers short/factual).

ACTIVITY 3 — PAGE 5

- Check with students that they understand the difference between skimming and scanning.
- For Q2, you can first ask students to underline words and phrases in the examples that indicate the type of information sought, e.g. *ideas for a friend's birthday present*, *a word*.

KEY

1. Skimming involves looking for the key points and overall message of a text. Scanning involves looking for specific information or details in a text.
2. **Skimming:** a, c, e **Scanning:** b, d, f

EXAM SKILLS: LEXICAL WORDS — PAGE 6

- Ask students to read the text in the box. You can explain that as lexical words are the words that carry content/meaning in a sentence, it will no longer make sense if we take them out. Function words, in contrast, are small words (e.g. articles, negative particles and prepositions) which add meaning but are not essential to understanding the main ideas in the text.
- Explain that lexical words can help students to find answers in Reading Part 1, even when they don't understand the whole sentence or text.

ACTIVITY 4 — PAGE 6

- Explain that there are different categories of words, referred to as parts of speech. You can elicit from students the names of different parts of speech.
- Tell students that most lexical words are nouns, adjectives, verbs or adverbs.
- After students have completed Activity 4, you can consolidate their learning by asking them to find examples of each type of lexical word (i.e. nouns, adjectives, verbs and adverbs) in the Honeycomb Hives leaflet.

KEY

adjective: a word that describes a person, place or thing   **adverb:** a word that describes an action   **noun:** person, place or thing   **verb:** an action

ACTIVITY 5 — PAGE 6

- Ask students to look at the photo and tell you what they see. You can take a note of their responses but do not write them on the board.
- Tell students to read the sentence and cross out the words that are not essential to its meaning. Note that although *was* is a verb, it does not describe an action.
- Check answers, and then ask students to list the lexical words: *small, striped, bee, smelled, flower, bright, red, flew, quickly, plant*.

KEY

1. The, and, the, which, was, and, towards, the
2. The remaining words are adjectives, an adverb, nouns and verbs (lexical words). They give meaning to the sentence and the sentence does not make sense without them.

> **TEACHING TIPS**
>
> **Hint Q4:** Point out the importance of lexical words in providing meaning. You can ask if any of the deleted words could be changed or left out of the sentence. Most of them could, for example:
>
> *The small, ~~and~~ striped bee smelled ~~a~~ bright red flower ~~which was bright red, and~~ then flew quickly ~~towards the~~ to (it) plant.*
>
> Now ask students if they can think of any words which would fit in the sentence in place of the lexical words they identified. Point out that if the lexical words change (for example *small > big, smelled > saw*), the meaning changes.

READING PART 1 | **UNIT 1: READING PREPARATION** | 5

EXTENSION

Provide students with some additional sentences (e.g. from the Honeycomb Hives leaflet on page 5) and ask them to delete all the words that are not lexical words.

EXAM SKILLS: SORTING INFORMATION
PAGE 6

- Ask students to read the text in the box. You can explain that visiting places of interest is a recurring topic in this part of the exam and that being able to sort different types of information will improve their understanding of these types of texts.
- Explain that even when they don't understand every sentence or word in a text, sorting information can help them to find answers.

ACTIVITY 6   PAGES 6–7

- Ask students to think of a place that they would like to find out more about. Alternatively, you could suggest a place for them. Ask students to consider what sorts of information they would need or want when planning a visit to this place. Try to elicit the information categories in the box.
- Check that students understand what a *category* is (a group of things that are all of the same type or connected by a common topic). Look at the questions in the first example and have students come up with some more questions for the category. Alternatively, choose another category from the box and have students come up with questions for that category.
- Ask students to think about the place they have chosen and decide which categories from the box they need to research. You could also ask them to come up with alternative categories. Then ask students to write questions for each category to help guide them in finding relevant information (see Key below for suggestions).
- Before students begin their research, ask them to look at the London Zoo table in the second example. Point out that they can use a similar table to sort the information they find. To illustrate this, elicit from students the five categories of information in the table (first and second columns: activities, third column: target audience/who the place will appeal to, fourth column: costs, fifth column: positives, sixth column: potential negatives).

- When students have prepared their questions, give them some time to do the research (if you choose to use the table). Remind them to skim and scan for the information they need and to sort it into their chosen categories.

KEY

Sample questions and answers are provided in the Student Book for the activities and costs categories.

Other suggested categories and questions:

Accessibility: *Who can experience ... ? Is it wheelchair-friendly?*

Food and drink: *Is there a café/restaurant? Is the food expensive?*

Animals: *Are pets allowed? Is it suitable for dogs?*

TEACHING TIPS

- If students do not have access to the internet in class, you could bring some printed material (e.g. travel magazines or leaflets) to class or ask students to do so.
- You could suggest that students research a place they have visited on a school trip.

EXTENSION

This activity could be extended into project work to be completed over several lessons.

PRACTICE TIME: READING PART 1   PAGES 7–9

- This section provides students with exam practice. The exam will have a similar text, layout and tasks.
- Ask students to read the exam instructions (i.e. the rubrics). Point out that they need to read these instructions carefully so that they are very clear about what they need to do.
- Remind students about their recent work on skimming, scanning, lexical words and sorting information, and then ask them to read the exam hints.

KEY

1 J   2 E   3 D   4 A   5 C   6 F   7 I   8 G   9 H   10 B

UNIT 1: READING PREPARATION

READING PART 1

TEACHING TIPS

Hint Q1: Key lexical words in Paragraph J include *hungry*, *refreshment* and *drinks*. They link with *snacks* and *drinks* in Q1.

Hint Q2: Key lexical words in Paragraph E include *look*, *magnified photographs*, *detail* and *poster-size images*. These words suggest getting a *closer view* from Q8.

Hint Q3: Paragraphs B and D both refer to *bees* and *time*, but D uses the word *globally*, which matches the lexical word *world* in the question.

Hint Q4: Paragraph A contains the lexical words *hi-tech* and *21st century*, matching the word *modern* in the question.

Hint Q5: Words in Paragraph C matching the lexical word *clothing* are *outfit*, *headgear*, *gloves* and *boots*.

Hint Q6: This question refers to *Honeycomb Hives' own bees*, and the adjective *own* is repeated twice in Paragraph F.

Hint Q7: A key phrase in the question is *tasty treats*. This could match words in both Paragraph J (*refreshment*, *home-baked bread*, *honey*) and Paragraph I (*pot of delicious honey*). Another key word is *purchasing*. Paragraph I is the better match because it includes the word *delicious*, suggesting a treat, and the words *gift shop* and *buy*.

Hint Q8: The Q8 key words *see* and *world* are both used in Paragraph G.

Hint Q9: Paragraph H uses the lexical word *children* twice, matching the word *younger* in the question.

Hint Q10: The question asks about *bees in the past*. Paragraph B contains the words and phrases *museum*, *periods in time* and *through the ages*.

HOW DID YOU DO? — PAGE 9

- Go through the Practice Time answers with the class and tell students to mark their work.
- Ask students what went well and what went less well, and how they think they could improve their performance.

VOCABULARY AND GRAMMAR

VOCABULARY ACTIVITY 1 — PAGES 9–10

- This activity revises one type of lexical word: adjectives.
- Ask students to skim the definitions and tell you if there are any words they don't understand.
- Tell students to read the Honeycomb Hives leaflet on pages 7–8 again to find adjectives matching the definitions provided.

KEY

1 hi-tech **2** authentic **3** protective **4** rare
5 fascinating **6** energetic **7** specially-designed
8 cutting-edge **9** cosy

DIFFERENTIATION

Strengthen: Paragraph hints for each could be given to students (Q1: Paragraph A; Q2 and Q3: Paragraph C; Q4: Paragraph D; Q5: Paragraph E; Q6: Paragraph F; Q7 and Q8: Paragraph G; Q9: Paragraph J).

Challenge: Students could write sentences using each adjective.

VOCABULARY ACTIVITY 2 — PAGE 10

- This activity reinforces the work on adjectives. Make sure that students understand what a synonym is. You could refer them to the definition in the Glossary on page 244.

  synonym a word that has the same or nearly the same meaning as another word

- Ask the class for any synonyms they know to check for understanding.
- Tell students to match the adjectives from Activity 1 to the synonyms listed. They can use dictionaries to help them if necessary.
- Check answers with the class.

KEY

1 authentic **2** protective **3** specially-designed
4 hi-tech **5** cutting-edge **6** rare **7** fascinating
8 cosy **9** energetic

VOCABULARY ACTIVITY 3 — PAGE 10

- Ask students to work individually to choose the best option. Encourage them to try to complete the activity without looking back at the definitions in the previous activity.
- When they have completed the activity, encourage students to compare their answers with a partner.
- Confirm answers with the class.

KEY

1 cutting edge, high-tech **2** authentic, elaborate, cosy **3** specially-designed, protective **4** fascinating, energetic

READING PART 1 — UNIT 1: READING PREPARATION

GRAMMAR ACTIVITY 4 — PAGE 11

- Tell students that this activity revises another type of lexical word: nouns.
- Revise countable and uncountable nouns with students. You can point out that countable nouns have both a singular and plural form (e.g. *gift* and *gifts*), while uncountable nouns have no plural form.
- Now ask students to sort the nouns into the table according to whether they are countable or uncountable.

KEY

Countable nouns	Uncountable nouns
give	furniture
hive	bread
tour	advice
shop	honey
museum	clothing

EXTENSION

- Ask students to identify countable and uncountable nouns. Remind them that some nouns can be both countable and uncountable, with different meanings. You can use the words from the lists below.

  Countable *boat, book, child, coin, dog, horse, hour, house, minute, moment, painting, picture, piece, shop, thing*

  Uncountable *advice, bread, clothing, equipment, furniture, honey, information, money, pasta, rice, rubbish, sleep, stuff, water*

  Both *cheese* (countable when talking about types of cheese), *coffee* (countable to mean *a cup of coffee*), *fish* (countable when talking about types of fish), *paper* (countable when it means *newspaper*), *people* (countable when it means *tribe* or *race*), *time* (countable in phrases like *How many times have I told you?*; uncountable when talking about the amount of time needed to do something, as in *How much time will it take?*).

- Suggested activity formats:

  Team work Line up and take turns to throw a paper/foam ball at one of three targets (labelled *Countable*, *Uncountable*, *Both*) on the wall/board.

  Individual or pair work Note down the answers on a sheet of paper.

  Class work Ask students to hold up their left or right hand (or both) depending on the answer.

GRAMMAR ACTIVITY 5 — PAGE 11

- Explain to students that the letter contains a number of deliberate errors related to countable and uncountable nouns. Their task is to identify and correct these errors.
- Tell students that they might have to make some words singular or plural, or correct corresponding verbs (e.g. *the books* are, *the information* is) or quantifiers (e.g. many *shops*, a lot of *honey*).
- Check answers with the class and ask students to explain the errors (e.g. *information* is uncountable in English).

KEY

See annotated letter below.

Dear Klaus,

Thank you for your letter asking me about my recent holiday to Penang. The best part was my visit to Penang National Park. The information online ~~aren't~~ isn't very reliable, so I will tell you all about it here. Many ~~peoples~~ people come to visit the park and there are ~~tour~~ tours in many languages. Generally, in Malaysia there are many bilingual people compared to other countries. Everyone ~~are~~ is/Everyone's also very ~~friendlies~~ friendly!

There ~~are~~ is some good advice I can give you if you are planning to go and visit the nature park. I recommend going early in the morning because then there are ~~less~~ fewer crowds. You will see ~~much~~ many/a lot of fine views so remember to take your camera!

There is a tea room and café where you can buy delicious Malaysian ~~snack~~ snacks. There ~~are~~ is also an excellent gift shop, if you want to do some ~~shoppings~~ shopping. I bought a really cute poster of a monkey eating some ~~breads~~ bread.

I hope you found my ~~informations~~ information helpful. Come to visit soon!

Best wishes,

Hilda

8 UNIT 1: READING PREPARATION — READING PART 1

TEACHING TIPS

Point out or elicit from students that:

The noun *information* is uncountable so the verb is in singular form. We normally talk about *some information*, but we can also refer to *pieces of information*.

The noun *people* is already plural. The singular form is *person*.

We are a talking about more than one tour. The word *tour* is countable, so we use the plural *tours*.

The pronoun *everyone* also takes a singular verb because it refers to a group of individuals.

As *friendly* is an adjective, it doesn't have a plural form.

The noun *advice* is uncountable so takes a singular verb. We normally talk about *some advice*, but we can also refer to *pieces of advice*.

The noun *crowd* is countable. In its plural form it takes the quantifier *few*, not *less*, which is used with uncountable nouns.

The noun *view* is countable. In its plural form it takes the quantifier *many* or *a lot of*, not *much*, which is used with uncountable nouns.

The noun *snack* is countable. It should be in the plural form because we are a talking about more than one snack.

The noun *shopping* is uncountable, so there is no plural form.

Bread is uncountable, so there is no plural form.

The noun *information* is uncountable in English (see above), so there is no plural form.

SAMPLE ANSWER FOR ACTIVITY 6:

Dear Klaus,

Thank you so much for your **letter**! I am so happy that you are thinking about visiting England. Of course I can give you some **tips**. In London we have lots of **art galleries** and **parks** and of course many **museums**! You can drink (coffee) in a **café**, or walk along the River Thames. Just don't try to swim in the (water). If you have (time) you can also go shopping for (clothes) in the many **shops**. I hope you find this (information) helpful!

Best wishes,

Maria

DIFFERENTIATION

Strengthen: You could give students the Sample answer as a model to help them plan and write their own texts.

Challenge: Ask students to write a reply to Klaus and to include mistakes related to countable and uncountable nouns. Encourage them to include at least five mistakes. Have students swap letters and find the mistakes.

GRAMMAR ACTIVITY 6 — PAGE 12

- Go over the task with students and explain that they have to write a letter (80–100 words) using countable and uncountable nouns, suggesting local activities for a visiting guest. As a class, think of some appropriate activities and write students' ideas on the board.
- Tell students to write their letters. When they have finished, ask them to exchange letters with a partner and check each other's work, paying particular attention to correct use of countable and uncountable nouns, and to any corresponding verbs or quantifiers.

KEY

See Sample answer below. Countable nouns are in bold and uncountable nouns are circled.

GRAMMAR ACTIVITY 7 — PAGE 12

- Before students attempt this task, ask them to read Grammar Reference page 254.
- Encourage students to work in pairs to find the correct sentences.

KEY

1 b 2 b 3 b 4 a 5 a 6 a 7 a 8 b 9 a 10 a
11 a 12 a 13 b 14 b 15 a

GRAMMAR ACTIVITY 8  — PAGE 13

- Tell students that, for Q1, they need to complete the news article extract by writing the articles *a*, *an* or *the* in the gaps or indicating no article (-). They then need to do the same for the interview in Q2.
- When students have completed the activity, play the recording and ask them to listen and check their answers.

KEY

1 **1** a/the **2** an **3** a **4** the **5** (-) **6** (-) **7** The
2 **1** (-) **2** (-) **3** a **4** a/the **5** the **6** the **7** the **8** (-)
   9 a **10** the **11** a/the **12** the **13** an **14** the **15** the

EXTENSION

If students require additional practice with *a* and *an*, you can play the game *I'm going on a picnic*. Instructions:

- Students form a circle. The first player (usually the teacher), begins a sentence with *I'm going on a picnic and taking an …* and completes it with a noun beginning with *a*, e.g. *I'm going on a picnic and taking an apple*.
- The second player then repeats the sentence, adding a noun beginning with *b*, e.g. *I'm going on a picnic and taking an apple and a bike*.
- Play continues through the alphabet. If a player is unable to remember the previous items, they are eliminated. If the players reach *z*, they can begin again from *a*.
- Help students by supplying vocabulary if needed. For example, if they are struggling with *z*, suggest *a zebra*.
- Throughout the game, draw students' attention to and correct any errors with *a* and *an*.

GRAMMAR ACTIVITY 9 — PAGE 13

- Before students attempt this task, ask them to read Grammar Reference page 256.
- Ask students to read the conversation and fill in the gaps with *some* or *any*. You can remind students that we use *some* for positive sentences and questions where we suspect the answer to be *yes*, and *any* for negative sentences and questions where we are not sure of the answer.
- When students have completed the activity, check their answers.

KEY

1 some **2** some **3** any **4** any **5** any **6** some
7 some

SELF-EVALUATION — PAGE 14

Tell students to look at the Self-evaluation table and tick the boxes that are true for them. Ask them if there are any topics they don't feel confident about yet.

UNIT 1: READING PREPARATION

READING PART 2

OVERVIEW

Topic: Celebrities, fame and entertainment
Exam skills: Select relevant detail from the text, identify synonyms
Assessment Objectives: 1B, 1C, 1D
Vocabulary: Nouns: celebrities and fame
Grammar: Use the present simple and present continuous
Practice text type: Newspaper article: 'The shadow side of celebrity'
Additional resources: audio player (internet access)

PREPARING THE WAY — PAGE 15

- Ask students to read the chapter topic title and elicit from them what they understand about the concepts of celebrity, fame and entertainment.
- Ask students to read the four questions and discuss them in pairs or small groups. For the second question, if students have never met a celebrity, you can suggest they talk about a celebrity they would like to meet. If students need more support, you could write some sentence structures on the board (see Key below) and ask them to produce brief written responses before discussing their ideas.
- Tell students to imagine they are going to have a party and they need to invite five celebrities, living or from the past. Once they have chosen their celebrities, explain that they need to write two sentences to explain their reasons for choosing each celebrity.
- When students are ready, have them discuss their celebrities and reasons in groups.
- Take feedback from the class and see if some students have chosen the same celebrity. You can also see if students agree/disagree with the choices others have made.

Background information

The photo shows a red carpet, often associated with fame and celebrity. The red carpet suggests the high status that comes with being a celebrity, but the chapter will look at some of disadvantages of being a celebrity as well. A key concept for students to think about is privacy.

KEY

Suggested sentence structures for discussion:
The advantages / disadvantages of being famous / a celebrity are …
I met / saw a celebrity at …
I think / don't think celebrities deserve privacy because …
I think the most well-known celebrity of all time might be … He / She is / was famous for …

EXTENSION

You can use these questions for discussion or writing activities, as individual work or in pairs, in class or for homework.
Do all celebrities have talent?
Are celebrities overpaid?
Would you want to become famous overnight? Why, or why not?
If you could choose to be famous for anything at all, what would it be?
Who are the five most well-known celebrities in your country?
Is there a difference between a famous person and a celebrity?
Are the stars of reality TV shows celebrities?
Which celebrity would you most want to meet?
Who is a celebrity from your country who has made a come-back?
If you were a celebrity, what would you do with your five minutes of fame?

ACTIVITY 1 — PAGE 15

- Tell students they are going to listen to a recording about a football team. Elicit the meaning of *press conference* (a meeting in which someone gives information to news reporters and answers questions). Ask students what topics they think might be discussed.
- Ask students to read the questions and check understanding of vocabulary such as *score a goal*. Then play the recording for students to listen and note their answers.

READING PART 2 | **UNIT 1: READING PREPARATION** | **11**

- Check answers with the class. Ask students what they heard that helped them to answer each question. Play the recording again so they can check anything they are not sure of. You can pause the recording just after each answer is provided. You could also refer students to the Audioscript on page 286.

AUDIOSCRIPT: Student Book page 286

Announcer: Welcome to the Ridgefield United Press Conference. The manager can now take questions.

Reporter: José, congratulations on your team's <u>victory</u>.

José: Thank you. We are playing very well at the moment and we are getting the results that we deserve.

Reporter: There was some controversy about the penalty kick in the first half.

José: Yes, the referee, unfortunately, is not performing as well as we are. The important thing is <u>the other team didn't score any goals</u> and we have three points, so we are feeling pretty pleased with ourselves.

Reporter: <u>Fred Sandilands doesn't seem to be playing for the team at the moment.</u> Lucas Harger was in goal today.

José: That's right, <u>Freddie isn't on the team at the moment</u>. Maybe next week. Right now, Lucas is playing and he is doing a great job.

Reporter: Can you tell me why Freddie is not playing for the team?

José: I am sure you know there are lots of stories about him in the newspapers at the moment. He's a little distracted by all the media attention. So, he isn't playing for us right now.

Reporter: All right. Now, let's talk about the future. Especially the club's transfer policy.

José: <u>Journalists always want to know which players are coming in the future. They never want to talk about the players we already have! We have some excellent players. We are working and we are improving …</u>

Reporter: Yes, but people are talking about a transfer which …

José: I do not want to talk about transfers. I know the player you are talking about. At the moment, he is playing for another club. I have nothing more to say.

Reporter: All right, but is it true that <u>you are offering over 100 million euros …</u>

José: I do not want to talk about transfers. Next question, please.

KEY

(Answers underlined in Audioscript above.)

1 yes **2** no **3** no **4** the present **5** he wants to talk about the players the team has now **6** one million euros

FOCUSING ON THE EXAM — PAGE 16

- Ask students to read the text in the box and tell you what they think will be challenging about this part of the exam.
- The Reading Part 2 Assessment Objectives are:
  Assessment Objective 1B: Understand in detail a range of texts, identifying finer points of detail. Students need to use the scanning skills they practised in Reading Part 1 find specific details in the text.
  Assessment Objective 1C: Distinguish between facts, ideas and opinions.
  Students need to be aware of the nature of the material they are presented with, e.g. whether it contains facts, opinions, or both.
  Assessment Objective 1D: Identify a writer's viewpoint and attitude, stated and implied. Students need to recognise suggested as well as directly stated opinions.
- Explain that Reading Part 2 carries 15 marks and is based on a long text.
- Go through the different types of tasks in Reading Part 2. Make sure students understand what these involve. You can point out that some variation is possible, e.g. sentence and summary completion tasks may require students to write two to four words in each gap.
- Tell students that in this chapter they will learn about and practise two important exam skills: selecting information, and identifying synonyms. These skills will help students meet Assessment Objectives 1B, 1C and 1D.

EXAM SKILLS: SELECTION — PAGE 16

- Explain that you are going to focus on the skill of selecting important information (i.e. the information needed to answer a question or complete a task).
- Draw students' attention to the two types of information (factual, abstract) and offer some examples to illustrate the difference between them, e.g. *Milk comes from cows./Cows are friendly and nice., Coffee is grown in Brazil./Coffee tastes good*. You could then elicit some examples from students.
- You could suggest that students use highlighters or coloured pens to help them identify and highlight important information in texts.

UNIT 1: READING PREPARATION

READING PART 2

ACTIVITY 2 — PAGES 16–17

- Ask students to read the email quickly the first time, then elicit some adjectives to describe Rachel Ritz. You could also ask them how they think the recipient of the email might feel after reading it.
- Before they read the email again, direct students to the questions. Ask them what two types of information they need to look for (Rachel Ritz's demands, and information about personality, ideas and feelings). Check whether there are any words in the email that students do not know, and then ask them to complete Q2.
- For Q3, to help students write their email, tell them to look at the information they have highlighted about Rachel's demands.

KEY

2a She requires a personal hair stylist and make-up artist, three large rooms (painted light blue) for her entourage, candles, fresh fruit, access to a swimming pool, and 25 security guards. The key words are highlighted in the annotated letter below.

2b Suggested answer:
Rachel Ritz is particular. She likes attention and is concerned about her appearance. Phrases or sentences about personality, ideas and feelings are underlined in the annotated letter below.

3 See Sample answer below.

TEACHING TIPS

You can point out to students that *friendly* is an adjective, not a noun. Adjectives in English do not have to agree with the noun. We never change adjectives (for example to make them plural).

Dear Sir or Madam,

I am writing to you because I am Rachel Ritz's personal assistant. Ms Ritz is going to perform at your venue this evening. As you know, Ms Ritz is the <u>most popular and beautiful</u> singer of our generation. There are a number of items which Ms Ritz feels are essential to her comfort <u>and security</u>. I am sure your studio will do everything to make Ms Ritz's stay at the studio as pleasant as possible.

Ms Ritz requires the attention of a personal hair stylist and make-up artist before she appears on stage. They must arrive at least three hours before the performance. Ms Ritz also requires three large rooms for her entourage before and after the show. These must be entirely light blue. This is <u>Ms Ritz's favourite colour</u> and it <u>helps her to relax</u> before a show. Please paint the walls, the ceiling and the floor light blue. Please make sure the curtains and all the furniture is light blue too. Please also provide honey-scented candles and a fruit basket with a selection of healthy, fresh fruit in her room. Ms Ritz has radiant skin because of all the fresh fruit she eats. She also needs access to a light blue swimming pool (28°C).

We require at least 25 security guards on duty in the stage area and dressing rooms. This is very important, because Ms Ritz gets headaches when she feels unsafe.

We trust you will make the arrangements and we look forward to seeing you later.

Yours sincerely,

Joe Dimarco

SAMPLE ANSWER FOR QUESTION 3:

Dear all,

Rachel Ritz's manager has written to me saying we have to provide a hair stylist, make-up artist, three large rooms, light blue everything, fresh fruit, candles (honey-scented), a swimming pool and 25 security guards. If she doesn't get these things, he says she will have a headache and won't sing.

Good luck, everyone!

Nicky

EXAM SKILLS: IDENTIFYING SYNOYNMS — PAGE 17

- Ask students for examples of synonyms or offer some examples of synonyms using different parts of speech, e.g. *start*: *begin*, *commence*; *big*: *large*, *enormous*; *lady*: *woman*, *female*.
- To emphasise the importance of synonyms, point out to students that when they are answering a question, they need to look for words in the text that have the same meaning as words in the exam question.
- You could also point out that using synonyms is important in the writing part of the exam, as students often copy the wording of the bullet points/task rather than using their own words.

READING PART 2 — UNIT 1: READING PREPARATION

ACTIVITY 3 — PAGES 17–18

- Ask students to work in pairs to read the paragraph and find synonyms for the underlined words. Tell them that they can use a dictionary.
- Check students' answers to Q1. To help students with Q2, tell them that it includes synonyms of underlined words in the paragraph, i.e. employee (assistant), sing (perform) and important (essential). Point out that students will need to refer back to the email in Activity 2 to find the answers.
- Check students' answers for Q2, making sure that they understand how identifying synonyms can help them to find answers in a text.

KEY

1 Suggested answers:
   assistant: helper, employee **perform:** sing, entertain **essential:** necessary, vital, crucial **security:** safety, well-being
2 a Joe Dimarco
   b at the music studio's venue/on stage
   c Rachel Ritz may not sing if her demands are not met.

TEACHING TIPS

Dictionaries will be helpful for this task. Remind students that some synonyms may be grammatically incorrect or may not fit the context.

ACTIVITY 4 — PAGE 18

- Ask students to work in pairs. Very able students can work individually. Elicit or provide a list of ten common lexical words (e.g. *to rush*, *middle*, *small*, *worried*, *anger*, *cheerful*, *enjoyed*, *sad*, *grand*, *ill*) and ask students to try to find synonyms for them in a dictionary or thesaurus.
- You could make the activity into a competition and tell the class that the first pair or individual who finds ten synonyms wins.
- You could extend the activity by asking students to write example sentences using each pair of words.

KEY

Suggested answers: to rush/to hurry, middle/centre, small/little, worried/anxious, anger/rage, cheerful/jolly, enjoyed/liked, sad/depressed, grand/impressive, ill/unwell

PRACTICE TIME: READING PART 2 — PAGES 18–21

- This section provides students with exam practice. The exam will have similar texts, layout and tasks.
- Explain the exam instruction (rubric) to students so that they are very clear about what they need to do.
- Remind students about their recent work on selection of detail and synonyms, and tell them to read the Exam Hints.
- Ask students to read through the questions on pages 19–21 and make sure they understand the instructions.
- Because this is the first Part 2 exam practice they have done, you could go through the first answer in each section with students.

KEY

11 (constant) media attention (line 6) **12** media attention (line 11) **13** (celebrities looking) unglamorous (line 15) **14** (develop) unusual methods (line 27) **15** identical (line 30) **16** (the) paparazzi (line 32) **17** 2012 (line 35) **18** (free) publicity (line 38) **19** smartphones (line 45) **20** (the) positives (line 49) **21** B **22** C **23** A **24** B **25** C

TEACHING TIPS

Hint Q21: While A, C and D are mentioned in the article, the key is the superlative *biggest*, which correlates with *best of all* in the article.

Hint Q22: Only the correct option is evidenced in the text.

Hint Q23: B is mentioned but only as additional information.

Hint Q24: The celebrity names should help students identify the relevant part of the text. The word *interest* is used in the text, which should help students identify the answer.

Hint Q25: In the article, *never disappear* is another way of saying *forever*.

14 UNIT 1: READING PREPARATION — READING PART 2

HOW DID YOU DO? PAGE 21

- Go through answers with the class and tell students to mark their work.
- Ask the class what went well and what went less well, and how they think they could improve their performance.

VOCABULARY AND GRAMMAR

VOCABULARY ACTIVITY 1  PAGE 21

- Tell students to read Q1 and ask them what information they need to listen for (the interviewer's name, Rachel's opinion of her admirers, how Rachel describes herself, where the interviewer heard about Rachel's record deal, what Rachel hopes to be in her new career).
- Play the recording. Then give students time to answer the questions and compare their answers with a partner before you check their answers. Answers/clues are underlined in the Audioscript below.
- Ask students to look at the list of words and phrases in Q2. Elicit the part of speech of the words (nouns) and check that students know what the words mean. Play the recording again and tell students to circle the words they hear. Then check students' answers.

AUDIOSCRIPT: Student Book page 286
Jeremy: Hello and welcome to Celeb Chat. I'm your host Jeremy Miles. Today we're chatting with overnight reality TV sensation and singer, Rachel Ritz. Rachel, please, tell us a little bit about the last six months and your experience with stardom.
Rachel: Hello, Jeremy. Well, it's amazing, really. All the fans are incredible and I'm really enjoying all the publicity. It's like a fairy tale.
Jeremy: So, everything's going well? You're not finding it difficult to deal with the lack of privacy?
Rachel: Oh, no. I'm an extrovert. And the paparazzi don't really disturb me; they go after the bigger celebrities.
Jeremy: Well, you're getting there, aren't you? I heard a piece of gossip about you, actually.
Rachel: Oh?
Jeremy: Yes, I heard this week on social media that you're signing for a major record deal, is that true?
Rachel: Oh, yes!
Jeremy: So, you're going to make the leap from reality TV star to singer? What amazing career opportunities you've had!

Rachel: I'm going to try! It's something I think I have a lot of talent for, so if people like it – that's brilliant.
Jeremy: Great, good luck with that and thanks for coming on the show. Can we have a huge round of applause for Rachel Ritz?

KEY

1 (See Audioscript with notes for answers underlined and highlighted above.)
  a Jeremy Miles **b** incredible **c** an extrovert
  d on social media **e** singer

2 (round of applause)   (social media)
   (talent)   (privacy)
   (paparazzi)   TV drama
   (a piece of gossip)   (publicity)
   introvert   incompetence
   a fact   (extrovert)
   (stardom)   (reality TV)

DIFFERENTIATION

Strengthen: For Q1, tell students to listen out for key lexical words as these will help them find the answers. For Q2, remind students that the answers may not appear in the same order on the page as they do in the recording.
Q2: Ask students to circle the words they think they heard first time around before you play the recording a second time.

VOCABULARY ACTIVITY 2 PAGE 22

- For Q1, ask students to work individually to match the words and the definitions.
- Check answers with the class.
- For Q2, elicit the four words/phrases from Activity 1 which were not used: *introvert*, *a fact*, *TV drama*, *incompetence*. Put students into pairs and ask them to define the words/phrases and to think of possible antonyms for them. For example, *introvert* (a shy, quiet person and its antonym is extrovert); *a fact* (something that is true and has happened and its antonym is lie, untruth, fiction); *TV drama* (usually a narrative story based on real life or fictional situations, and some may consider reality TV programmes its antonym); *incompetence* (inability to do something successfully and it could be considered an antonym of talent).

KEY

1 a talent **b** reality TV **c** paparazzi **d** privacy
  e round of applause **f** stardom **g** extrovert
  h social media **i** a piece of gossip **j** publicity

READING PART 2 — UNIT 1: READING PREPARATION

VOCABULARY ACTIVITY 3 — PAGE 22

- Ask students to work in pairs. Give them a short time to work together to check they understand the meaning of any words they don't know in the sentences.
- Ask students to fill in the gaps with words from the list in Activity 1 on page 21. As an extension activity, you could ask students if they can think of any synonyms to fill the gaps.

KEY

1 **a** publicity **b** piece of gossip **c** privacy, social media, paparazzi **d** talent **e** reality TV, a round of applause **f** stardom, extrovert

VOCABULARY ACTIVITY 4 — PAGE 23

- Ask students to work in pairs. Ask them to read the questions and give them some time to discuss their ideas and to make brief notes. Remind students to give reasons for their opinions (for the third bullet, you can ask them to explain why they use/do not use social media).
- Ask each pair to prepare to report back to the class on the results of their discussion, including any areas in which they strongly agreed or disagreed with their partner.

KEY

Students' own answers.

VOCABULARY ACTIVITY 5 — PAGE 23

- Before students begin this task, you could give them a short time to read Grammar Reference pages 261–262 to revise the rules for formation and use of the present simple.
- Ask students to work in pairs to complete the sentences.

KEY

1 handle 2 wears 3 take 4 are
5 do not/don't want 6 likes

GRAMMAR ACTIVITY 6 — PAGES 23–24

- Tell students to look at the words and symbols in brackets. Explain what the symbols mean: + means the sentence is positive; – means the sentence is negative; ? means the sentence uses a question form.
- Give students a short time to complete the sentences with the present simple form of the verbs in brackets.
- To help students complete the activity, ask them to remind you of the main features of the present simple, e.g. subject/verb agreement, question forms.

KEY

1 We accept 2 Do they know 3 She does 4 I am
5 Rachel does not/doesn't regret, she hopes
6 Don't you want 7 Isn't it 8 She carries
9 Ricardo's flying/Ricardo is flying

GRAMMAR ACTIVITY 7 — PAGE 24

- Ask students some questions about their daily routines to get an idea of a typical day for students.
- Ask students to write about their favourite celebrity's daily routine. They could use their imagination or, as an extension activity, do some research.
- You could provide students with some sample sentences to help with writing about the structure of the celebrity's day (see Key below).

KEY

See Sample answer below.

SAMPLE ANSWER FOR ACTIVITY 7:

Rachel Ritz wakes up at six o'clock every morning. She does yoga and then she has a hot shower. She normally has a light breakfast and chooses her outfit for the day. She then practises singing for two hours. After that, she has a late lunch with friends. She often goes to dinner parties in the evening. She doesn't like to stay up late and tries to go to bed by 11 p.m.

GRAMMAR ACTIVITY 8 — PAGES 24

- Before students begin this task, you could give them a short time to read Grammar Reference page 262 to revise the rules for formation and use of the present continuous.
- Ask students to form sentences in the present continuous using the words provided. Remind them to reread their final sentences to check that they make sense.

KEY

1 We are getting the results that we deserve./We deserve the results that we are getting.
2 People are talking about a transfer.
3 The referee is not performing as well as we are./We are not performing as well as the referee.
4 Lucas is playing and he is doing a great job.
5 Is it true that you are bidding over a million euros?

GRAMMAR GAME: PICTIONARY — PAGE 24

- Tell students to get into groups and follow the instructions to play the game. You will need several sheets of paper for each group of students.
- You could prepare some sentences in advance for students to use. Suggested sentences:
  The dog is eating its dinner.
  The boy is laughing with his friends.
  The frogs are hopping into the water.
  The man is taking a photograph.
  The teacher is shouting at the class.
  The cat is chasing a mouse.
  The birds are eating apples.
  The motorists are driving over the bridge.
  The mouse is running away from the cat.

GRAMMAR ACTIVITY 9 — PAGE 25

- Elicit when we use the simple present and the present continuous, and revise the formation of each. If necessary, you can refer students once again to Grammar Reference pages 261–262.
- Give students some time to read and choose the correct sentences.
- Check students' answers. You could ask them to explain their answers.

KEY

1 a   2 a   3 a   4 b   5 b   6 a   7 a

GRAMMAR ACTIVITY 10 — PAGES 25–26

- To help students complete the task, you could go through each of the sentences first, identifying which tense is needed.
- You could tell students that they will need to write at least two words in each gap. You can ask them when they will need to write more than two words (for negative sentences and questions).
- Ask students to complete the sentences using the correct tense for the verbs and the information in brackets.

KEY

1 Does Rachel look   2 Chris updates
3 I do not/don't know   4 are you thinking
5 Do you believe   6 I don't have
7 does everyone like   8 he is/he's relaxing
9 Are you working   10 Janet is not/isn't coming

SELF-EVALUATION — PAGE 26

Tell students to look at the Self-evaluation table and tick the boxes that are true for them. Ask them if there are any topics they don't feel confident about yet.

READING PART 3

OVERVIEW

Topic: History and time
Exam skills: Verify information (true, false or not given), identify facts, ideas and opinions
Assessment Objectives: 1B, 1C, 1D
Vocabulary: Phrasal verbs
Grammar: Use comparative and superlative adjectives
Practice text type: Newspaper article: 'Amazing discovery of the Biggest Dinosaur Ever'
Additional resources: audio player, atlas, world map or globe (internet access)

PREPARING THE WAY   PAGE 27

- Tell students to read the chapter topic title and, as a starting point, elicit from them which historical events in their own country they think are the most important. Write these on the board in the form of a timeline, showing approximate dates.
- Then ask students to read and discuss the questions relating to history and ideas about the past. You could provide students with key words and phrases (e.g. *records*, *the past*, *historical figures*, *accuracy*) and ask them to produce brief written responses to the questions.

KEY

Suggested sentence structures for discussion:
History is usually recorded by ...
The personalities of those living long ago may be ...
It is useful to learn about history because ...
I think the most significant event of all time is ...

TEACHING TIPS
The final question may need to be dealt with sensitively in light of students' experiences and alternative viewpoints.

EXTENSION

- You could ask students to copy the timeline you have drawn on the board and research events to add to it. You may want to extend this research task or ask students to choose one historical event in their own country and find out more about it. They could then present their findings to the class.
- Alternatively, you could ask students to work in pairs or groups to find out about the main historical events in another country. Each pair or group could research a different country. Findings could be presented to the class or turned into classroom display material.
- If students enjoy drama, they could form groups to act out or form tableaux of well-known scenes from history and the rest of the class would have to guess the scene.

ACTIVITY 1   PAGE 27

- Ask students to look at the picture and elicit the meaning of *painting* (as a noun and a verb) and *gallery guide* (a *gallery* contains paintings and other artworks and a *guide* shows these works to visitors and talks about them).
- Explain that the painting depicts the historical figure King Canute. Ask students where they think he is and what he is trying to do.
- Ask students to read the questions and underline the key words. Explain that listening out for these key words will help them find the information to answer the questions.
- Before you play the recording, check the meaning of *robes* (clothes), *wealth* (money, or things that make you rich), *status* (how important someone is), *command* (to tell someone what to do), *the waves* (the sea), *legend* (an old well-known story) and *humble* (not proud, modest).
- Play the recording and ask students to listen and take notes. Then give them some time to write their answers and compare their ideas with a partner.
- Play the recording again if necessary, pausing at the appropriate places for students to check their answers. You could also refer students to the Audioscript on page 286.

UNIT 1: READING PREPARATION
READING PART 3

AUDIOSCRIPT: Student Book page 286

Gallery guide: This is an image of King Canute. King Canute was the ruler of Denmark, Norway and England <u>more than 1000 years ago</u>. He is a ruler with a very interesting story and people have given many different versions of it over the years. <u>His date of birth is thought to be around the year 995 and he died in 1035</u>, aged about 40. As you can see, the picture shows him standing at the edge of the sea surrounded by his servants and advisors. You will notice in the picture that he's wearing very rich and brightly-coloured robes. This, of course, is <u>because he was a king and therefore had high wealth and status</u>. There <u>have been many paintings of King Canute over the centuries</u>. This picture dates from around 1850. It is a well-known representation of Canute, even though it was painted so long after his life.

A legend about King Canute says that <u>he once tried to command the waves.</u> Here the sea is rising around his feet and he is getting wet. The legend says he did this <u>to show that, even though he was the king, he could not control the forces of nature</u>. This is why some people remember him as a humble ruler.

Unfortunately, there are not many records about the event, so <u>it is difficult to know whether or not this story about King Canute is actually true</u>. We don't know if he really did try to stop the tide. However, people still use the legend to talk about trying to stop the unstoppable. <u>The tale is still popular, even now, because it is a good illustration of a fact</u>: there are some things that we cannot change.

KEY

(See Audioscript with notes for answers underlined.)
1 more than 1000 years ago / from 995 to 1035 **2** As king, he had high wealth and status. **3** Yes, there are many paintings of him. **4** He is trying to command the waves to show that Nature is more powerful than a king. **5** We don't know. **6** It is a good example of a fact and teaches us that there some things we cannot change.

EXTENSION

- You could ask students to locate Norway, Denmark and England using an atlas, world map or globe. Then ask them to research King Canute and his kingdom comprising these countries.
- Alternatively, ask students to find some other famous stories about kings, queens or other rulers from their own country or other parts of the world.

FOCUSING ON THE EXAM   PAGE 28

- Ask students to read the text in the box and tell you what they think will be challenging about this part of the exam.
- The Reading Part 3 Assessment Objectives are:
  Assessment Objective 1B: Understand in detail a range of texts, identifying finer points of detail.
  Assessment Objective 1C: Distinguish between facts, ideas and opinions.
  Assessment Objective 1D: Identify a writer's viewpoint and attitude, stated and implied.
- Explain that Reading Part 3 carries 20 marks and is based on a longer text, such as long prose passages (possibly from academic sources), reports or articles.
- Go through the different types of tasks students may have to complete in Reading Part 3. Make sure students are aware of the range of possible formats and advise them to spend time reading the instructions and questions carefully before they start writing.
- Tell students that in this chapter they will learn about and practise verifying information and identifying facts, ideas and opinions. These skills will help them meet Assessment Objectives 1A, 1B and 1C.

EXAM SKILLS: VERIFYING INFORMATION (TRUE, FALSE OR NOT GIVEN)   PAGE 28

To consolidate students' understanding of how to approach this task type and to clarify their understanding of the 'not given' option, you could write some true, false and not given statements on the board, e.g.
There are 20 students in class today.
The classroom has two windows.
At two o'clock it will rain.
Ask students to identify whether the information contained in the statements is true, false or not given.

DIFFERENTIATION

Strengthen: This activity could be conducted in students' native language first.
Challenge: Ask students to come up with their own statements for others in the class to identify as true, false or not given.

READING PART 3 | UNIT 1: READING PREPARATION

ACTIVITY 2 — PAGE 28

- Tell students that they are going to do some research about a dinosaur and produce both true and (deliberately) false statements about it.
- Students will need access to information about dinosaurs, ideally from the internet, but it could be from books on the topic if these are available. Alternatively, you could print information prior to the lesson and distribute it.
- Go over the activity steps with students to check that they understand what they have to do. In groups, ask students to decide whether they will research Tyrannosaurus rex or Brontosaurus (sometimes known as Apatosaurus).
- Give students time to complete Q1 and Q2 in their groups. When they have prepared their statements, ask them to swap statements with another group and guess whether they are true or false.
- Once the groups have checked their guesses, ask students to work individually to complete Q5. Alternatively, you could set this question as a homework task.

KEY

Students' own answers. Suggested answers for Q1:

Tyrannosaurus rex

Tyrannosaurus rex had long sharp teeth as a special feature.

Tyrannosaurus rex ate meat/other dinosaurs.

Tyrannosaurus rex weighed about nine tonnes.

Tyrannosaurus rex was 4.6–6 metres tall.

Tyrannosaurus rex lived in North America and Asia.

Tyrannosaurus rex became extinct about 65 million years ago.

Brontosaurus

Brontosaurus had a very long thin neck/small head as a special feature.

Brontosaurus ate plants/vegetation.

Brontosaurus weighed about 30 tonnes.

Brontosaurus was 4–5 metres tall.

Brontosaurus lived in North America/Colorado.

Brontosaurus became extinct about 65 million years ago.

EXTENSION

Ask students to design their own dinosaur. They need to provide set of information about it, following the structure of Q1 if desired. They could produce a fact file about their dinosaur or prepare a PowerPoint presentation.

EXAM SKILLS: IDENTIFYING FACTS, IDEAS AND OPINIONS — PAGE 29

- Activity 3 helps students learn the difference between facts, ideas and opinions. This skill will be of use to them in the exam.
- You could tell students that ideas in this context could be taken to mean suggestions or thoughts. You may want to provide an example of a fact, idea and opinion, e.g. *The temperature today is xx degrees.* (fact), *I love warm weather.* (opinion), *Let's have a picnic.* (idea).

ACTIVITY 3 — PAGE 29

- Ask students to read the statements about dinosaurs in Q1 and, with a partner, decide if the statements are facts, ideas or opinions.
- Check answers with the class. Then ask students to copy the table and add to it at least two more examples in each column.

KEY

Fact: Dinosaurs laid eggs. **Idea:** Let's go the Natural History Museum. **Opinion:** Dinosaurs are cute.

TEACHING TIPS

Hint Q1: To help students with this activity, you can tell them to use the following language structures to help make clear the difference between facts, ideas and opinions. Tell them to use:

- *is/are* to talk about facts. They suggest certainty.
- *will/going to* for ideas. They suggest intention.
- *like/dislike, prefer/hate/love* to talk about opinions. They suggest preferences and feelings.

UNIT 1: READING PREPARATION — READING PART 3

ACTIVITY 4 — PAGE 29

- Ask students to study the picture carefully before writing their six sentences. You can elicit or tell the class that the dinosaur shown is Tyrannosaurus rex. They will already know some facts about it from Activity 2.
- Note we do not use the definite article with dinosaur names because we use their Latin names. We would normally include the definite articles with animal names, e.g. *The blue whale is bigger than the sperm whale.*
- Remind students that facts are about things that can be measured or proven, whereas opinions are a point of view and may not be objectively true or accurate.

KEY

Students' own answers. Suggested sentences:

Facts

Tyrannosaurus rex would have been large compared to a human.

Tyrannosaurus rex had sharp teeth.

Tyrannosaurus rex could stand on its back legs.

Opinions

Tyrannosaurus rex looks terrifying!

Tyrannosaurus rex was the meanest dinosaur of all.

Tyrannosaurus rex was very clumsy.

PRACTICE TIME: READING PART 3 — PAGES 29–32

- This section provides students with exam practice. The exam will have a similar text, layout and task. Note that the instructions are more complex in Reading Part 3 so students may need more support in understanding what they have to do.
- Go over the rubrics with students and draw their attention to the Exam Hints.
- Advise students to read each set of questions before returning to the article as they work their way through the paper so that they know what information to look out for. You can tell them that underlining key words in the questions, where appropriate, and then looking for these or their synonyms in the text, will help them to answer the questions.
- For Q26–Q30, remind students to use lexical words to help them locate the relevant information.
- For Q31–Q40, remind students that they should take the words directly from the text.
- For Q41–Q45, tell students that crossing out the words in the box as they work through the summary will reduce the number of possible answers for the remaining gaps.

KEY

26 T   27 T   28 F   29 T   30 NG   31 32 rhinos (line 9)
32 77 tonnes (lines 5–6)   33 fascinating (line 15)
34 travelled to (line 18)   35 desert (in Patagonia) (line 26)   36 dinosaur anatomy (line 33)   37 species (line 36)   38 ancient wood (line 43)   39 weight (line 49)   40 (very) complex process (line 49)
41 existence   42 gigantic   43 specimens
44 accuracy   45 estimated

TEACHING TIPS

Hint Q26: This is stated in line 8 and referred to several times throughout the article.

Hint Q27: In line 25, some students may be able to recognise *unearthed* as a synonym for *found*, and all should be able to match the phrase *farm worker*.

Hint Q28: Although students may not know the word *herbivore*, lines 45–46 provide the definition *plant-eater*.

Hint Q29: Identifying *rare* (line 51) as a synonym of *unusual* will guide students to the correct answer (line 51).

Hint Q30: This is not suggested in the article as it contains no direct references to scientific advances. At the same time, the information is not necessarily false.

HOW DID YOU DO? — PAGE 32

- Go through answers with the class and tell students to mark their work.
- Ask the class what went well and what went less well, and how they think they could improve their performance.

READING PART 3 — UNIT 1: READING PREPARATION

VOCABULARY AND GRAMMAR

VOCABULARY ACTIVITY 1 — PAGES 32–33

- Ask students to underline the phrasal verbs in the article on pages 29–30. Tell them that looking at these verbs in context will help them work out what they mean.
- As an extension activity, you could ask students to choose three of the phrasal verbs that are new to them or that they find the most difficult and use them to write sentences.

KEY

draw on: use **look after:** take care of
come from: originate in **come across:** find unexpectedly or without intention **look for:** search for **look up:** research, consult other sources
turn out: happen in a particular way, usually unexpectedly **reflect on:** think about for a long time

DIFFERENTIATION

Strengthen: Help students to understand the vocabulary in the definitions (*use, take care of,* etc.) if necessary before they attempt the task.
Challenge: Ask students to create their own phrasal verb matching activity, either from memory or by researching further phrasal verbs.

EXTENSION

Write the following sentences on the board and ask students to choose one and act it out.
1 A person reflecting on something.
2 A person coming across some money.
3 A person looking for a lost dog.
4 A person looking after a baby.
5 A person looking up a word.
6 A person coming home from the shops.
Other students have to guess which sentence they chose.

VOCABULARY ACTIVITY 2 — PAGE 33

Before students attempt the activity, ask them to read through the blog post and identify any words they don't know. Help with understanding.

KEY

1 reflect on 2 look up 3 come from 4 reflect on
5 draw on 6 come across 7 turn out 8 look after

GRAMMAR ACTIVITY 3 — PAGE 34

- For Q1, you can tell students that there are 17 adjectives in the blog post.
- For Q2, remind students that articles preceding the adjectives may need changing (e.g. *an interesting > a fascinating*).
- The synonyms below are suggestions, but other answers are possible.
- You can tell students that not all of the adjectives need to be replaced. They should keep in mind that the aim of the activity is to make the text more entertaining.

KEY

See annotated blog post below. Q1: adjectives underlined. Q2: Suggested synonyms highlighted.

MY DAY WITH DINOSAURS

Today, we need to **1** reflect on ideas about moving the newly-discovered bones back to the museum. I'm sure (certain/positive) that if we talk about it we can agree on something. It may also be helpful (useful/valuable) to **2** look up how they've moved big (large) bones like this in the past. It's amazing (incredible) to think that this time last week we didn't know that such an interesting (a fascinating) dinosaur skeleton existed. What a great (amazing) day for palaeontologists everywhere when that farm worker made his incredible (extraordinary) discovery! This new (fresh) find deepens our research, which is really nice (rewarding) for me.

It is good (great) to think that someone just found these bones, yet they turned out to be so important (significant). Where does luck like this **3** come from? It makes you **4** reflect on the role that chance plays in scientific (technical) work. We really can **5** draw on a whole (complete/entire) new (current/recent) set of data for future research; already it has such important (vital) implications and as time goes on we may **6** come across even more reasons to recognise its significance. It is a real (true) honour to excavate these remains and I think that in the future they may **7** turn out to be even more important (crucial) than we now realise. We now just have to make sure we **8** look after these bones as carefully as we can!

UNIT 1: READING PREPARATION — READING PART 3

> **TEACHING TIPS**
>
> **Hint Q2:** The compound word *newly-discovered* is functioning as an adjective here. You can tell students to concentrate on the one-word adjectives.

GRAMMAR ACTIVITY 4 — PAGE 34

This activity is designed to help students practise using comparative adjectives. The pictures have been chosen to provide a variety of qualities to contrast.

KEY

Students' own answers. Suggested answers:
The dinosaur looks fiercer than the puppy.
The puppy looks friendlier than the dinosaur.
The dinosaur is bigger than the puppy.
The puppy is cuter than the dinosaur.
The dinosaur is more dangerous than the puppy.
The puppy is more appealing than the dinosaur.

GRAMMAR ACTIVITY 5 — PAGE 34

- Elicit rules for forming comparative and superlative adjectives or refer students to Grammar Reference pages 278–279.
- Ask students to copy and complete the table. You could encourage any students who finish quickly to add more adjectives to the table.
- Have students check answers in pairs before checking with the class.

KEY

Adjective	Comparative adjective	Superlative adjective
hard	harder	hardest
intelligent	more intelligent	most intelligent
stupid	stupider	stupidest
lazy	lazier	laziest
beautiful	more beautiful	most beautiful
near	nearer	nearest
far	further	furthest
simple	simpler	simplest
easy	easier	easiest
calm	calmer	calmest
delicate	more delicate	most delicate
good	better	best
bad	worse	worst
talented	more talented	most talented

GRAMMAR GAME: SURVEY TIME — PAGE 35

- Elicit from the students what a *survey* is (when you ask lots of people the same questions to find out about their habits or opinions as a group).
- Explain to students that they are going to carry out a survey to find out some facts about their classmates.
- You could ask students to work in pairs to discuss what questions they can ask to find out the information they need (*How far do you live from our school? How old are you? How many brothers and sisters do you have? How old are they? Do you have a pet? How old is it? How tall are you?*) Elicit what these are and write them on the board.
- Ask students how they plan to record the information they gather. You could suggest that they use a table with columns headed *Name*, *Age*, *Distance from school*, *Number of brothers and sisters*, *Age of brothers and sisters*, *Age of pet*, *Height*. Encourage them to prepare this table before they begin.
- When students are ready, put students into groups and have them survey their group members first. They then can leave their groups and begin to survey the class.
- Take feedback and elicit some answers from the survey.

READING PART 3 | **UNIT 1: READING PREPARATION** 23

TEACHING TIPS

Depending on the time you have available, you might want to set the number of classmates that students have to speak to, e.g. eight or ten, before they can collate their information and complete the question sheet.

KEY

1 ug / ly **2** ar / tic / u / late **3** fas / ci / nat / ing
4 in / fur / i / a / ting **5** con / fu / sing **6** fast
7 ri / dic / u / lous **8** sim / ple **9** bored
10 help / ful

GRAMMAR ACTIVITY 6   PAGE 35

- Read through the list of adjectives with the class and check that students understand the meaning of all the words. This is also an opportunity for you to model the pronunciation of any new words.
- Encourage students to say the words aloud as they try to work out the number of syllables and correct their pronunciation as necessary.
- When you check answers with the class, say the words aloud and ask students to repeat after you.

SELF-EVALUATION   PAGE 35

Tell students to look at the Self-evaluation table and tick the boxes that are true for them. Ask them if there are any topics they don't feel confident about yet.

UNIT 2: WRITING PREPARATION

WRITING PART 4

OVERVIEW

Topic: Food and drink
Exam skills: Identify and use formal and informal register, consider relevance and word limits in the exam
Assessment Objectives: 2A, 2B, 2C
Vocabulary: Collocations: food and drink
Grammar: Use the present perfect
Practice text type: Informal email: cooking a birthday meal
Additional resources: audio player, dictionaries (internet access)

PREPARING THE WAY   PAGE 38

- Tell students to read the chapter topic title and elicit from them what their favourite foods are.
- Ask students about traditional food in their countries and whether or not they are healthy. You could also ask them whether they like cooking or whether they know how to cook.
- Ask students to read the questions about food and discuss them in pairs.
- If students are able to sustain a class or small group discussion, you can ask them to discuss each of the questions in more detail.
- If students need more support for their discussion, you could write some key words and phrases and some sentence structures on the board (see Key below). You could then ask them to produce brief written responses and compare their ideas with a partner or in groups.

KEY

Suggested key words and phrases:
nutritious, unhealthy, priority, delicious, family meal, family gathering, socialise, together
Suggested sentence structures for discussion:
Food / eating should be …
Eating with friends / family is important because …
I like / prefer … because …
If I had to choose, I would choose …
The reason I would choose … is …

Background Information

The topic of food and drink has universal appeal so it is not difficult to form and express opinions about it. The topic also lends itself to a range of research projects to extend students, and real-life applications (e.g. understanding menus, ordering food, paying bills) which students can role-play and practise.

EXTENSION

Ask students to research the food and food-related customs of the country they named in response to the third question. Suggested research questions could be:
What are the main ingredients of dishes from this country? Why is this?
What are this country's best known dishes?
How is food served and presented in this country?
Are there lots of small dishes or one big one?
Are meals served with a particular accompaniment such as salad or rice?
Do people eat one dish at a time or all together? Do adults and children eat separately or together? At what times of the day do people eat?

ACTIVITY 1   PAGES 38–39

- Read the words in the box aloud to the class to model the pronunciation of any new vocabulary. You could then ask students to work in pairs to put the adjectives and nouns into the correct columns in the table.
- For Q2, you could challenge students to see who can add the most new words to each column within a given amount of time. Ask students to share their words and write them on the board in columns. You could then take a class vote on the most unusual adjective and noun.
- Have students choose one of the categories from the box and create a menu. Go over the menu with the class and make sure that students understand each part. You may want to limit students to three or four items per section. When students have finished, put them into pairs and have them role-play a waiter and a customer.

KEY

1

Adjectives	Nouns
sliced	*watermelon*
delicious	*honey*
tasty	*coffee*
home-baked	*bread*
fresh	*fruit*

2 and 3 Students' own answers.

EXTENSION

- Ask students to come up with ideas for a new restaurant and to design an advertisement (e.g. a leaflet, a flyer) for it. The advertisement could mention features such as:
  the menu/type of food served
  the reputation of the chef
  the service/staff
  the décor
  online reviews received
  any other special features, e.g. food is ordered electronically at the table, staff are dressed in national costume, the restaurant can be hired for private parties.
- As a follow-up activity, students could write a customer review of one of their classmates' restaurants.

FOCUSING ON THE EXAM — PAGE 39

- Ask students to read the text in the box and tell you what they think will be challenging about this part of the exam.
- You could point out to students that the Writing Part 4 Assessment Objectives (2A, 2B, and 2C) all relate to accuracy and control. Key assessment features are punctuation, spelling, use of the correct register and word choice.
- The Writing Part 4 Assessment Objectives are:
  Assessment Objective 2A: Demonstrate appropriate use of paragraphing, punctuation and spelling.
  Assessment Objective 2B: Write in a range of registers to fit the context.
  Assessment Objective 2C: Demonstrate a control of a range of vocabulary and structures.
- Explain that Writing Part 4 carries 10 marks and includes a range of informal text types, e.g. email, letter to a friend. Tell students they will be given a context and that they need to follow instructions carefully and cover all points in the question. Make sure that students understand what this task involves.
- Tell students that the organisation of their response is also important, and they can gain or lose marks according to the way their work is structured.
- Tell students that in this chapter they will learn about and practise writing in the correct register, using appropriate punctuation, spelling, vocabulary and structures. These skills will help them meet Assessment Objectives 2A, 2B and 2C.

EXAM SKILLS: REGISTER — PAGE 39

- Go through the information about register with the class and explain that candidates often lose marks in this part of the exam by writing in a register that is too formal. Tell students that this section will help them to understand the difference between formal and informal register by contrasting examples of each.
- Tell students the definitions for the highlighted words in the Register box can be found in the Glossary on page 244.
- Ask students to tell you when we use an informal register (when talking or writing to friends, family and people we know well). Ask students to look at the features of informal language listed and elicit or give examples of each one, e.g.
  We'd really like you to come. (contraction)
  I'm writing to tell you why I wasn't there. rather than *I am writing to explain my absence.* (simpler vocabulary)

ACTIVITY 2 — PAGE 40

- Tell students that Q1 asks them to assess the register of two sentences. You can point out that both are grammatically correct but only sentence **a** would be appropriate for Writing Part 4 in terms of register.
- Elicit from the class which features of sentence **a** make it informal and which features of sentence **b** make it formal or informal, referring back to the Register box on page 39 as necessary.
- Emphasise the importance of appropriateness (i.e. suitability for context) rather than responses being right or wrong. Point out that sentence **a** would be suitable for use in an email between friends, a common context for Writing Part 4. This is what is expected in the exam even if in other parts of the world a different register may be used in this context.
- For Q2, ask students to work in pairs to sort the phrases into the correct columns.

26 UNIT 2: WRITING PREPARATION — WRITING PART 4

KEY

1 **a** is informal **b** is formal

Sentence **a** is shorter, contains contractions, simpler vocabulary, and has a friendlier tone. The tone in sentence **b** is more distant and polite, suggesting that the writer and recipient know each other less well than in sentence **a**.

2 **Informal:** I don't like him much./Why don't you try this?/I need help with this.

Formal: The man does not impress me./I would suggest this action./I require additional support.

EXTENSION

- For more practice in understanding differences in register, you could conduct the following activity. It requires students to think about how they would use language differently depending on who they were talking to.
- Put the students into groups of four and assign these roles: Student 1, Student 2, Teacher, Observer.
- Student 1's task is to give two separate accounts of a recent, enjoyable weekend, first, to Student 2 and then to the Teacher. Student 1 should include details about:
  where he/she spent the weekend
  what he/she did
  why he/she enjoyed it so much.
- Student 2 and the Teacher need to listen to Student 1 in turn. They should also ask Student 1 some follow-up questions.
- The Observer should observe and note down specific examples of how Student 1's register changes depending on who they are talking to.

ACTIVITY 3 PAGE 40

- For Q1, ask students to number the greetings from 1 (very informal) to 5 (very formal). You could also ask them to draw the continuum line and to place the listed greetings along it correctly, writing the letters rather than the words if they prefer. Ask them to repeat this process for the closings in Q2.
- When you elicit answers, ask students to justify their choices and to try to explain the differences between the words in level of formality. If they have made any mistakes in their original ordering, this process should help to correct them.

- For Q3, after students have discussed in pairs, elicit which greeting and closings students could use in Writing Part 4.

KEY

1 1 a Hi 2 d Hello 3 e Dear 4 b Greetings
   5 c To whom it may concern
2 1 d See you soon 2 b Take care 3 e Best wishes 4 c Yours truly 5 a Yours sincerely
3 **Greetings:** a, b, d, e **Closings:** b, d

ACTIVITY 4 PAGE 41

- You could begin this activity by asking students why postcards tend to be informal (because we usually send them to friends and family).
- Tell students to read the postcard and underline any phrases that they think are too formal.
- Before students rewrite the underlined words and phrases using less formal equivalents, you may want to point out that synonyms (covered in Chapter 2) do not always have the same register. For example, *exquisite* and *lovely* can mean the same thing, but only *lovely* is appropriate for an informal message. The same is true of *exceptionally healthy* and *well*.

KEY

1 See postcard with unsuitably formal phrases underlined below.

<u>Warmest greetings</u> Ravi!

How are things? I hope you're <u>exceptionally healthy</u>. I am having an <u>exquisite</u> time here in Italy. It's a beautiful country and the food is yummy. There are also <u>numerous spectacular locations</u> to visit. Have you <u>had any thoughts</u> about what we could do <u>upon my return</u>? <u>I regret</u> that it may be ages until we see each other again.

Lots of love,

Jason

WRITING PART 4 UNIT 2: WRITING PREPARATION

SAMPLE ANSWER FOR QUESTION 2:

Hi Ravi!

How are things? I hope you're <u>well</u>. I am having a <u>great</u> time here in Italy. It's a lovely country and the food is yummy. There are also <u>lots of</u> <u>amazing</u> places to visit. Have you <u>decided</u> what we could do <u>when I get back</u>? <u>It's a shame</u> that it may be ages until we see each other again.

Lots of love,

Jason

TEACHING TIPS

Hint Q1: Encourage students to respond to the bullet points as early as possible in their response. Emphasise that they should avoid including extra material since it will not gain them additional marks.

Hint Q2: Discourage students from memorising long openings and endings. They risk losing marks for this as fewer words (within a very small word limit) are left to address the bullet points and to use a range of relevant vocabulary.

EXAM SKILLS: RELEVANCE AND WORD LIMIT   PAGE 41

- Tell students that including irrelevant material can cause them to lose marks in the exam. Explain that they can avoid this by studying the bullet points with the details they are supposed to include in their answer very carefully. They should not miss out anything that is asked for, nor include irrelevant details.
- Emphasise to students that the word limit is very important and they should not write more than 100 words.

ACTIVITY 5   PAGES 41–42

- Give students some time to read the question. Then tell them to close their books and ask them what the word limit is (75–100 words) and what three points their message should cover (why they want to start a new hobby, which two hobbies they are considering, questions to ask for their friend's opinion).

- Tell students to read the two sample answers and then to discuss the questions in Q1 in pairs. You could then ask some pairs to share with the class their ideas about which sample answer is the best one and why.
- Give students some time to write their own answer to the exam question. Then ask students to exchange texts with a partner and to check each other's work for relevance and word length.

KEY

1 Student A's response would score the highest mark. It covers most points (but only mentions one, not two hobbies as was required) in under 100 words. Student B's response is too long and covers only the first point within 100 words.

Student B wrote 179 words. The examiner would stop marking after *problems* (line 9).

Student B could start his email with *I am thinking of taking up a new hobby*. The details that come before this phrase aren't relevant.

2 Students' own answers.

PRACTICE TIME: WRITING PART 4   PAGE 43

- Tell students to read the question to find out what they have to do. You could also draw their attention to the Exam Hints and After Exam Check boxes.
- You could write the word limit on the board as well as the three points that students' emails should cover.
- Ask students what the register of the language in their emails should be (informal) and then draw their attention to the Watch Out! box. You could elicit from students some examples of text speak (i.e. language they would use in phone texts) to avoid.

UNIT 2: WRITING PREPARATION — WRITING PART 4

KEY

Students' own answers. See Sample answer below and the Writing Guide.

SAMPLE ANSWER FOR PRACTICE TIME:

Dear Adah,

I've had a great idea. I'm going to cook you a birthday meal! You did me such a huge favour by lending me your bike last week, so I want to make you something really special.

I think a vegetarian curry would be perfect. It's healthy, not too difficult to cook and we'd both enjoy it.

I just want to check, are you allergic to anything? Would it be better if I avoided using peanuts in the sauce, for example? Mmm, I can taste that Naan bread already!

See you soon,

Mona

(94 words)

HOW DID YOU DO? PAGE 43

- Read your answer. Did you include information about each of the three bullet points in your answer? Did you write a suitable number of words? Do you think your spelling, punctuation and grammar is correct? Did you write in a suitable register?
- Ask the class what went well and what went less well, and how they think they could improve their performance.

VOCABULARY AND GRAMMAR

VOCABULARY ACTIVITY 1 PAGE 43

- Before students listen to the recording, draw their attention to the photo and remind them that unit topic is food and drink. Explain that visual clues and background knowledge will help them understand the dialogue.
- Ask students to read Q1 and then play the recording for them. Remind them to make notes as they listen to the dialogue. (The relevant information is underlined in the Audioscript below).

- You could ask students to write answers to the questions using their notes. Then give students a minute or so to compare their answers with a partner before checking the answers with the class.
- Draw students' attention to the word lists in Q2. Ask them to create the collocations (two or more words that are often used together, e.g. junk food, set menu), using a word from each column. You can tell them that all of the collocations are used in the dialogue. Play the recording again for students to listen and check their answers.

AUDIOSCRIPT: Student Book pages 286–287

Jane: I'm glad we've already booked a table! It's pretty crowded for a weekday, isn't it?

Hassan: I agree. I've heard several times that it's the best place for fine dining in this area! No wonder it's popular.

Jane: You're right there. I've eaten here twice. The food was delicious both times – so mouth-watering!

Hassan: Even the cutlery is stylish. Look at this knife and fork! And the way they've decorated the dining room … They must have hired an interior designer!

Jane: Probably! And the service is excellent, don't you think?

Hassan: I certainly do. Right, let's see what's on the menu.

Jane: Ooh! I've just seen what I'd like to order …

Hassan: Well, you're right; this does look good, but it feels as if there's something a bit strange about the fish.

Jane: I was just going to say that!

Hassan: It's got a sort of metallic taste to it.

Jane: Yes. Almost as if it's past its expiry date …

Hassan: I'm not sure I want to keep eating it. I don't want to get food poisoning.

Jane: Me neither. Should we ask them to take it back, do you think?

Hassan: The head chef would be really upset if we did that. I've heard that he takes a lot of pride in his work.

Jane: But we can't make ourselves ill just to avoid upsetting him! And the fish is definitely odd. I think we should ask for a full refund. If that's not possible, they should at least bring us a different main course.

WRITING PART 4 — UNIT 2: WRITING PREPARATION

KEY

1 They are in a restaurant. The fish tastes strange and has a metallic taste as if it's past its expiry date. Both Jane and Hassan are worried about getting food poisoning. They discuss returning the food, asking for a refund and ordering a different main course.

2 dining room, full refund, mouth-watering, expiry date, food poisoning, main course, knife and fork, head chef, fine dining

DIFFERENTIATION

Strengthen: Pre-teach some of the key vocabulary that students will hear in the recording. For example, you could write the words *cutlery, metallic, expiry date, food poisoning, odd, course, refund* on the board and elicit or explain what they mean.

Challenge: Ask students to use the collocations from Q2 to write sentences of their own.

VOCABULARY ACTIVITY 2 — PAGE 44

- Ask students to match the collocations and the definitions.
- Check answers with the class. You could elicit from students some sentences using the collocations.

KEY

1 full refund 2 knife and fork 3 expiry date
4 food poisoning 5 main course 6 fine dining
7 dining room 8 mouth-watering 9 head chef

VOCABULARY ACTIVITY 3 — PAGE 44

- Tell students to look at the title of the text and ask why people read restaurant reviews (to decide whether they want to eat at a restaurant or not). Ask them to work in pairs to read the review and fill in the gaps.
- Check answers with the class. Ask students whether they think Jane's review is fair and to explain why.

KEY

1 fine dining 2 mouth-watering 3 dining room
4 (a) head chef 5 main course 6 expiry date
7 food poisoning 8 knife and fork 9 full refund
10 fine dining

GRAMMAR ACTIVITY 4 — PAGE 45

- Before students begin work on this section, you might like to give them time to read Grammar Reference pages 262–263 to revise the formation and use of the present perfect tense.
- Check that they understand the structure of the present perfect by demonstrating some present perfect positive and negative sentences and questions. Then ask the class to look at the table. Play the first part of the dialogue from Activity 1 again and for students to complete the table.
- Play the first part of the dialogue several times if necessary, pausing after each present perfect verb.
- Check answers with the class.

KEY

Verb	Verb form in dialogue	Time phrase
book	we've booked	already
hear	I've heard	several times
eat	I've eaten	twice
decorate	they've decorated	no time phrase
see	I've (just) seen	just

GRAMMAR ACTIVITY 5 — PAGE 45

- Ask students to look at the verbs in the word box and check that they know their past participle forms. Then ask students to complete the sentences with the present perfect form of the verbs given. You could point out to students that two of the sentences are negative.
- Have students check answers in pairs before checking answers with the class.

KEY

1 has gone 2 Has ... ever been 3 have not/haven't completed 4 has broken 5 have not/haven't seen

GRAMMAR ACTIVITY 6 — PAGE 45

- You could ask students to complete this activity in pairs. Encourage them to look at the individual words provided for each sentence and to guess what each sentence is about before they begin.
- Check answers with the class by calling on pairs to read the sentence aloud for the class.

KEY

1 It has often caused problems./Often it has caused problems./It has caused problems often. **2** How much money have you spent? **3** They haven't had this meal before. **4** Thanks, but I've already eaten./Thanks, but I've eaten already. **5** I've been ill for the last two weeks./For the last two weeks, I've been ill.

TEACHING TIPS

Hint Q1: Although *Often it has caused problems.* and *It has caused problems often.* are also considered correct, you should encourage students to place adverbs of frequency between the modal verb and past participle in the present perfect tense.

Hint Q4: The adverb of frequency *already* can go at the end of the sentence, but again encourage students to place it between the modal verb and past participle in the present perfect tense. Also note that *I've already eaten, but thanks.* is also a possible answer.

GRAMMAR ACTIVITY 7 — PAGE 46

- Remind students of the meaning of the symbols in brackets: + means the sentence is positive; – means the sentence is negative; ? means the sentence uses a question form.
- Elicit the difference between the first, second and third person forms of the present perfect (*you/we/they have* vs *he/she/it has*) and go over the past participles of the verbs in brackets.
- Students can do the activity individually but compare their ideas with a partner before you check answers with the class.

KEY

1 Why hasn't/haven't Barcelona lost yet this year? (*hasn't* is more likely to appear in American English)
2 She has flown before.
3 We have done the reports.
4 Abed hasn't found the answer yet.
5 Has she written the email to headquarters?
6 Why haven't they eaten breakfast?
7 I haven't tried that.
8 Has Britta finished lunch yet?
9 We've finished the exercise! We can use the present perfect!

GRAMMAR GAME: *I HAVE NEVER EVER ...* — PAGE 46

- Tell students to follow the instructions to play the game. You could demonstrate how to play first by describing things you have never done using sentences beginning *I have never ever*. When you are satisfied that students have got the idea, put them into groups to play.
- You could write some verbs on the board to prompt students, e.g.
  I have never:
  read   seen   eaten   drunk   bought   slept
  tasted   climbed   listened to   danced   played
  met   swum (in)   camped   learned (to)   cooked

SELF-EVALUATION — PAGE 47

Tell students to look at the Self-evaluation table and tick the boxes that are true for them. Ask them if there are any topics they don't feel confident about yet.

WRITING PART 5

OVERVIEW

Topic: Colours
Exam skills: Consider context, purpose and audience when writing
Assessment Objectives: 2A, 2B, 2C
Vocabulary: Idioms: colours
Grammar: Use the past simple
Practice text type: Formal letter: school sports day
Additional resources: audio player (internet access)

PREPARING THE WAY — PAGE 48

- Tell students to read the chapter topic title and elicit from them what comes to their mind when they think about different colours.
- Ask students to read the questions about colours and discuss them in pairs. If need more support for their discussion, you could write some adjectives and suggested sentence structures on the board (see Key below). You could then ask them to produce brief written responses and compare their ideas with a partner or in groups.
- Colour is an accessibile topic in that it is something everyone has experience of and can express an opinion about. However, talking about the effect of colours involves using more abstract language. To help students, you could model this using the suggested sentence structures in the Key below.

Background Information

The photograph shows the Hindu festival of Holi, which is celebrated in India and Nepal to mark the arrival of spring and to celebrate love and the victory of good over evil. During the festival, people go out into the streets and throw coloured powders and paints at each other. Non-Hindu people around the world are starting to celebrate this colourful festival because it has such universal appeal.

KEY

Suggested adjectives for talking about colour:

dynamic, relaxing, positive, negative, warm, cool, sunny, cheerful, powerful, creative, healing, gloomy

Suggested sentence structures for discussion:

My favourite colour is ... because it makes me feel ... it reminds me of

The colour ... best represents my personality because ...

In ... culture, the colour black is associated with ...

People normally wear ... when ...

The colours I would choose would be ... because ...

Some animals can't see ...

EXTENSION

Students could conduct a class survey using the first, second and fourth questions. The results could be presented in the form of a table or graph.

ACTIVITY 1 — PAGE 48

- Tell students to look at the colour grid. Say the names of the colours aloud and have them repeat after you to practise their pronunciation of any new words.
- For Q1, you could set a short time limit, e.g. one or two minutes, for students to list all the objects they see around them that match each of the colours in the grid.
- Ask students to share their lists. If there are any colours that students cannot see around them, elicit names of any objects or things which are of this colour.
- For Q2, elicit the meaning of the word *rainbow* and give students a few minutes to discuss the questions about rainbows in pairs. You could then ask each pair to share their ideas with the class.

KEY

Students' own answers.

32 UNIT 2: WRITING PREPARATION — WRITING PART 5

FOCUSING ON THE EXAM — PAGE 49

- Ask students to read the text in the box and tell you what they understand for this part of the exam. Writing Part 5 requires students to produce an article, a letter or a report using a semi-formal register, so elicit what they think will be challenging for them.
- Ask students to read the text in the box and tell you what they think will be challenging about this part of the exam.
- Tell students that, as for Writing Part 4, the Writing Part 5 Assessment Objectives (2A, 2B, and 2C) all relate to accuracy and control. Again, punctuation, spelling, use of appropriate register (semi-formal, in this part of the exam) and word choice are important, as is organisation (e.g. paragraphing). Students are also assessed on their use of grammatical structures.
- The Writing Part 5 Assessment Objectives are:
  Assessment Objective 2A: Write using the correct paragraphing, punctuation and spelling.
  Assessment Objective 2B: Write in a range of registers to fit the context and the audience.
  Assessment Objective 2C: Demonstrate a control of a range of vocabulary and a variety of grammatical structures.
- Explain that there is more variety in terms of form for Writing Part 5 than for Writing Part 4. Students may be asked to write an article, a letter or a report. There are also more marks available in Writing Part 5 (20) than in Writing Part 4 (10).
- Tell students that a specific context, purpose and audience will be provided, and the exam skills focus for this chapter focuses on these when writing.

EXAM SKILLS: CONTEXT AND PURPOSE — PAGE 49

- There are definitions in the Glossary on page 244 for words used in this section:
  purpose what something is intended to achieve
  layout the way in which writing and pictures are arranged on a page
  genre a particular type of art, writing, music, etc., which has certain features that all examples of this type share
- Ask students to read the information in the box. Emphasise that they will need to think carefully about the purpose of a piece of writing and the audience (who it is written for) as these are important factors in determining what type of text to produce. You can point out that there are three types of writing that may be required in this part of the exam: letters, reports and articles.
- You could also point out to students that, as Writing Part 5 is a semi-formal task, they need to develop a neutral style which is not familiar, but not excessively formal either.

ACTIVITY 2 — PAGE 49

- This activity is designed to test students' existing knowledge of the three genres of writing that they may be asked to produce in the exam. As well as language use, they need to be aware of features of layout. Showing students authentic examples of letters, articles and reports will help them develop this awareness.
- For Q1a, you can prompt students to consider what each text type looks like and how it is laid out on the page. They should think about the specific layout for the beginning and ending and the use of features such as headings and sub-headings, lists and paragraphs. For Q1b, you can ask students to think about whether the writer is likely to express facts or opinions. You may want to suggest that students organise their notes for Q1 in a table (see Key below).
- For Q2, suggest that students think about when they themselves might write letters, reports or articles and for what kind of audience.

KEY

1

Genre	What to include	What to avoid
letter	a formal opening e.g. Dear Ms X some kind of **closure** a focus on information (within the context of **Part 5**; this is not true of all letters)	your address the address of the person you are writing (not required in the exam)
report	clear organisational features e.g. sub-headings (bullet points may be useful but may not let you demonstrate a sufficient range of grammatical features) a neutral tone	a long introduction an emotional tone humour

WRITING PART 5
UNIT 2: WRITING PREPARATION

| article | clear organisational features e.g. paragraphs a headline/title a focus on information | columns/pictures *Dear Sir/Madam* anything that sounds as if you are making a speech |

Letters:
Layout: must have opening and closing. Normally includes the sender's address at least, but note that these are not needed in the exam.
Language: informal or semi formal.

Reports:
Layout: In paragraphs. May include sub-headings or bullet points.
Language: Semi formal / less personal tone. May include technical language.

Articles
Layout: Headlines, subheading, captions if there are photos, normally follow style of publication. Note that photos, captions, and in most cases subheadings are not required in the exam.
Language: Formality varies, depending on publication. Not too informal. Likely to be about an issue/opinions - no real narrative content.

2 Suggested answers:
Letters
Audience: friends, the editor of a newspaper or school magazine, a teacher, a head teacher.
Context: a response to a job advert, for a classroom assignment, to tell a friend about a life event, to provide an opinion about an event in your home city.
Reports for teacher for homework, for head teacher, to be published in school magazine
Articles: for school magazine, class magazine, or newsletter

ACTIVITY 3 — PAGES 49–50

- Before students read texts A and B, you may want to teach or elicit the meaning of *droplet* (a small drop), *prism* (an object that separates white light into colours) and *breathtaking* (demonstrate by drawing in your breath). If students find the language in the texts difficult, you could read them aloud with the class and explain any complex phrases.
- You could ask students to discuss the questions in pairs, then share their answers with the class, supporting their answers with reasons.

KEY

more factual A
more imaginative B
from a personal account B
from a Science textbook A

ACTIVITY 4 — PAGE 50

- Elicit from students or remind them what lexical words are (the nouns, verbs, adjectives and adverbs which carry the main meaning of a text). Ask them to work in pairs to choose the six most significant lexical words from each text in Activity 3 and write them in the table.
- Check answers with the class and write the lists of words on the board for each text type.
- For Q2, elicit from the students which list would be most suitable for each of the purposes given and why. The for Q3, ask students which list would be most suitable for a report and why.

KEY

1 Text B suggested lexical words: forget (verb), rainbow (noun), truly (adverb), breathtaking (adjective), sight (noun), stopped (verb)
Text A suggested lexical words: tiny (adjective), droplets (noun), form (verb), minute (adjective), prisms (noun), refract (verb)
2 creative writing: B giving information: A
giving personal history: B explaining facts: A
3 A

EXAM SKILLS: CONSIDERING AUDIENCE — PAGE 51

- Tell students that this section focuses on preparing students to adapt their writing for specific audiences.
- You could point out to students that we adapt the way we talk and write every day, depending on who we are talking to. Go through the examples given in the box with students. You could also ask them to come up with some examples of their own.

34 UNIT 2: WRITING PREPARATION — WRITING PART 5

ACTIVITY 5 — PAGE 51

- Put students into pairs to ask and answer the three questions, adapting their responses according to audience.
- Take feedback from the class on this experience and elicit examples from students of the language and expressions used. Remind students that adapting language is just as important in writing as it is in speech.

KEY

Students' own answers.

EXTENSION

- Tell students to make a list of three conversations they have had in the last 24 hours with three different people. Ask them to write down some brief examples of statements they made.
- Ask students to work with a partner and discuss how this language would change if they were conveying the same information but to a different person or group of people. For example, if one statement was made to a friend, how would the same statement be made to a teacher, a police officer, a famous person or a small child?

ACTIVITY 6 — PAGES 51–52

- Tell students that this activity will help them write an article in Writing Part 5 by drawing attention to the key features of this text type.
- Ask students to read Text C and then complete Q1. Go over the answers with the class. Students can then discuss the points in Q2 in pairs. You could ask them to share their ideas for the third question with the class.

KEY

1 article, semi-formal, informative
2 The title means that the teams will play, whatever the weather.
  The audience for the text is local people, especially those with an interest in football and/or the schools involved.

The semi-formal register is suitable because the text is for a wide audience rather than an individual who is known to the writer personally. At the same time, the context (likely a school newspaper), the topic (a school football match) and the purpose (to inform but also to entertain) are not extremely serious, so use of a formal register would not be appropriate.

PRACTICE TIME: WRITING PART 5 — PAGE 52

- Tell students that they will now have the opportunity to practise the exam task. Remind them to look at and follow the Exam Hints and the After Exam Check boxes. If you think it would be helpful, read these aloud with the class after they have had some time to read through the question.
- Elicit from the students which type of text they are being asked to produce (a letter) and elicit or remind them of the letter format conventions they should follow. You could write these on the board along with the three content points that the letter should cover and the word count.
- Give students some time to write their letters. When they have finished, ask them to exchange their letters with a partner and check each other's work against the marking criteria (word count, correct layout and register, covering all the points asked for). Ask students to award each other a mark out of 20 based on how well they think their partner has met these criteria.

KEY

Students' own answers. See Sample answer below and the Writing Guide.

SAMPLE ANSWER FOR PRACTICE TIME:

Dear Ms Amari,

As you are aware, we had to cancel this year's Sports Day because a sudden heavy rain soaked the field and track, making it unfit for play. This rain had not been forecast, so it took everyone by surprise.

The students were extremely disappointed as many of them, especially the runners, had trained very hard. Students of course accepted the circumstances, but were very upset, as they had looked forward to the event for many months.

WRITING PART 5 — UNIT 2: WRITING PREPARATION

In light of this, we would like to reschedule the Sports Day for Thursday 12 July. I have checked the school calendar and there no events or other school trips planned for that day. We will hold the Sports Day on the sports field, and the event will take place from 9.00 a.m. to 1.30 p.m.

I hope this sounds acceptable.

Best regards,

K. Funai
(School Sports Club Representative)

(*148 words*)

HOW DID YOU DO? — PAGE 53

- Read your answer. Did you include information about each of the three bullet points in your answer? Did you write a suitable number of words? Do you think your spelling, punctuation and grammar is correct? Did you write in a suitable register?
- Ask the class what went well and what went less well, and how they think they could improve their performance.

VOCABULARY AND GRAMMAR

VOCABULARY ACTIVITY 1 — PAGE 53

- Before students do this task, ask the class if they know what an idiom is (a phrase that has a particular meaning that is different from the meanings of each word on its own). Then ask them to reread Text C and underline the colour idioms from the activity.
- Ask students to listen to the recording and choose which of the three definitions provided for each idiom is the best match.

AUDIOSCRIPT

1 When the Green Road School football team left school this morning, the students who had to stay indoors were green with envy because it was a beautiful day.
2 The temperature had fallen dramatically during the morning and some of the spectators complained that they were blue with cold!
3 Supporters from both schools were watching the ball intently as players chased it, everyone eager to create a golden opportunity to make the score 2–1.
4 Double rainbows happen once in a blue moon. Everyone cheered and then started playing again.
5 Later on, though, the losing team, St Mark's College, went home red-faced after Green Road scored two goals in the last five minutes.

KEY

1 b 2 a 3 c 4 a 5 c

VOCABULARY ACTIVITY 2 — PAGE 53

- Ask students to work in pairs to match this new set of colour idioms to their definitions.
- Elicit answers from the class. Then ask students to write an example sentence using each idiom. You could ask each pair of students to share their sentences with the class.

KEY

1 see red: feel extremely angry
roll out the red carpet: make extensive preparations for a visit from someone important
show (your) true colours: reveal your real personality and intentions
pass with flying colours: do exceptionally well in a test or exam
2 Students' own answers.

VOCABULARY ACTIVITY 3 — PAGE 54

- Before they begin this activity, ask students to make a list of the colour idioms they have covered in Activities 1 and 2. Then have students complete the diary entry with those idioms.
- When students have finished, check their answers.

KEY

1 blue with cold 2 red-faced 3 green with envy
4 once in a blue moon 5 showed her true colours
6 golden opportunities 7 see red 8 roll out the red carpet 9 passed with flying colours

36 UNIT 2: WRITING PREPARATION — WRITING PART 5

GRAMMAR ACTIVITY 4 — PAGE 54

- Ask students how we form the past simple tense of regular verbs (normally by adding *-ed*). You can tell students that the focus of this activity is on pronunciation of *-ed* endings.
- Explain to students that the *-ed* ending produces three different sounds depending on the final sound of the verb we add it to. The final sound of the verb *-ed* is pronounced as:

  -ed when the verb ends in *t* or *d*, e.g. *needed, visited.*

  -t when the verb ends in an unvoiced consonant (*c, k, f, p, ss, gh, ch, sh* or *x*), e.g. *laughed, washed.*

  -d when the verb ends in a vowel sound or a voiced consonant (*b, g, j, l, m, n, r, w, v, y* or *z*), e.g. *played, retired.*

- You could complete the activity as a class, saying the verbs in the past simple aloud for students to listen and write in the correct columns in the table. When you check answers, ask students to repeat after you.

KEY

Verb *-ed* sound	Verb *-t* sound	Verb *-d* sound
wanted	washed	loved
shouted	danced	retired
visited	coughed	tried
started	relaxed	allowed
directed	liked	played
needed	watched	begged
mended	hoped	closed
irritated	worked	cleaned

EXTENSION

- Ask students to work in pairs or groups to place the following verb endings into a similar table:

  -t, -d, -p, -k, -f, -gh, -sh, -ch, -ss, -c, -x, -l, -n, -r, -g, -v, -s, -z, -b

- This can be done by writing down the verb endings on pieces of paper and having the students sort them into piles, by using a board or with pen and paper.

  -ed sound: *-t, -d*

  -t sound: *-p, -k, -f, -gh, -sh, -ch, -ss, -c*

  -d sound: *-x, -l, -n, -r, -g, -v, -s, -z, -b*

GRAMMAR ACTIVITY 5 — PAGE 55

- Before students attempt this task, you could ask them to read the past simple section of Grammar Reference pages 263–264 to review its structure and use with finished time periods (e.g. *yesterday, last week*) as a speaking activity.
- Ask students to complete the activity individually or in pairs. Remind them to pay attention to whether or not a sentence is positive, negative or a question.
- When you check answers with the class, ensure students understand the difference between *lie* (tell an untruth) and *lie* (as in lie down), and correct any errors in their answers. For pronunciation practice, you could ask students to read aloud the completed sentences.

KEY

1 We met **2** I woke **3** We didn't have **4** the Miami Dolphins won, the Buffalo Bills lost **5** I lied **6** He lay **7** You kept up, I was **8** We held, it didn't change **9** I wrote **10** didn't you paint

GRAMMAR ACTIVITY 6 — PAGE 55

- Give students a short time to prepare for the task, perhaps by writing some notes. You could ask them to make a mind map of the word *holiday* with branches (e.g. *beach, sightseeing, eating, shopping, hotel*) to help them generate ideas and vocabulary.
- Start the activity by telling students about your last holiday, using the past simple and drawing the beginning of a mind map on the board.
- When students are ready, ask them to take turns to tell their partner about their holiday while he or she takes notes. The listening student should try to ask at least two follow-up questions to find out more information. When students have finished, ask them to tell the class about their partner's holiday.

KEY

Students' own answers.

GRAMMAR ACTIVITY 7 — PAGE 55

- Elicit from students the difference between the past simple and the present perfect (finished time periods are used with the past simple, while unfinished time periods are usually used with the present perfect).
- Ask students to fill in the table with the time expressions in the box. Check answers with the class and try to elicit an example sentence for each time expression.

KEY

Past simple	Present simple
yesterday	today
last month	this week
1996	ever
the 90s	this year

EXTENSION

Ask students to add two additional time periods in each column (e.g. *last week* and *2010* for past simple; *this month* and *so far* for present perfect).

GRAMMAR ACTIVITY 8 — PAGE 56

You could ask students to complete the activity in pairs, keeping in mind the difference between finished time periods and unfinished time periods. You could ask students to circle the time expressions in the sentences first to help them.

KEY

1 She broke her foot last week. 2 He has never tried Korean food before. 3 Did you go to the party on Saturday? 4 She has never eaten at that restaurant. 5 Why did you leave France to live here? 6 I spent yesterday making the cake. 7 What time did you arrive? 8 I slept all afternoon last Tuesday. 9 I've started the project but I haven't finished. 10 I painted the room in 2015.

GRAMMAR ACTIVITY 9 — PAGE 56

- Before students complete the sentences, you could ask them to circle any time expressions and make a note of the tense with which they are normally used.
- Then ask them to complete the activity with the appropriate verb forms, paying attention to whether the sentences are positive, negative or questions.

KEY

1 She ate 2 I've twisted 3 Emi hasn't cooked 4 Did you read / Have you read (the current time of day makes a difference here) 5 Ramin has been 6 They ate 7 have you lived 8 Did you like / Tim went 9 They haven't watched 10 Paul has been / I arrived

GRAMMAR GAME: TIME EXPRESSIONS — PAGE 57

- Ask students to follow the instructions to play the game. For the time expressions, students could choose from *last week*, *before*, *on Saturday*, *ever/never*, *yesterday*, *this morning*, *in 2015*, *recently/lately*.
- After students have finished preparing their cards in pairs, put the students into small groups to play the game. Make sure each group has a set of time expression cards and verb cards.
- You could demonstrate how to play by taking a card from each pile yourself and eliciting possible sentences using the verb and the time expression you have drawn.

SELF-EVALUATION — PAGE 57

Tell students to look at the Self-evaluation table and tick the boxes that are true for them. Ask them if there are any topics they don't feel confident about yet.

WRITING PART 6

OVERVIEW

Topic: Speech and communication
Exam skills: Find equivalent expressions for given phrases, identify and paraphrase relevant information in a text, make inferences/predictions about the content of a text, summarise information
Assessment Objectives: 2A, 2B, 2C, 2D
Vocabulary: Verbs: communication
Grammar: Use past continuous and past simple, and *would* and *used to*
Practice text type: Summary (Scientific journal: 'How babies talk')
Addtional resources: dictionaries (internet access)

PREPARING THE WAY — PAGE 58

- Tell students to read the chapter topic title and ask them to think of situations where it is easy or difficult to communicate, e.g. talking to your boss, giving bad news, watching a football game with friends.
- Ask students to read the questions about speech and communication and discuss them in pairs. If students are able to sustain a class or small group discussion, you can ask them to discuss each of the statements in more detail.
- If they need more support for their discussion, you could write some key words and phrases and sentence structures on the board (see Key below). You could then ask students to produce brief written responses and compare their ideas with a partner or in groups.

KEY

Students' own answers. Suggested answers:
Key words and phrases: *facial expression*, *emotion*, *direct contact*, *visual cues*, *distance*
Suggested sentence structures for discussion:
Virtual interaction is more ... but less ... than face-to-face interaction.
I prefer communicating by ... because ...
Sometimes I'm in the mood for communicating by ... but other times I'd rather ...
My friends and I socialise by ... in ...
Social media is ... We often/don't often speak/send/exchange ...
I think/don't think I could survive for more than ... without ... because ...

EXTENSION

Students could research an aspect of speech and communication and present their findings. You could provide them with some suggested topics, e.g.
The history of language, spoken and/or written.
Languages in the world with unusual features.
Languages which are in danger of disappearing.
Language change – how new words enter a language and why words leave it.
The creation of archives to preserve different accents and/or dialects.

ACTIVITY 1 — PAGE 58

- If possible, give students the questions in advance so that they have the chance to find out the answers from older family members.
- Ask students to discuss the questions in pairs. You could then ask students to share with the class any interesting facts they learned about their partner.
- You could also ask them what the differences are between the way they learned to speak their first language as babies and as a child and learning English now.

KEY

Students' own answers.

WRITING PART 6 | **UNIT 2: WRITING PREPARATION** | 39

ACTIVITY 2 — PAGE 59

- Ask students to work in pairs to discuss the list of qualities and rank them according to how important they are in contributing to what makes a person easy to talk to and a good conversationalist (someone who is good at talking to others).
- You could ask students to select the top five most important qualities or to rank the whole list. Consider printing the statements on paper or card and cutting them up into separate slips which could then be moved up and down in the rank order as discussions developed.
- Give students some time to discuss in pairs before you check their ideas a class. Take a class vote on what they consider the top five most important qualities to be. Encourage them to give reasons for their answers.

KEY

Students' own answers.

FOCUSING ON THE EXAM — PAGE 59

- Ask students to read the text in the box and tell you what they think will be challenging for them. You may want to check that they understand the phrases *draw inferences* (use what is implied rather than stated to form an understanding about something) and *make predictions* (use available information to make guesses about the future) before asking what they think will be challenging about this part of the exam. Tell students that the Assessment Objectives for Writing Part 6, like those for Writing Parts 4 and 5, focus on accuracy, organisation and word choice. However, students also need to meet Assessment Objective 2D.
  Assessment Objective 2D: Summarise information provided in text form for a given purpose and audience.
- Explain that Writing Part 6 carries 25 marks and requires students to write a summary based on a text. Make sure that students understand what this task involves.
- To help them achieve this objective, explain to students that in this chapter they will learn about and practise two important exam skills: paraphrasing and summarising. These skills will help them meet Assessment Objective 2D.

- Point out to students that the criteria for the Writing Parts 4 and 5 still apply here. They must consider purpose and audience, cover all the bullet points in the question, and use the correct register.

EXAM SKILLS: FINDING EQUIVALENT EXPRESSIONS — PAGE 59

- Explain to students that successfully presenting given information in a different ways involves substituting words (perhaps using synonyms and altering grammatical structures).
- Point out that changing inflections (the tense or form of a word, whether a word is singular or plural) on words is better than copying them. However, students should aim to introduce their own vocabulary choices to access the higher mark bands.
- You may also want to explain to students that it will not be possible to substitute all key words because there may be no appropriate synonym.

ACTIVITY 3 — PAGE 59

- Draw students' attention to the Exam Hint and, if necesary, encourage them to refer back to the pages listed to revise synonyms and antonyms.
- To help students get started, elicit or suggest some possible answers to Q1, e.g. *There's a good chance that we'll be late.*
- Ask students to work on the sentences in pairs and then share their answers with the class. You could write the most successful sentences on the board and go over them with the class.

KEY

Students' own answers. Suggested answers:
1 There's a good chance that we'll be late.
2 I've never had a slower rail journey in my life!
3 Meet me at seven at my house.
4 It is completely dry in the desert.

UNIT 2: WRITING PREPARATION — WRITING PART 6

EXAM SKILLS: PARAPHRASING AND SUMMARISING — PAGE 60

- There are definitions in the glossary on page 244 for words used in this section:

  inference something that you think is true, based on information that you have

  prediction a statement about what you think is going to happen, or the act of making this statement

  paraphrase to express in a shorter, clearer or different way what someone has said or written

  summarise to make a short statement giving only the main information and not the details of a plan, event or report

- Ask students to read the information in the box. To make sure that they understand the difference between paraphrasing and summarising, you can tell them that paraphrasing involves saying the same thing using different words, whereas summarising involves giving an overview of the main points.
- You may want to explain that summarising the passage provided involves understanding its main idea.
- Point out that summary they write will need to focus on the bullet points. Emphasise that students need to ensure they address the bullet points using information from the text only. They should not introduce information they happen to know from elsewhere.

ACTIVITY 4 — PAGES 60–61

- Explain to students that this activity breaks down a Writing Part 6 summary task into steps to guide them through it. They do not actually have to produce a summary for this activity.
- Draw students' attention to the bullet point below the picture of dolphins and point out that, in the exam, they will have to address three bullet points in their summary.
- Before students read the extract, ask them to read the instructions in the box below the picture. Elicit what information must be included in the summary (one way in which dolphins are able to find out information about their environment) and then ask them to complete Q1.
- You could go through Q2 and Q3 with students as a class or ask them to work in pairs or groups.

KEY

1 The relevant section begins at *Some of these sounds* and finishes at *giving the dolphin important information*.
2 a makes: produces
    sound: noise
    bounces off: rebounds
    whatever: anything/everything/all the things that
    surroundings: environment
  b The noun phrase *a clicking sound* could be shortened to *clicks*.
  c *sound* and *whatever is*
3 a Suggested answer: The student has changed the subject from *sounds* to *dolphins* and substituted *environment* for *surroundings*.
  b Suggested answer: Changing the subject in sentences is helpful for both (e.g. *were being used* can now be *use*).

ACTIVITY 5 — PAGE 61

Read the sample answers aloud with the class. Then ask students to compare them and answer the questions in pairs before checking answers with the class.

KEY

Students' own answers. Suggested response:
- Student B's response is better because it uses more word substitution than Student A's.
- Student B's response moves further away from the text by introducing new language, e.g. *nature of their surroundings* in place of *their environment*, *The sounds strike any object* in place of *bounces off whatever*.
- Student A's is more like a paraphrasing of the original because it substitutes words while relying on the sentence structure of the original. Student B's is more like a summary of the original because it reorganises main ideas from the original.

PRACTICE TIME: WRITING PART 6 — PAGES 62–63

- Tell students that they now have the opportunity to practise a full-length Writing Part 6 exam task. Read the task aloud with the class and tell students to underline the key words in the bullet

WRITING PART 6
UNIT 2: WRITING PREPARATION

points. Encourage them to highlight the corresponding relevant information in the text as they read.
- Remind students to follow the Exam Hints and to use the After Exam Check box to check their work. Also draw their attention to the Watch Out! box which reminds students to focus solely on providing the information required by the three bullet points.

KEY

Students' own answers. See Sample answer below.

SAMPLE ANSWER FOR PRACTICE TIME:

Before the age of nine months all babies, no matter which countries they come from, sound the same. After nine months, the sounds babies make begin to change. At that time, they still cannot produce words, but the noises they make are clearly those of the languages around them.

Experts disagree about child language development. Skinner, for example, thought babies copied the speech of their parents or other people around them. Chomsky, on the other hand, thought babies were pre-programmed to speak. Given enough stimulation, he thought their language would develop naturally. Bruner believed that parents were vital because their feedback allowed the child to learn.

Where a child grows up in a bilingual or multilingual family, I predict they would learn all the languages they are exposed to successfully. I also think they would learn languages better the earlier they hear them.

(143 words)

DIFFERENTIATION

Strengthen: Go through the passage with students to help them locate the information they need to address the three bullet points.
Challenge: Encourage students to attempt the task under exam conditions by setting a time limit.

HOW DID YOU DO? — PAGE 63

- Read your answer. Did you include information about each of the three bullet points in your answer? Did you write a suitable number of words? Do you think your spelling, punctuation and grammar is correct? Did you write in a suitable register?
- Ask the class what went well and what went less well, and how they think they could improve their performance.

VOCABULARY AND GRAMMAR

VOCABULARY ACTIVITY 1 — PAGE 63

- Ask students to discuss the different communication verbs with a partner. Then ask students to find the verbs in the article on page 62. Explain that all of the verbs appear in the article, although some may appear in different forms, e.g. *debates* is a noun in the passage.
- For Q2, encourage students to try and work out the meaning from context, but to use dictionaries for extra help as needed.
- Check answers with the class, if possible eliciting example sentences for each word.

KEY

Students' own answers.

VOCABULARY ACTIVITY 2 — PAGE 63

- Ask students to complete the sentences.
- Elicit the answers and encourage students to explain the reasons for their choices.

KEY

1 tell 2 speak 3 talk 4 say

VOCABULARY ACTIVITY 3 — PAGE 64

Ask students to match the words to the definitions as directed. Make sure they understand that only six of the ten verbs from the box are used.

KEY

1 emphasise 2 communicate 3 reject 4 copy
5 debate 6 praise

UNIT 2: WRITING PREPARATION — WRITING PART 6

VOCABULARY ACTIVITY 4 — PAGE 64

Ask students to choose the correct option from the pairs provided. You could then ask some students to read the sentences aloud to the class to check answers.

KEY

1 emphasise 2 talking 3 communicate 4 say
5 debating 6 speak 7 rejects 8 praises 9 tell
10 copying

VOCABULARY ACTIVITY 5 — PAGE 65

Encourage students to attempt this activity without looking at the verbs on page 63.

KEY

1 praise 2 talk 3 copy 4 debated 5 say 6 rejected
7 told 8 communicate 9 emphasise 10 spoken

VOCABULARY ACTIVITY 6 — PAGE 65

- After students have completed this activity and you have checked their answers, you could ask them to write a sentence using each of the verbs.

KEY

say: something about
speak: to someone
tell: someone, a story, an anecdote, me
talk: to someone

GRAMMAR ACTIVITY 7 — PAGE 65

- Before students complete this task, you might like to give them a short time to read the information about formation and use of the past continuous on Grammar Reference page 264.
- You could go over the first sentence with the class to demonstrate that there may be more than one possible order for the words.

KEY

1 What were you doing when Paul called?/When Paul called, what were you doing?
2 I was sleeping while we were travelling./While we were travelling, I was sleeping. 3 Sarah was running late for work when she dropped her phone./When Sarah dropped her phone, she was running late for work. 4 The band was playing well, but nobody was dancing./Nobody was dancing, but the band was playing well.

> **TEACHING TIPS**
>
> Tell students to note that when we use the 'when' clause first, we must add a comma after it.

GRAMMAR ACTIVITY 8 — PAGE 66

- Tell students that this activity tests their understanding of when to use the past simple and when to use the the past continuous.
- Ask students to attempt to match the situations with the appropriate tenses in pairs and then refer to Grammar Reference pages 263–264 to check any points they are unsure about.
- You could illustrate the point in Q2 with an example sentence in which a longer background action is interrupted by a shorter one, e.g. *I was walking when I met my friend*. For Q6, you could demonstrate two simultaneous actions of equal duration in a sentence, e.g. *I was reading my book while my sister was talking on the phone*.

WRITING PART 6 | **UNIT 2: WRITING PREPARATION** 43

KEY

1 past simple   2 past simple   3 past continuous
4 past simple   5 past continuous   6 past continuous

GRAMMAR ACTIVITY 9 — PAGE 66

- Give students a short time to review the structures of the two tenses and to remind themselves that the past simple uses *did* in questions and negatives whereas the past continuous uses *was* and *were* and the *-ing* form of the verb.
- Elicit the answer to the first question and explain that, in this case, both tenses are possible depending on whether the person was in the middle of lunch at 1 p.m., or started lunch at 1 p.m.
- Ask students to complete the other sentences in pairs and then check answers with the class.

KEY

1 She was eating / She ate   2 were you chatting   3 Rose wasn't doing   4 The coffee tasted   5 I didn't see, I went   6 Femi broke   7 did you have   8 The doctor forgot, I had.   9 You were being, I spoke.   10 I told / I was telling.

EXTENSION

- This activity can be used as a warm-up game for *used to*. Write three true sentences about yourself on the board and one false sentence, e.g.
  I used to have long hair.
  I used to live in Spain.
  I used to play piano every week.
  I used to eat seafood.
- Tell students to ask you questions to try to determine which sentence is the lie (you can invent information to answer these questions). You can then get students to vote on which sentence is false. Ask students to write their own sentences (three truths and a lie) and play the game in groups.

GRAMMAR ACTIVITY 10 — PAGE 67

- Ask students to review Grammar Reference page 267 briefly and clarify the difference between *would* and *used to*.
- Tell students to work through the sentences and identify and correct any errors. You could let them know that half of the sentences are correct and half are incorrect.

KEY

1 correct   **2** correct   **3** I didn't <u>use</u> to eat so many vegetables.   **4** I <u>used to</u> have a dog when I was a child.   **5** correct   **6** I never <u>used to</u> / I <u>would never</u> play video games before I moved here.
7 correct   **8** He <u>didn't always use to</u> have showers.   **9** My friend <u>used to</u> fly his kite when he was a boy.   **10** correct

GRAMMAR GAME: WHAT WERE YOU DOING …? — PAGE 67

- Go through the instructions with students. You can demonstrate how to play by asking and answering questions with a strong student until you find a time when you were both doing the same thing.
- Ask students to play the game in pairs. When they have identified three occasions when they were doing the same thing, you could get them to swap partners.

SELF-EVALUATION — PAGE 67

Tell students to look at the Self-evaluation table and tick the boxes that are true for them. Ask them if there are any topics they don't feel confident about yet.

UNIT 3: LISTENING PREPARATION

LISTENING PART 1

OVERVIEW

Topic: The world of work
Exam skills: Understand the overall message of a spoken text, identify details in a spoken text
Assessment Objectives: 3A, 3B
Vocabulary: Nouns: the world of work
Grammar: Use *wh-* questions and question tags
Practice text type: Conversation: five people talking about restaurants
Additional resources: audio player (internet access)

PREPARING THE WAY — PAGE 70

- Tell students to read the chapter topic title and ask them what jobs they have done or would like to do in future.
- Ask students what are different ways that people communicate at work or in a work setting (meetings, job interviews, chatting with colleagues, talking to the boss).
- Ask students to read the questions about work and discuss them in pairs. If students are able to sustain a class or small group discussion, you can ask them to discuss each one in detail.
- If students need more support, put some key words and phrases on the board (see Key below) and ask them to produce brief written responses and compare their ideas with a partner or in groups.
- You could ask follow-up questions to extend the discussion. For example, you could ask students to give more detail about their ideal job and why this kind of work is appealing and what steps they would need to take to work towards being able to follow this career in future.
- Take feedback from the group and find out what kind of jobs students think they might like to do in future.

KEY

Students' own answers.
Suggested sentence structures for discussion:
Ideally, I would like to be a ... work in the ... industry.
What makes a job fun is having the opportunity to ...
The purpose of work experience is to try ...
Work experience is for + -ing
Useful words and phrases: *to have the opportunity to (do something), to experience, skills, abilities, responsibilities, earn money (a salary)*

EXTENSION

Suggested activities:
- Interview their parents about jobs they have done.
- Interview different members of the school staff about their work (with permission) and write job profiles for them.
- Use a careers advice website.
- Mime a range of different careers for the rest of the class to guess.
- Role-play a job interview.

ACTIVITY 1 — PAGE 70

- Tell students to work in pairs, and ask them to look at the photos. They should take turns to describe each picture, e.g. *There is a group of people. / Some people are sitting round a table. They are talking to each other. On the table there are ...* and use this as the basis for hypothesising about what the people are doing and how they are feeling.
- There is no definite right or wrong answer, other than that the pictures show work-based discussions.
- Take feedback from the class and write the students' ideas on the board.

LISTENING PART 1 | **UNIT 3: LISTENING PREPARATION** 45

KEY

1 Both groups look as if they are working collaboratively in some way, although the seating arrangement in the first picture looks more hierarchical, i.e. there seems to be one leader. Alternatively, he may be being interviewed.
Students' own answers. Suggested answers: Some people are working together./A group of colleagues is having an informal meeting.

2 Students' own answers. Suggested answers: The people are feeling relaxed. They are interested in the discussion. The seating in that picture is less formally arranged, so the situation may be less intimidating.

3 Students' own answers. Suggested answer: I had a job interview when I started my job at the café. I was very nervous because it was the first interview I'd ever had. I was sure I'd say something wrong. The manager was very friendly, though, and she made me feel at ease. She didn't ask many questions and it was all over with quite quickly.

FOCUSING ON THE EXAM — PAGE 71

- Ask students to read the text in the box and tell you what they think will be challenging about this part of the exam.
- The Listening Part 1 Assessment Objectives are:
  Assessment Objective 3A: Understand the overall message of a spoken passage.
  Assessment Objective 3B: Identify essential and finer points of detail in spoken material.
- Explain that Listening Part 1 carries 10 marks and includes a range of short listening texts.
- Go through the range of different question types, including various types of multiple-matching or multiple-choice tasks as well as short-answer questions. Make sure that students understand what this task involves.
- Remind the students that, as in all parts of the exam, it is very important that they set aside the time to read the instructions carefully and follow them correctly. For example, in short answer questions, students are usually asked to write two, three or four words for each answer. They should not write more than the number of words asked for or they will lose marks.
- Tell students that in this chapter they will learn about and practise two important exam skills: listening for the overall message of a text and identifying specific details. These skills will help them meet Assessment Objectives 3A and 3B.

EXAM SKILLS: LISTENING FOR THE OVERALL MESSAGE — PAGE 71

- Ask students to read the information in the box about listening for the overall message or read it together as a class. Then ask students to cover the text and tell you what they need to do when listening to a passage for the first time in order to get the overall idea.
- Emphasise that it is important for students not to panic and lose concentration if there seem to be lots of words they don't understand. They should try to focus on what they do understand and try to build meaning from this.

ACTIVITY 2 — PAGE 71

- Tell the class that it is important to make a distinction between hearing and listening. Ask students to consider how overwhelmed they might feel if they listened carefully to every single sound. In order to avoid this, 'tuning out' some sounds, i.e. hearing them but not listening to them, is sometimes necessary.
- After the discussion activity, ask students to fill in the gaps to check their understanding of the verbs to hear and to listen. Check answers with the class and clarify any problems the students are having.
- Ask students to work in pairs to discuss the listening skills needed for the sentences in Q2. Elicit and discuss answers with the class.

KEY

1 Suggested answer: Listening is more attentive than hearing, which can be accidental. A useful comparison might be made between this verb pair and *to see* and *to watch*.

2 **a** hear **b** listened **c** heard **d** heard **e** listening **f** listened

3 Listening for details: b, e, f
Listening for the overall message: a, c, d

46 UNIT 3: LISTENING PREPARATION — LISTENING PART 1

> **TEACHING TIPS**
>
> **Hint Q2:** As well as selecting the correct verb in terms of meaning, students will need to use the correct inflection/tense, etc.

ACTIVITY 3 — PAGE 72

- For Q1, encourage students to cover a range of different contexts and functions when they make their lists, e.g. being woken up for the day, being greeted by friends, on the bus, in the canteen at lunchtime, in the classroom during lessons. Ask students to consider the purpose of the speaker: Who was the speaker interacting with? What did he/she hope the listener would 'do' with the information (if anything)?
- For Q2, ask students to be honest in evaluating the extent to which they think they were actively listening to the speaker in the different situations they listed in Q1. This activity may encourage students to consider their own listening practices and processes in a different way.
- For Q3, ask students to compare their lists and discuss the similarities and differences. Also ask them to consider why they listen more carefully to some types of speech than others.
- When you take feedback, find out if partners share the same listening priorities. You could ask students if they think the same would be true among students who don't know each other well. Elicit the reasons why students listened to some types of speech more than others.

KEY

Students' own answers.

EXAM SKILLS: LISTENING FOR DETAIL — PAGE 72

- Ask students to read the information in the box about listening for detail or read it together as a class. Then ask students to cover the text and tell you what they need to do. Point out that the equivalent skill in reading is scanning a text, a skill they learned about in the first unit. As with scanning they are trying to find very specific information.
- Elicit the main points: students should listen attentively for facts. Times, dates, places and names may all be helpful, but students should

read the question carefully so that they know exactly what to listen for.
- Highlight the importance of using the correct format for writing detail, e.g. using capital letters for names.

ACTIVITY 4 — PAGE 72

- Tell students that this listening activity requires them to listen carefully for detail to match the information they hear to a written description – in this case related to different jobs.
- Play the recording, more than once if necessary, and ask students to match the speakers with the jobs. Take feedback from the class and ask them to tell you any words and phrases that helped students to identify each job. (See the key words and phrases underlined in the Audioscript.)

AUDIOSCRIPT: Student Book page 287

1. The training for this job is long, but I think it's worth it. I help people every day. The most rewarding thing for me is treating young children and helping them to get well again.
2. My company has built bridges all across Portugal. We are well-known for using environmentally-friendly materials. My personal responsibilities include technical planning and working on site.
3. Sometimes I'm really busy, sometimes not so much. For example, last week I played in four concerts in three different cities, but next week I have none. I do practise for several hours a day, though, and I occasionally give lessons – on three different instruments!
4. I'm working on a case about gender discrimination. It's about an employee. She was unfairly treated because she is a woman. That's not right, is it? I help people fight for their rights and that's rewarding.
5. I get a lot of inspiration from my travels. I look carefully at the very different styles of dress, the variety of fabric, the different use of colour. I think people like my clothes because they're original.
6. My training is intensive. I work out in the gym for three hours every day. I also work with my trainer every day for at least three hours – normally on the tracks. I also have to be very careful with my diet.

LISTENING PART 1 | **UNIT 3: LISTENING PREPARATION** | **47**

KEY

(Clues underlined in Audioscript.)

designer 5 **musician** 3 **athlete** 6
doctor 1 **lawyer** 4 **engineer** 2

PRACTICE TIME: LISTENING PART 1
PAGES 72–73

Section A

- Students now have the opportunity to practise some exam tasks. Remind students to spend time reading the question carefully. Because this is the first Listening Practice Time, they may need some additional support with understanding the exam rubric.

- Check that they understand what they have to do and point out the instructions given for what to do if they change their mind about which box to cross (so that they don't panic if this happens in the exam). The task is to identify which type of eating place each speaker is talking about. As in the previous activity, students will need to understand details in order to establish this.

- Read the list of options aloud with the class and make sure they understand what each type of place is. Elicit what sort of food you might eat there.

- Remind the class to look at and follow the Exam Hints and the After Exam Check boxes. If you think it would be helpful, read these aloud with the class after they have had some time to read through the question.

- Before you play the recording, you might want to pre-teach the more demanding words and phrases: *peckish* (hungry), *selection* (a choice of different things), *to struggle to do something* (to do something with difficulty and only by trying very hard), *to grab something to eat* (to quickly get something to eat), *to linger over a meal* (to take time over eating a meal and not hurry).

- Play the recording twice for students to answer the questions. Tell students that in the exam they will also get the opportunity to hear the audio twice.

AUDIOSCRIPT

1 <u>This is a good place for a break when you're tired of carrying all your bags around</u>. They serve great coffee and cakes, as well as several kinds of snacks in case you're feeling peckish and you can eat and drink in such attractive surroundings. There are flowers and ferns everywhere and the whole setting is really pretty and well-designed.

2 There's not always a great range, but if your priority is to <u>get on with your journey as quickly as possible</u>, it definitely helps with that. It's a convenient way of <u>breaking up long trips</u> – apart from anything else, it <u>provides a change from driving</u>.

3 We had a wonderful meal there and there was a really great selection of dishes on offer. <u>Many places only offer meals that contain meat, so we often struggle to find good restaurants, but this place was a great exception</u> and we'll definitely go back!

4 I always stop off here on my way to work. I get a special 'green' drink, made from <u>apples, green pepper and cucumber</u>, and I think it's delicious! <u>The fruit and vegetables are all very fresh</u> so it's a healthy start to the day. I also like it because you often see the same customers <u>every morning</u> and it's nice to say hello to them as well as to the <u>vendor</u>, of course. He's been at the same spot for fifteen years and is a real character.

5 This is very <u>convenient if you want to grab something quickly when you don't have the time to get out of the car</u>, let alone linger over a meal. It might not be the healthiest food in the world, but some of it does come in a slightly healthier form, like the range of sugar-free drinks. <u>It does have the disadvantage of leaving the car a bit smelly</u>, though.

KEY

(Clues underlined in Audioscript.)

1 G **2** A **3** B **4** F **5** C

48 UNIT 3: LISTENING PREPARATION — LISTENING PART 1

SECTION B 🔊 PAGE 73

- Ask the class to read the rubric and check that students understand what they have to do. Point out that 'no more than four words' means that one-, two-, three-, or four-word answers are acceptable as long as they contain the information required. However, if students write more than four words, they will lose marks.
- Tell students to read the questions and underline the key words. Ask them to think about what kind of information they will be listening for in each case, e.g. a length of time for Q6, adjectives describing personal qualities for Q9.
- Remind the class to look at and follow the Exam Hint and the After Exam Check boxes. If you think it would be helpful, read these aloud with the class after they have had some time to read through the question.
- Before you play the recording, you might want to check the vocabulary related to work, e.g. *staff* (the people that work in a place), *apprenticeship* (a scheme where a person learns a job by doing it), *briefing* (a special meeting to give people information about something), *shift* (a set number of hours, usually eight, within the 24 hours of a day and night in which a person works), *dedicated* (serious and committed). Also check *cleanliness* as it's a key word and students might not recognise that it is related to the adjective *clean* because the pronunciation changes. Some of this vocabulary is reviewed in Vocabulary Activities 1 and 2 in the next section.
- Play the recording twice for students to answer the questions. Tell students that in the exam they will also get the opportunity to hear the audio twice.

AUDIOSCRIPT

Lena: This is probably your first time doing work experience and I'd like to welcome you all to my restaurant. My name is Lena and I've been running this restaurant for <u>over twenty years</u>.

I'm also the manager, so it matters a lot to me that we keep our customers happy. That means providing excellent food and excellent service, and that's only made possible by having a team of really dedicated staff.

Your work experience will last for one week and at the end of that time there may be <u>a job</u> available for anyone who has really impressed me, so you could have the chance to join our dedicated team!

You could also make an application for one of our chef apprenticeships if you're interested in learning to cook.

As this is a restaurant, our first priority is <u>cleanliness</u>, so trainees must wear the uniforms we provide and you need to attend a hygiene briefing provided by Bob, our assistant manager. Our uniforms are made of cotton so that they're practical as well as comfortable and we will provide you with a clean one every day – twice a day if you are doing two shifts! You must also be <u>polite at all times</u>, not just in your dealings with customers, but also in the way you communicate with other staff. A friendly workplace is a happy workplace, isn't it?

You'll need to learn about the different kinds of pizzas we make: thin crust, deep crust, vegetarian and so on. You'll also need to learn how to advise customers who have allergies. One of the great things about working here is that you get your meals provided. If you're not keen on eating pizza every day, don't worry, we also serve <u>delicious salads</u>. Whether you're preparing food in the kitchen, serving customers, or washing up, you'll all have a role to play in our success and providing you with delicious free food is our way of saying thank you for your efforts!

Finally, remember that we sometimes need to take on new full-time and part-time staff, so work hard and you may be offered a contract and become part of our team!

KEY

(Clues underlined in Audioscript.)

6 (for) over twenty years **7** a job **8** cleanliness
9 polite (at all times) **10** (delicious) salads

HOW DID YOU DO? PAGE 74

- Go through answers with the class and tell students to mark their work.
- Ask the class what went well and what went less well, and how they think they could improve their performance.

VOCABULARY AND GRAMMAR

VOCABULARY ACTIVITY 1 PAGE 74

- This activity helps build student vocabulary about the topic area of work and jobs. It is a matching activity, similar in format to other activities students have already done.
- Ask students to skim the definitions and tell you if there are any words they don't understand.
- Ask students to do the task in pairs and then check answers with the class.

LISTENING PART 1 | **UNIT 3: LISTENING PREPARATION** 49

KEY

1 work experience 2 full-time 3 application
4 contract 5 apprenticeship 6 staff 7 uniform
8 workplace 9 briefing 10 manager 11 trainee
12 customer 13 part-time

DIFFERENTIATION

Strengthen: It will make the activity easier if students do not match the definitions in the order they are printed, but instead start with those they find easiest – this will mean they are working from a smaller range of possible answers.

Challenge: Ask students to write three (or more) example sentences for three (or more) words that are new to them or that they find more difficult.

VOCABULARY ACTIVITY 2 — PAGE 75

Ask students to do the task and check answers with the class.

KEY

1 trainee 2 briefing 3 customer 4 application
5 work experience 6 uniform 7 part-time
8 contract 9 full-time 10 apprenticeship
11 manager 12 staff 13 workplace

VOCABULARY ACTIVITY 3 — PAGE 75

- Put students into pairs for this activity. Encourage students to use as much work-related vocabulary from the previous two activities as possible in their discussions. If they haven't had any work experience yet, they can focus on work experience they would like to do.
- Give pairs a few minutes to discuss the questions with their partner before taking feedback from the group. Find out the various different types of work experience the class has had and write the jobs or workplaces on the board.

KEY

Students' own answers.

GRAMMAR ACTIVITY 4 — PAGE 76

- Start by asking students to cover the questions and elicit some typical answers. Then ask students to do the activity and match with the answers given.
- If students have difficulties with the task, encourage them to look at the wording if the question and think about whether the answer should be a place, a person, a time, a reason, etc.

KEY

What are you doing later? Having dinner.
Where are you eating dinner? In town.
Why didn't you eat at home? I didn't have any food in the house.
Who did you eat with? With my family.
How are you finding the meal? Quite pleasant.
When are you eating dinner? At seven.

GRAMMAR ACTIVITY 5 — PAGE 76

- This activity is designed to draw students' attention to the relation between tenses and time periods. Start by reading the time expressions aloud with the class and elicit whether they refer to past, present or future.
- For Q1, give students a few minutes to form the questions, using a variety of different *wh-* words and compare their ideas with a partner. Check answers with the class. Answers will vary, but the most likely tenses for each time period appear below. Accept any correct variants the students offer and correct any tense mistakes they make.
- When students are ready, put them into pairs to take turns to ask and answer the questions they have prepared in Q1.

UNIT 3: LISTENING PREPARATION — LISTENING PART 1

KEY

1 Students' own answers. Suggested questions:
What are you doing at the moment? Where is she working at the moment?
How do you normally get to school? How do you get to school normally?
What did you eat yesterday? Where did the boss go yesterday?
Where are you living this year? Where will you go on holiday this year?
When will you go to school tomorrow? What are you studying tomorrow?

KEY

Students' own answers. Suggested answers:
1 You live near here, don't you?
2 You don't know the answer, do you?
3 You're older than me, aren't you?
4 They're confused, aren't they?
5 She's smart, isn't she?
6 He isn't serious, is he?
7 You've been to the shops, haven't you?
8 He has been to England already, hasn't he?
9 You haven't finished the exercise yet, have you?
10 He hasn't slept enough, has he?

GRAMMAR ACTIVITY 6 — PAGE 76

- As with the previous activity, this activity is designed to draw students' attention to the relation between tenses and time periods.
- Ask students to identify the tense of each sentence before attempting the activity, and also whether the tag is positive or negative.
- Ask students to create their own possible beginnings to the sentence.
- Students' answers will probably vary significantly, but should always correspond to the tense of the question tag. In addition, if the tag is positive, the beginning will be negative. If the tag is negative, the beginning will be positive.

GRAMMAR ACTIVITY 7 — PAGES 76–77

- This activity is designed to help students discover examples of inversion outside of questions. There is a definition in the Glossary on page 244:

  inversion is the act of changing something so that it is the opposite of what it was before, or of turning something upside down

- Draw students' attention to the first example of an inversion circled in the text and ask them to identify the six further examples.
- Check answers with the class and point out the addition of the auxiliary verbs *do* or *did* for the inversions of present simple and past simple phrases.
- Ask students to make a list of the words preceding inversion in the text (*under no circumstances*, *little*, *no sooner*, *not until much later*, *nowhere*, *hardly*, *never*) and ask what they have in common (they all have negative meanings).

LISTENING PART 1 **UNIT 3: LISTENING PREPARATION** 51

KEY

1 See circled words below.
2 See underlined phrases below. Suggested answers:
Under no circumstances had I suspected needs *how* or *that*.
Little did I know needs *that*.
No sooner had I arrived needs *than*.
Not until … did they show me does not need extra phrases.
Nowhere … was there anything does not need extra phrases.
Hardly had I started needs *than*.
Never had the time passed needs an adverb.

Under no circumstances had I suspected how intense my first work experience would be. After I sent the application, I was invited for an interview and they accepted me. I was so happy! Little did I know that it would be one of the most challenging weeks of my life.

No sooner had I arrived than they put me in the kitchen and told me to start arranging the toppings on the pizzas! I don't have any qualifications at all, so I thought they would teach me how to do things on my first day without any pressure, but they just threw me straight in. Not until much later that week did they show me a video about all the correct cooking methods. Nowhere, at any point, was there anything written down to help me.

Anyway, hardly had I started working when they told me that my shift was over! I couldn't believe it. Apparently, I had been working for five hours – it felt like five minutes. Never had the time passed so quickly. So even though it was very challenging, in the end I really enjoyed everything.

GRAMMAR ACTIVITY 8 PAGE 77

- Ask students to identify the sentences as past, present or future and to work out when they are going to need to add an auxiliary verb for the inversion and, if so, which one they will need to add.
- Ask students to write the inversions. Then have them compare their ideas with a partner once they have finished writing.

KEY

1 No sooner had I seen Venice than I fell in love with the city. (*did I see* also acceptable)
2 Under no circumstances will I talk to him again.
3 Little did I know what would happen.
4 Not until later did I realise my mistake.

SELF-EVALUATION PAGE 77

Tell students to look at the Self-evaluation table and tick the boxes that are true for them. Ask them if there are any topics they don't feel confident about yet.

UNIT 3: LISTENING PREPARATION

LISTENING PART 2

OVERVIEW

Topic: Pets
Exam skills: Identify detail in a spoken text, identify viewpoints and attitudes in a listening text
Assessment Objectives: 3B, 3D
Vocabulary: Collocations: health and training
Grammar: Use prepositions of time, place and movement
Practice text type: Presentation: a man giving advice about dog training
Additional resources: audio player, dictionaries (internet access)

In my opinion, animals do/don't have personalities because …
Humans can't/don't … whilst animals can …
I think/don't think/don't know if animals dream because …
Laws should exist to protect animals against …
If I could be an animal, I would be a …
Useful words and phrases: *personality, the ability to …, instinct, cruelty, neglect, to communicate by/with … wings, tails, claws, sense of hearing, sight, smell*

PREPARING THE WAY   PAGE 78

- Tell students to read the chapter topic title and ask them what different pets they know and whether or not they have or have had a pet.
- Ask students what they know about different types of pets, e.g. how to take care of them, what they eat, how much they cost. If there are students who have never had a pet, ask them why and what kind of pet they would like to have.
- If students are able to sustain a class or small group discussion, you can ask them to discuss each of the questions in detail. This is a topic about which students may feel strongly and it may generate some heated discussion, so some sensitivity may be needed.
- If students need more support, put some key words and phrases on the board (see Key below) and ask them to produce brief written responses and compare their ideas with a partner or in groups.
- Take feedback from the group and find out what kind of pets students have at home and what the class's general attitude towards animals and animal welfare is.

KEY

Students' own answers.
Suggested sentence structures for discussion:
I think … make the best pets because they are/have/can/don't …

EXTENSION

Suggested activities:
- Ask students to bring in pictures of their own pets, past and present, and write descriptions of them.
- Debate the merits of different species of pet. Weigh up companionship/cost/intelligence/level of demand/ease of maintenance and so on.
- Research animal welfare laws in students' own country or in others; explore and explain contrasts and differences.
- Write or read a story with an animal at its centre.
- Write a review or evaluation of a film involving animals.

ACTIVITY 1   PAGE 78

- As well as being relevant to the topic of pets, this activity also allows students to revise the grammar topic of superlative adjectives.
- Go through the photos with the class and elicit the word for each animal (rabbit, tortoise, dog, budgerigar, parrot, hamster, goldfish, cat/kitten). Explain that the these are the most common types of animals kept as pets and ask if anyone in the class has another type of animal.
- Check understanding of the adjectives in the box and elicit from students the different ways in which superlatives can be formed.
- Compare results with the class at the end of the activity and find out which animal wins the most categories.

LISTENING PART 2 | **UNIT 3: LISTENING PREPARATION** | 53

KEY

Students' answers may vary. Suggested answers:
a cutest **b** slowest/oldest **c** most intelligent/cleverest **d** prettiest **e** best at talking/loudest **f** fluffiest/cutest **g** best at swimming **h** cutest/most intelligent/cleverest

FOCUSING ON THE EXAM — PAGE 79

- Ask students to read the text in the box and tell you what they think will be challenging about this part of the exam.
- The Listening Part 2 Assessment Objectives are:
  Assessment Objective 3B: Identify essential and finer points of detail in spoken material.
  Assessment Objective 3D: Identify a speaker's viewpoint and attitude, stated and implied.
- Explain that Listening Part 2 carries 10 marks and is based on a longer listening text, often a monologue of some kind such as a presentation, lecture or radio broadcast.
- Go through the different type of tasks for Listening Part 2 mentioned in the box. Make sure students understand what this task involves.
- Remind students that, as in all parts of the exam, it is very important that they set aside the time to read the instructions carefully and follow them correctly. For example, they may need to complete sentences within a specified number of words.
- Point out that there is time allocated for reading the question before students hear the recording, but that they will be expected to write their responses as they listen. This is why it's important for students to be well-prepared and clear about what they are listening for.
- As in the other listening tasks, they will hear the recording twice.
- Tell students that in this chapter they will learn about and practise two important exam skills: identifying specific details and identifying implied viewpoints and attitudes. These skills will help them meet Assessment Objectives 3B and 3D.

EXAM SKILLS: IDENTIFYING DETAIL — PAGE 79

- Ask students to read the information in the box about listening for detail or read it together as a class. Then ask students to cover the text and elicit the main points back from the class. Point out again that the equivalent skill in reading is scanning a text, a skill they learned about in the first unit.

- Draw students' attention to the point about listening for key words and ask them how to identify the key words for each task. Elicit that they will be able to find key words in the question and that it is useful to underline these.

ACTIVITY 2 — PAGE 79

- Tell students to read Q1 and identify the context of the recording (a pet show). Ask them what they think happens at pet shows (pet owners *show* their animals to an audience and can be awarded prizes in different categories, e.g. for looking good, performing certain tasks).
- Before playing the recording, ask students to think about the different sorts of animals people keep as pets and the words that might be used to describe them. You might also want to check some of the vocabulary, e.g. *jungle* (a forest in hot, tropical countries where the trees grow close together, such as the Amazon jungle), *contender* (someone who is taking part in a competition), *show off something* (show something in a way that tries to get people to admire it), *exception* (something that is different from all the others).
- Play the recording the first time and elicit what the four animals are. Then give students time to read the questions for Q2 and check understanding of vocabulary. Play the recording again for students to complete the activity and check answers with the class.

AUDIOSCRIPT: Student Book page 287

1 First up in the arena, we have one fine creature! He can <u>fly</u> high above the <u>jungle treetops</u> and there's no way you could miss his amazing <u>bright colours</u> …

2 And next! Please welcome one of nature's most <u>elegant animals</u>. <u>Ancient Egyptians worshipped them</u> as a god and <u>a black one might bring you bad luck if you're superstitious</u>! This beauty is only three months old, but she's already outshining all others in her category …

3 OK, now here's one <u>fluffy</u> friend that will have you <u>'jumping'</u> with excitement! Those <u>long ears and strong legs</u> are just perfect for this little guy to hear you from a mile away and run off at any sign of danger! And who says that this one only eats carrots? This fine specimen eats a whole lot more …

4 If you're a <u>water</u> fan, you'll love this next contender! This <u>golden</u> female just loves to shake her <u>tail</u> and show off her colour. Some people say that these creatures don't have much memory, but this lady is an exception, I can tell you …

54 UNIT 3: LISTENING PREPARATION — LISTENING PART 2

KEY

(Clues for Q1 underlined in Audioscript.)
1. parrot, cat, rabbit, goldfish
2. 1c 2a 3b 4b

TEACHING TIPS

Hint Q1: It may be helpful, after the activity, to provide students with a copy of the Audioscript to get students to underline the lexical words so that they can see how helpful they are in identifying the answer. For example, in the first script: *fine creature, fly, high, jungle treetops, amazing, bright colours*. Even without understanding the sentences as a whole, the lexical words suggest that the correct answer is parrot.

Hint Q2: Tell students to read the questions before they listen. Also advise them to use the second time they hear the recording to confirm their first answers.

EXAM SKILLS: IDENTIFYING VIEWPOINTS (STATED AND IMPLIED) — PAGE 79

- Check that students understand the difference between stated and implied. There are definitions in the Glossary on page 244 for words used in this section:

  to state to formally say or write a piece of information or your opinion

  implied not stated openly, but understood to exist or to be true

  viewpoint a particular way of thinking about a problem or subject

  Elicit or tell the class that when something is *implied* it is not said directly but indicated by tone of voice, context and other remarks that the speaker makes on the subject. The lexical words will help students to identify factual detail and explicitly stated viewpoints. However students will need to think more carefully about what they hear to understand implied meaning.

- Ask the class to read the information in the box or read it together with the group. Then ask students to cover the text and tell you the main points.

- Elicit that thinking about the impact the speaker is trying to have on the listener will help students to work out implied meaning.

ACTIVITY 3 — PAGE 80

- This activity is designed to help make students aware of the different kinds of information they are hearing.

- Ask students to discuss Q1 in pairs for a short time and then elicit definitions of stated vs implied meaning. Give some more examples of your own, e.g. *It is cold today.* vs *I should probably put on another jumper.*

- When you think students have got the idea, ask them to put the statements into the correct columns and check answers with the class.

KEY

1. Stated information is said directly. Implied information is hinted at.
2. **stated information:** b, d
   implied information: a, c

ACTIVITY 4 — PAGE 80

- Although there are several stages to this activity, the audioscript is relatively short so students do not have a large amount of information to process.

- Make sure students understand the context. Explain what a dog trainer if necessary, then give students time to look through the table. Answer any questions they have about vocabulary.

- Students will need to consider each of the four pieces of information from the recording twice – once to decide whether it is true or false, and the other to decide whether it has been stated or implied. They will then need to use the correct symbol to complete the table.

- Before you play the recording, explain what a dog *lead* is (you can draw one on the board). Play the recording twice for students to complete the table and check answers with the class.

- Play the recording a third time for students to consider which words or phrases helped them answer the question and note these down.

AUDIOSCRIPT: Student Book page 287

Dog Trainer: Dogs enjoy activity and most dogs need several walks a day. That's <u>good news for dog owners like me who love hiking</u>. <u>Older dogs may need shorter walks</u> but they will still enjoy a change of scene. It is important that you exercise your dog in a safe place and that you always know where it is. <u>Even if your dog behaves well off-lead, other dogs might not!</u>

Walking your dog at night will bring its own challenges. Some dogs may not be seen very easily so it is important to make them visible to others in some way.

LISTENING PART 2 — UNIT 3: LISTENING PREPARATION

KEY

(Clues underlined in Audioscript.)

1 T ✗   2 T ✓   3 T ✗   4 F ✓   5 T ✗

Students' own answers. Suggested words and phrases underlined above.

PRACTICE TIME: LISTENING PART 2
PAGES 80–81

- Students now have the opportunity to practise some exam tasks. Remind them to spend time reading the two tasks carefully and check that they understand what they have to do.
  Point out the instructions given for what to do if they change their mind about which box to cross in the second task so that they don't panic if this happens in the exam.
- Students are going to hear a short talk about dog training. Before playing the recording, you might want to check the meaning of the more specialised vocabulary items related to this topic, e.g. *breed* (a type or race of dog), *agility training* (training that gets the dog to move around, run, jump and perform different tasks), *to stick to something* (to continue doing it and not change), *territory* (a place or area that is considered to belong to someone), *come to heel* (when a dog comes to walk or sit just behind its owner), *shift* (move), *reinforcement* (the process of making something stronger), *obedience* (the fact that people or animals do what they are told to do).
- Remind the class to look at and follow the Exam Hints and the After Exam Check boxes. If you think it would be helpful, read these aloud with the class after they have had some time to read through the question.
- When students are ready, play the recording twice so they can complete and check each task.

AUDIOSCRIPT

Sean: Hi, I'm Sean Daly. I'm a professional dog trainer and I'm going to give you some tips for training your dog successfully.

Let's start with some ground rules. It's really important that you <u>show your dog who's in charge right from the start</u>. For example, once he or she develops bad habits, it can be very difficult to break them. It may be tempting to let your dog sit on the sofa next to you, especially when they're a puppy, <u>but once the dog sees the sofa as their territory, it can be very difficult to shift them</u>. You don't want to end up with your clothes and <u>furniture</u> covered in dog hair!

You need to be firm with your dog, but you also need to be consistent. <u>If you start feeding the dog every time you eat, they'll come to expect it. Some dogs make a real nuisance of themselves at meal times</u> – again, it's much better not to let them get into bad habits.

You can train your dog to do many things, but <u>you must be prepared to put in the hours</u>. You'll be working together a lot and that will definitely improve the bond between you. You should also remember that <u>you'll need to be patient</u>. If you can manage that, then you should certainly see positive results.

Remember that dogs learn through positive reinforcement – if you <u>praise them for obeying a command</u> like 'sit', for example, they will associate praise with obedience and are more likely to sit on command. As well as 'sit', there are lots of other commands you can teach your dog. Some dogs can be trained to fetch items and many can also be taught to 'stay' and to <u>come to heel</u> when the owner tells them to. It's a pleasure to watch a well-trained dog and, of course, some dogs even go on to do agility training, which is the area most of my work is focused on. Agility training involves the dog having to run around obstacles, jump over small hurdles and travel through specially-made tunnels. Agility training is often associated with certain breeds, such as collies and Alsatians and it's true it's ideal for these dogs. Other breeds can do agility training too and benefit from it, but collies and Alsatians are perfect candidates because they tend to be very clever and to have <u>high energy</u> levels. The most important thing is that the activities are appropriate for the dogs' health, age and general fitness level. <u>It's always wise to check with your dog's </u><u>vet</u> before starting your dog on any kind of training programme.

One thing that's crucial with agility work – and indeed with any kind of training – is the relationship between a dog and its owner. I feel that this cannot be neglected. <u>There has to be mutual trust and this is something that is built up gradually over time. I would say, don't expect to get instant results!</u> Remember that any kind of training needs to be tailored to the individual dog, and older dogs and younger ones will tire out quite easily.

The best dog I've ever trained for agility is my current dog, Wolfgang, who is a Carpathian Shepherd dog. He was a rescue dog and wasn't in the best state of health. The rescue centre had looked after him really well, but his life on the streets before had left him severely underweight.

As time went on, though, he built his strength up and I started realising what <u>an amazing mind</u> he had. <u>Wolfgang is definitely the cleverest dog I've known.</u> Before long he was winning prizes and trophies all over the country. It just shows you: anything is possible!

KEY

(Clues underlined in Audioscript.)

11 start   12 sofa/furniture   13 meal times
14 time (and) patience   15 commands   16 heel
17 high energy levels   18 vet   19 C   20 B

UNIT 3: LISTENING PREPARATION

LISTENING PART 2

DIFFERENTIATION

Strengthen: Allow students to listen to the recording an additional time, so that they get more used to the task and format.

Challenge: Ask students to write a summary of the passage, suitable for a Part 6 Writing task. Bullet points could be linked to: training puppies, general training and agility work. The third point should be inference or prediction-based to mimic a Part 6 Writing task.

KEY

1 **a** iv **b** ii **c** i **d** vi **e** viii **f** vii **g** ix **h** x **i** iii **j** v
2 **i** c refuge for animals   **ii** b Praising   **iii** i extremely thin   **iv** a negative behavioural patterns   **v** j (very) well-suited   **vi** d physical power and enthusiasm   **vii** f immediately   **viii** e have confidence in each other   **ix** g teaching of new skills   **x** h physical condition

HOW DID YOU DO?   PAGE 81

- Go through answers with the class and tell students to mark their work.
- Ask students what went well and what went less well, and how they think they could improve their performance.

VOCABULARY ACTIVITY 2   PAGE 83

- This activity helps students to consolidate their understanding of collocations from the previous two activities.
- Ask students to read and complete the sentences individually. Then have them compare their ideas with a partner before checking answers with the class.

EXTENSION

Write a letter to Sean Daly explaining the problems you are having in training your own dog using the methods he suggests.

KEY

1 instant results   2 severely underweight
3 ideal candidate   4 bad habit   5 mutual trust
6 energy levels   7 positive reinforcement   8 training programme   9 rescue centre

VOCABULARY AND GRAMMAR

VOCABULARY ACTIVITY 1   PAGE 82

- This activity revisits some of the text for the Audioscript and gets students to match information from it with similar statements. It tests students' understanding and helps consolidate their vocabulary.
- Tell students to work in pairs to read extracts a–j to familiarise themselves with their meanings. Tell them to pay particular attention to the bold words and to think of possible synonyms for them. Encourage them to use a dictionary to look up any of the words or phrases that they can't understand from the context.
- When students have completed Q1, ask them to underline the parts of the sentences that are similar to the bold words in the extracts.
- Check answers with the class.

DIFFERENTIATION

Strengthen: Write the collocations on the board for students to select the answers from. You could add two or three extra ones as distractors to increase the level of difficulty.

Challenge: Ask students to select three collocations that are new to them or that they find the most challenging and write example sentences.

GRAMMAR ACTIVITY 3   PAGE 83

- This is a straightforward gap-fill activity consolidating students' knowledge of prepositions of time.
- Ask the students to complete the questions in pairs. They can check Grammar Reference page 281 if there's anything they are not sure of.
- Confirm answers with the class.

LISTENING PART 2 — **UNIT 3: LISTENING PREPARATION** 57

KEY

1 in **2** at **3** on **4** in **5** at **6** at **7** in **8** in

GRAMMAR ACTIVITY 4 — PAGE 84

- This activity allows students to revise prepositions of place and movement in context. You can tell students that there is sometimes more than one possible answer.
- Ask the students to complete the speech in pairs and check anything they are not sure of on Grammar Reference pages 281–282.
- Confirm answers with the class. The answers given below are the most obvious ones but variations are possible.

KEY

1 to **2** in **3** to **4** into **5** around/round **6** over
7 through **8** to **9** by/near/next to/behind
10 next to/behind/in front of/near
11 in/behind/next to/in front of/near/by

GRAMMAR ACTIVITY 5 — PAGE 84

- Tell students to ask you about any words they don't know the English for in the pictures. Check *log* in Picture c and *coral* in Picture d.
- Give students a few minutes to write one or two sentences for each picture using a range of prepositions.

KEY

Students' own answers. Suggested answers:

a The trainer is running beside his dog. The dog is nearly a metre above the ground.
b There's a dog behind the hamster. The dog is between the kitten and the rabbit.
c There are two carrots in front of the rabbit. The rabbit is crawling through a piece of wood.
d There's a fish in a shell. The fish is swimming out of a shell.
e The dog is running through the water. The dog is running towards a yellow ball.

GRAMMAR ACTIVITY 6 — PAGE 85

Ask students to read the sentences and complete them with the correct prepositions. Then check answers with the class.

KEY

1 a **2** c **3** b **4** d **5** a **6** b **7** c **8** b **9** b **10** a

GRAMMAR GAME: PLACE THE OBJECT — PAGE 85

- Follow the instructions in the Student Book to play the game. Demonstrate how to play with the whole class by giving example sentences and asking a student or students to put their pencil or other object in the locations you describe.
- When you are satisfied that students have got the idea, put them into pairs to play. At the end of the game, elicit from the class which student has won the most points in each pair and who has the most points overall in the class.

SELF-EVALUATION — PAGE 86

Tell students to look at the Self-evaluation table and tick the boxes that are true for them. Ask them if there are any topics they don't feel confident about yet.

UNIT 3: LISTENING PREPARATION

LISTENING PART 3

OVERVIEW

Topic: Games
Exam skills: Consider the difference between statements and implications, identify facts and opinions, including stated and implied opinions
Assessment Objectives: 3C, 3D
Vocabulary: Adjectives and adverbs
Grammar: Use adverbs of frequency and intensifiers
Practice text type: Interview: a writer talking about a book he has written
Additional resources: audio player (internet access)

PREPARING THE WAY — PAGE 87

- Tell students to read the chapter topic title and elicit from them what their favourite games are.
- Ask students what games are most popular in their countries. You can ask whether they grew up playing these games or if anyone in their family enjoys playing these games.
- If students are able to sustain a class or small group discussion, you can ask them to discuss each of the questions in detail. (You may need to explain that the term *gaming* in the second question means playing computer games).
- If students need more support, put some key words and phrases on the board (see Key below) and ask them to produce brief written responses and compare their ideas with a partner or in groups.
- Take feedback from the group and elicit the names of all the different kinds of games they can think of and have talked about. Write these on the board and find out which is/are the class's favourite game or games.

KEY

Students' own answers.
Suggested sentence structures for discussion:
A game can be ... whereas a sport ...
I like/don't like gaming because I find it ...
I enjoy/don't enjoy ...
The most popular games in my country are probably ...
Useful words and phrases: *indoors/outdoors, physical activity, board game, card game, computer game, players, competitive, fantasy, for fun, the winner, winning, take turns*

EXTENSION

Suggested activities:
- Produce a written project and/or spoken presentation on a sport or game, explaining features such as its history, rules, cost, equipment, competitive status.
- Design a new sport and produce a set of rules for it. Students could consider: the pitch or play area, equipment, e.g. hoops, court markings, number of players, how long the game is played.
- Design a new computer game. Write instructions explaining how to play it, including a summary of the story line, monsters encountered, rewards and so on.
- Alternatively, the new sport or computer game could be the basis of a spoken presentation, where students have to 'pitch' their ideas to others in the class; this could be done as a competition if desired.
- Students could write an article reporting on a school sports match or sports day event at their school, or one that they have watched.
- Students could write a personal account of a sporting or gaming event which went particularly well or badly, e.g. winning a hockey match, being defeated by a 'boss' multiple times in a computer game.

ACTIVITY 1 — PAGE 87

- Go through the dates in the box with the class and revise the pronunciation as necessary. Note that in Western calendars, AD (for the Latin phrase *Anno Domini* meaning 'in the year of the Lord' is often replaced by CE, 'common era'.
- Give students some time to identify the different types of games and think how to describe them. Then ask students to match with the dates.
- Check answers with the class. You can tell students that although the dates given here for when the games were first played are widely accepted, there is some disagreement around the origins of some of these games.

KEY

a (early version of chess) around AD 500
b (golf) 1400s   **c** (computer games) 1950s
d (ice hockey) 1700s   **e** (computer games on phones) 1990s   **f** (card game) 868

LISTENING PART 3 | UNIT 3: LISTENING PREPARATION

FOCUSING ON THE EXAM — PAGE 88

- Ask students to read the text in the box and tell you what they think will be challenging about this part of the exam.
- The Listening Part 3 Assessment Objectives are:
  Assessment Objective 3C: Understand a conversation where information is being negotiated and exchanged.
  Assessment Objective 3D: Identify a speaker's viewpoint and attitude, stated and implied.
- Explain that Listening Part 3 carries 10 marks includes a range of longer listening texts.
- Go through the different types of task in Listening Part 3 mentioned in the box. Make sure students understand what this task involves.
- Tell students that in this chapter they will continue to practise understanding information that is being negotiated and exchanged and identifying attitudes and viewpoints (stated and implied).

EXAM SKILLS: STATEMENTS AND IMPLICATIONS — PAGE 88

- There are definitions in the Glossary on page 244 for words used in this section:
  explicit expressed in a way that is very clear and direct
  implicit suggested or understood without being stated directly
- The focus here is on statements versus implications. Ask students to read the information in the box and elicit or tell the class what the difference is.
- Tell students again that when something is *implied* it is not said directly but indicated by tone of voice, context and other remarks that the speaker makes on the subject.
- Ask students why people sometimes don't say things directly and elicit that this is may be because they are trying to avoid giving offence and/or bad news.

ACTIVITY 2 — PAGE 88

- This activity requires students to match what is being said with what is being hinted at. Demonstrate the idea by saying a sentence such as, *It's very hot here, isn't it?* to imply that you want to open a window. Then try to get students to understand this implication by, for example, fanning your face, loosening your collar whilst looking pointedly at the window.

- Give students a minute to read through the sentences in Q1 and try to guess what words might go in the gaps. Then play the recording for students to listen and complete the sentences.
- For Q2, put students into pairs and ask them to match the completed sentences with the implied or hidden meanings in sentences a–f.
- Check answers with the class.

AUDIOSCRIPT: Student Book page 286

1 There's <u>a slight problem</u> with the antique vase I took to the auction house.
2 I managed to beat <u>my personal best</u> for push-ups at the gym today.
3 These cookies are really great. Your cooking <u>is definitely</u> improving.
4 You <u>might want</u> to reconsider that hairstyle.
5 I'm not sure an elephant <u>is really the</u> best pet for you at the moment.
6 I've <u>tidied up</u> the whole house because you didn't get round to it.

KEY

(Clues underlined in Audioscript.)
1 1 a slight problem   2 my personal best
   3 is definitely   4 might want   5 is really the
   6 tidied up
2 1 c   2 d   3 e   4 b   5 f   6 a

ACTIVITY 3 — PAGE 89

- Read the example given and, if possible, offer students some further examples of people expressing themselves indirectly, e.g. *Your cat certainly seems to enjoy his food.* could be a way of saying *I've never seen such an overweight creature in my life!*
- Ask students to think of three to five examples of their own of indirect ways to say that they want or need something or that something bad has happened.
- When they are ready, students take turns to read their sentences aloud for their partner to guess what they really want to say.

KEY

Students' own answers.

EXAM SKILLS: FACTS AND OPINIONS
PAGE 89

- Ask students to read the information in the box about facts and opinions. Tell students to close their books and summarise the information.
- Elicit that facts are objective and measurable and can be checked or verified, whereas opinions, which can be stated directly or implied, are subjective views.

ACTIVITY 4 PAGES 89–90

- Invite students to reflect on the context of the text before they start the activity, which is based on a report for a football match. Elicit the fact that if a reporter supports one team over the other, the report may be biased.
- Discuss with the class which aspects of a football match are factual, e.g. the number of players, the identity of the teams and referee, the length of the game, the number of goals scored. Contrast them with those aspects which are opinion-based, e.g. whether the victory was deserved, how well each team played, the competence and performance of managers, goalkeepers and individual players. These could be written on the board in two columns.
- To help students further, you could advise them to watch out for 'emotional' words and/or words that are opinion-based.
- Put the class into pairs to discuss the questions for Q1.
- Check answers with the class and then ask them to write a summary of the writer's opinions.

KEY

1 Students' own answers.
  Underlined words in the text below give clues about the writer's opinion.
2 Students' own answers. See Sample answer below.

SAMPLE ANSWER FOR QUESTION 2:

Whe writer supports Mistley United. We know this because of the language he uses, even though he does not directly say <u>I am a Mistley United fan</u>. He praises the Mistley United team and uses positive words to describe them (like <u>Mighty</u>). The team lost the match, and the writer's language shows that he thinks this result was unfair. He also talks about <u>our lads</u>. Most of the opinions words in this text are adjectives and adverbs.

THE MIGHTY MISTLEY HAVE BEEN ROBBED!

Weeley Wanderers 3 – Mistley United 0

Weeley Wanderers edge cup final in complete sham.

The <u>glorious</u> Mistley United's series of victories came to an end today after a <u>calamitous</u> string of events led to an <u>undeserved victory</u> for Weeley Wanderers.

The heroic Mistley players battled <u>fiercely</u> for the whole 90 minutes, but ultimately were unable to take the win <u>they so thoroughly deserved</u>.

The first key moment of the game came in the tenth minute, when <u>our boy</u> Tom Mathews was <u>unfairly</u> sent off after the referee <u>wrongly</u> called for a handball when the ball <u>clearly</u> came into contact with his chest. <u>What a joke!</u>

And because of that, Weeley got a penalty and scored their first goal, <u>putting our lads up against the wall</u>.

Our luck <u>didn't get any better</u> when the next goal for Weeley came soon after: I blame the bad weather, several <u>questionable</u> decisions from the referee and an <u>oddly-weighted</u> ball. In the second half, things got <u>worse</u>. Manager James Humphries tried to save the day with some tactical and timely substitutions, <u>but unfortunately luck, rather than skill,</u> played a bigger part in the result.

The referee must have been <u>blindfolded</u> when he sent off Max Green, Mistley's <u>inspirational</u> captain. The <u>filthy</u> Weeley striker <u>deliberately</u> fell to the ground, he hadn't even been touched! In the final 15 minutes, we had <u>our heads in our hands</u> when Weeley scored again. I'd say the game was an utter <u>sham!</u>

A <u>tragic</u> day indeed, but heads up! Next year <u>that cup will be ours!</u>

LISTENING PART 3 **UNIT 3: LISTENING PREPARATION**

PRACTICE TIME: LISTENING
PART 3 🔊 PAGES 90–91

- Students now have the opportunity to practise some exam tasks. Remind them to spend time reading the two tasks carefully and point out that they do not need to write in full sentences for the first task. Words or short phrases will suffice, providing they give the necessary information.
- Point out the instructions given for what to do if they change their mind about which box to cross so that they don't panic if this happens in the exam.
- Students are going to hear an interview with the author of a book about the positive and negative effects of video games (or gaming). Before playing the recording, you may want to check the meaning of the more demanding vocabulary items, e.g. *multi-tasking* (doing several things at the same time), *spatial awareness* (the skill of understanding how objects within a particular space relate to each other and how to manipulate them and move them around), *reaction speed* (how quickly you react to what happens around you), *an impact* (an effect or result).
- Remind the class to look at and follow the Exam Hint.
- When students are ready, play the recording twice so they can complete and check each task.

TEACHING TIPS
Hint Q1: Advise students to read the questions first.
Hint Q2: Remind students to listen out for opinions as well as facts.

AUDIOSCRIPT
Monica: Today I'm very happy to welcome writer Lance Worthington here to the studio.
Lance: Thank you very much, Monica.
Monica: Now, Lance, you've just written a book about the impact of video games on young people. What got you interested in the topic?
Lance: I wanted to find out the truth. Video games were getting really bad press and I wondered what that was based on – something that was real, or just people's perceptions.
Monica: I see. Interesting. And what did you discover?
Lance: Well, I think people are right to be cautious. Any activity pursued to excess can be dangerous and video games are no exception.
Monica: Any activity?
Lance: Sure. Even something like fitness training would cause problems if you did too much of it.
Monica: True. So, what did you find out?
Lance: Well, interestingly, it was the notion of 'use' and 'overuse' that was most significant. There's nothing really bad about gaming itself – it's the fact that it can be so addictive that causes problems.
Monica: You say there's nothing really wrong with gaming, but some people would challenge that. Doesn't it sometimes cause a lot of anger, when players get frustrated about not winning? How can that be good for people?
Lance: Well, it may surprise you to know: studies have been done which suggest that one of the benefits of gaming is that players learn to tolerate anger and frustration. In fact, statistically, players' frustration levels can rise by as much as 80%. But I don't think that's a bad thing. We all have to deal with frustration sometimes. It's an important life lesson.
Monica: That's very interesting.
Lance: And again, I come back to my point about sensible usage. People need to be careful with how much time they spend on gaming. It's certainly the case that some people do get sucked into the gaming world and it has a negative impact on other areas of their life. Studies, work, relationships – all of these things can suffer.
Monica: Yes, I'm sure a lot of people would agree with you on that.
Lance: One thing I believe, however, is that even if gaming may have a negative impact on relationships, I don't think it necessarily has a negative impact on learning – at least if games aren't played to excess.
Monica: Oh? Can you say a bit more about that?
Lance: Well, it seems to me that 'learning' is a much wider concept than just what we learn in school and how to pass exams. Learning for me means firstly gaining a wider knowledge of the world we're living in.
Monica: Yes, I see what you mean, but how does that link with gaming?
Lance: Often games open you up to other cultures,

other worlds. <u>They show you different perspectives</u> and even different landscapes you wouldn't normally see. This is great, especially for widening young people's knowledge of the world!

Monica: I'm with you now. So, you're saying that gaming can enrich young people's experiences?

Lance: Exactly. I'd say secondly, that as well as developing your mind, gaming helps us to develop other, more physical skills, such as motor skills, hand-eye coordination …

Monica: Interesting. Can you say a bit more about that?

Lance: Well, when you're playing a game, <u>spatial awareness is key and how fast you can move your fingers and thumbs is also critical, of course! The speed of your brain sending impulses to your body is greatly improved through gaming</u>.

Monica: I suppose all of that makes sense. So, players have a lot going on at once and have to react quickly, don't they?

Lance: Yes, playing games can help to speed up reaction time, for example when multi-tasking. This is probably because video games operate on several levels simultaneously. You might be trying to solve a puzzle by moving three-dimensional objects while listening to spoken instructions, or while watching out for random enemies. It's all good training. Which is why a lot of research is being done into using games as a way of keeping the brain active as people get older.

Monica: So, there may be possible benefits we haven't really grasped yet?

Lance: That's correct, yes. But on the other hand, there may be problems we haven't uncovered yet too. We need to keep an open mind regarding negative impacts as well as positive. One issue is that young people nowadays tend to exercise less than was the case a few years ago. Video games can be unhelpful there, because …

Monica: Because teenagers are all busy sitting in their rooms glued to their games consoles <u>rather than going out and kicking a ball around a park</u>?

Lance: Exactly. There was a trend for games that encouraged you to exercise in your own home and <u>even had ways of tracking your progress, which could help you to gradually build up fitness levels</u>. But these are sadly not as popular any more. Now, at least there are games that get people outside, looking for clues and objects, so that's something!

Monica: <u>Yes, that's a great way to get people outside in the fresh air, isn't it?</u>

Lance: Exactly! So, I'm quite excited about the way gaming is going. It can definitely offer all sorts of benefits. <u>There are so many new ideas coming through all the time</u>. Personally, I think the gaming industry will make positive contributions to society in general.

Monica: Well you've convinced me at least! I'd like to thank you for your time and wish you all the best with the upcoming book launch!

Lance: Thanks Monica. It's been a real pleasure.

KEY

(Clues underlined in Audioscript.)

(Note students' answers may vary.)

21 to find out the truth about video games
22 even fitness training can be harmful if you do too much
23 gamers might get frustrated when they lose
24 coping with frustration is a valuable life lesson
25 too much gaming can make studies, work and relationships suffer
26 C 27 D 28 B 29 C 30 C

HOW DID YOU DO?   PAGE 91

- Go through answers with the class and tell students to mark their work.
- Ask student what went well and what went less well, and how they think they could improve their performance.

LISTENING PART 3 | **UNIT 3: LISTENING PREPARATION** | 63

DIFFERENTIATION

Strengthen: Give students a copy of the Audioscript afterwards and let them attempt the Practice Time again.

Challenge: Ask students to write the script for an interview between Monica and an interviewee who is very hostile to the idea of gaming (the interviewee could be an expert or an angry parent or both).

VOCABULARY AND GRAMMAR

VOCABULARY ACTIVITY 1 — PAGE 91

- Ask students what the rule is for forming regular adverbs (add *-ly* to the end of most adjectives; add *-ily* to adjectives that end in *-y*). Then ask them what they know about irregular adjectives (they change form, e.g. *good* changes to *well*). You could also direct students to Grammar Reference page 280.
- Ask students to work in pairs to write the adjectives for each of the adverbs.
- Check answers with the class and ask students what else they noticed about adverbs and adjectives while doing the activity (some adverbs and adjectives have the same form, e.g. *early*). Ask them if they know any other adjectives that don't change form, e.g. daily, hard, fast, close, likely.

KEY

especially – special	greatly – great
firstly – first	well – good
probably – probable	simultaneously – simultaneous
secondly – second	normally – normal
happily – happy	constantly – constant
quickly – quick	rarely – rare
certainly – certain	early – early
definitely – definite	

VOCABULARY ACTIVITY 2 — PAGE 92

- Give students some time to read the sentences and make sure they understand that they are taken from the interview with the writer of the book about video games they listened to earlier.
- Ask students to fill in as many of the missing adverbs as they can from memory and by process of logical deduction. Remind students that the adverbs may not all be used and none are used twice.
- Play the recording for students to listen and check their answers.

AUDIOSCRIPT

1 It can <u>definitely</u> offer all sorts of benefits.
2 It's <u>certainly</u> the case that some people do get sucked into the gaming world and it has a negative impact on other areas of their life.
3 This is great, <u>especially</u> for widening young people's knowledge of the world!
4 Learning for me means <u>firstly</u> gaining a wider knowledge of the world we're living in.
5 They show you different perspectives and even different landscapes you wouldn't <u>normally</u> see.
6 The speed of your brain sending impulses to your body is <u>greatly</u> improved through gaming.
7 This is <u>probably</u> because video games operate on several levels <u>simultaneously</u>.
8 I don't think it <u>necessarily</u> has a negative impact on learning.

KEY

(Clues underlined in Audioscript.)

1 definitely **2** certainly **3** especially **4** firstly
5 normally **6** greatly **7** probably, simultaneously
8 necessarily

UNIT 3: LISTENING PREPARATION — LISTENING PART 3

VOCABULARY ACTIVITY 3 — PAGE 92

- In this activity, students continue to practise with the adverb set.
- Tell students that some questions require them to make quite subtle distinctions, especially Q2 and Q7.
- Ask students to complete the activity individually, and then have them check answers in pairs before you check answers with the class.

KEY

1 simultaneously 2 probably 3 firstly 4 normally
5 especially 6 firstly (and) secondly
7 necessarily / definitely 8 greatly

TEACHING TIPS

Hint Q2: The answer is probably not *definitely* because the adjective *likely* suggests probability rather than certainty.

Hint Q7: The answer is more likely to be *necessarily* because *definitely* is normally used with absolutes (*it is definitely not true*, or *it is definitely true*) rather than limitation (*it is not definitely true* sounds strange, but both are possible in some contexts).

VOCABULARY ACTIVITY 4 — PAGE 93

- This activity consolidates students' knowledge of the adverbs they have been studying and helps students gain a clearer idea of meaning.
- Ask students to work independently to circle the correct options. Then have them check their answers with a partner before you check answers with the class.

KEY

1 greatly 2 simultaneously 3 probably 4 normally
5 especially 6 Firstly 7 certainly 8 necessarily

VOCABULARY ACTIVITY 5 — PAGE 93

- Revise the difference between adjectives and adverbs with the class. You could do this by asking *What are adverbs used to describe or give more information about?* (actions) *What are adjectives used to describe or give more information about?* (things).
- Check students' understanding by going through the first few sentences with class and eliciting whether the missing word is an adjective or an adverb.
- When you are confident that students are clear about the differences between adjectives and adverbs, ask them to work independently to complete the sentences with an appropriate adjective or adverb.
- Encourage students to compare their ideas with a partner before you check answers with the class.

KEY

1 certain 2 greatly 3 simultaneously 4 especially
5 probably 6 special 7 first, second 8 normally
9 probable 10 normal

GRAMMAR ACTIVITY 6 — PAGE 94

- Students will probably be familiar with adverbs of frequency so give them a short time to put the set given in order from most to least frequent before eliciting the answers from the class.
- Ask students how we form a question to ask about the frequency of something and elicit that we use the expression *How often?*

KEY

1 always 2 often 3 regularly 4 sometimes
5 rarely 6 hardly ever 7 never

LISTENING PART 3 | **UNIT 3: LISTENING PREPARATION** | 65

GRAMMAR ACTIVITY 7 — PAGE 94

- Before students attempt this speaking activity, direct them to Grammar Reference page 281 to revise how adverbs of frequency are used in sentences and questions.
- Check students' understanding of word order by writing these two sentences on the board:
  I go swimming. I don't go swimming.
  Then elicit where we would put the adverb of frequency in each place (before the main verb in the first sentence and between the auxiliary and the main verb in the second sentence).
- Put students into pairs to interview each other about how frequently they do the things in the list. Encourage students to give more detail in their answers by adding *once/twice/three times a week/year/month*, etc. For example, *I sometimes go for a walk at the weekend. I go walking with my father in the forest about once a month.*

KEY

Students' own answers.

GRAMMAR ACTIVITY 8 — PAGES 94–95

- Ask students to read Grammar Reference page 280 before attempting this activity. Check the meaning of *too much/many* versus *not enough* and the difference between *so, quite* and *very*.
- Ask students to work independently to choose the correct options to complete the activity. Then have them compare their answers with a partner before you check answers with the class.

KEY

1 d **2** a **3** b **4** b **5** d **6** a **7** c **8** d **9** a **10** b

GRAMMAR ACTIVITY 9 — PAGE 95

- The activity consolidates students' knowledge of the intensifiers they have been studying and helps them to gain a clearer idea of meaning.
- Ask students to work independently to circle the correct options. Then to check their answers, have them role-play the conversation with a partner before you check answers with the class.

KEY

1 really **2** quite **3** much too **4** a lot of **5** enough **6** some **7** very **8** so many **9** far too **10** Hardly any **11** extremely

SELF-EVALUATION — PAGE 96

Tell students to look at the Self-evaluation table and tick the boxes that are true for them. Ask them if there are any topics they don't feel confident about yet.

LISTENING PART 4

OVERVIEW

Topic: Shopping
Exam skills: Distinguish between essential and less important details
Assessment Objectives: 3B, 3D
Vocabulary: Verbs and expressions: shopping)
Grammar: Use separable and non-separable verbs and the passive
Practice text type: Interview: changes in shopping patterns
Additional resources: audio player (internet access)

PREPARING THE WAY   PAGE 97

- Tell students to read the chapter topic title and elicit from them whether or not they like to go shopping and why.
- Ask students how most people in their country do their shopping, e.g. at shopping centres, at markets. You could also ask how they like to do their shopping, e.g. online, with their friends, or what are the advantages of shopping online.
- Read through the questions with the class and make sure they understand all the vocabulary. Check the meaning of *chore* (a job or task that you have to do), *to be addicted to something* (to be unable to stop doing something and depend on it to feel good), *gift* (present). If students are able to sustain a class or small group discussion, you can ask them to discuss each of the questions in detail.
- If students need more support, put some key words and phrases on the board (see Key below). Ask the students to produce brief written responses and compare their ideas with a partner or in groups.
- Take feedback from the group and find out how many people in the class are enthusiastic shoppers, what their favourite shops are and how many students don't enjoy shopping.

KEY

Students' own answers.
Suggested sentence structures for discussion:
I love / enjoy / hate / can't stand shopping because ...
I think / don't think shopping is a skill because ...
People can become addicted to shopping when / if (they associate shopping with ...)
My favourite shopping place / shop is ...
I love / enjoy / hate / can't stand buying gifts for people because ...

ACTIVITY 1   PAGE 98

- Tell students to look at the pictures in pairs and match them with the words in the box. Tell them they can use a dictionary if necessary.
- Check answers with the class and discuss where and when students would see each of these signs and their purpose.

KEY

1 a parking   b sale   c barcode   d CCTV
2 a near a free car park or a parking area
   b on a label on an item for sale in a shop at a reduced price
   c on an item for sale, e.g. in a supermarket
   d in an area where there are CCTV cameras operating

FOCUSING ON THE EXAM   PAGE 98

- Ask students to read the text in the box and tell you what they think will be challenging about this part of the exam.
- The Listening Part 4 Assessment Objectives are:
  Assessment Objective 3B: Identify essential and finer points of detail in spoken material.
  Assessment Objective 3D: Identify a speaker's viewpoint and attitude, stated and implied.
- Explain that Listening Part 4 carries 10 marks and is based on a range of longer recordings, e.g. a monolgue, and that the recordings tend to be more academic and complex.
- Go through the different types of tasks in Listening Part 4 mentioned in the box. Make sure students understand what this task involves.
- Tell students that in this chapter the will continue to practise identifying the speaker's viewpoint and attitude, both stated and implied, and distinguishing the finer points of detail from the essential ones.

LISTENING PART 4 **UNIT 3: LISTENING PREPARATION** 67

EXAM SKILLS: IDENTIFYING IMPORTANT INFORMATION AND DETAILS   PAGE 98

- Ask students to read the information in the box and ask what the most important skill in this part of the exam is. Elicit that it is the ability to distinguish between what details are essential – the main message – and what details are optional.
- Ask students what the difference is between essential and optional details. Elicit that essential details are relats to factual information and optional details are related to personal preferences and opinions rather than facts.

ACTIVITY 2   PAGE 99

- This activity gives students practice in distinguishing between essential information and less important details within a practical context.
- Tell students to imagine that they are interested in buying the jumper in the picture. Ask them what they think they would need to know to make a firm decision.
- Give students a minute or so to discuss their ideas with a partner and then elicit ideas from the class.

KEY

Suggested answers:
Essential information: Size: 10, £10.00, women's jumper
Very important information: Condition is nearly new, colour is pale grey, Dry clean only, Genuine wool
Less important information: Made in Wales, can be worn with skirts or trousers

ACTIVITY 3   PAGE 99

- Direct students to the photo and ask them to describe what they see. Ask students what the man's job is and elicit that he is a flight attendant or air steward. Explain that they are going to read and listen to a flight attendant's announcement.
- Give the class some time to read the question and copy the table into their notebooks. You might also want to check the meaning of some of the more specialised vocabulary in the text, e.g. *detour* (a different way or route to go somewhere often taken in order to avoid a problem such as bad weather), *in-flight* (something that happened during a flight), *bargain* (a thing bought or offered for sale much more cheaply than is usual or expected), *goods* (things for sale), *reduction* (a lower price – from the verb to *reduce* – make smaller or less).

- Tell students that there is some information missing in the transcript, but they do not need to write the missing words. They should pay attention to the missing information as they listen and take notes in the table they copied into their notebooks.
- Play the recording the first time for students to listen and complete the first column in the table with the missing details. Repeat as necessary until students have all the missing information.
- Tell students to decide which details are essential and which are less important. Then have them mark the correct columns in the table.
- Check answers with the class.

AUDIOSCRIPT

Mark: Hello, everyone. My name is Mark and I'll be giving you some information about today's flight to Madrid, in sunny Spain. The first thing I need to tell you is that today's my birthday – isn't that cool? – and I should also mention that the journey will take three hours longer than expected, unfortunately, because we need to make a detour to avoid some storms, but that's not so bad as it will give you lots of extra time for in-flight shopping! We will be arriving at 16.00 hours local time, rather than 13.00 as planned, but I'm sure you won't mind once you hear all about the fantastic bargains we've got in store for you today! For example, we have over ten different kinds of perfume for sale – isn't that great?

There is some safety information that you'll be given soon, but before that, I want to let you know that the goods we have on board have all been reduced by 2% – we want to make sure you enjoy these massive reductions.

You need to put your seat belts on now, as the plane is about to be cleared for take-off, but don't forget to get your credit cards out ready – it won't be long until you can start shopping. I bet you can't wait!

KEY

(Clues underlined in Audioscript.)

Subject matter? Details?	Essential?	Less important?
1 destination – Madrid	✓	
2 birthday		✓
3 journey lengthened/delayed	✓	
4 landing later than expected	✓	
5 perfume for sale		✓
6 safety information	✓	
7 2% off sale		✓
8 put seat belts on now	✓	

UNIT 3: LISTENING PREPARATION — LISTENING PART 4

PRACTICE TIME: LISTENING PART 4
PAGE 100

- Students now have the opportunity to practise an exam task. Remind them to spend time reading the question carefully. Check that students understand what they have to do and encourage them to underline key words in the rubric (or make a note of it if they are not allowed to write in their textbooks) since these will help the students to sort the essential information from details as they listen.

- Tell students that they are going to hear an extract from an interview about shopping and shopping patterns or habits. The speaker will discuss the ways in which shopping habits have changed, particularly with the arrival of online shopping.

- Check the meaning of *consumer* (a person who buys, eats or uses something), *splash out* (spend lots of money), *to purchase* (to buy), *a purchase* (something a person has bought).

- Remind the class to look at and follow the Exam Hints and the After Exam Check boxes. If you think it would be helpful, read these aloud with the class after they have had some time to read through the question.

- Play the recording twice for students to complete the tasks and check their answers. Remind students to follow the instructions in the rubric by not writing more than three words. Check answers with the class.

AUDIOSCRIPT

Mike: Hello, my name is Mike Malone, host of the weekly radio show *Out and About*. Today I'm here with Sarah Hubbard, an expert on consumer culture, who'll be telling us all about what has changed in the world of shopping. Welcome to the show, Sarah.

Sarah: Hello, Mike.

Mike: So, Sarah, what is it that you do?

Sarah: Well, I study shopping patterns. Customers nowadays are very different to customers fifty years ago and shops that don't adapt to the changing shopping culture don't succeed.

Mike: I see. What is it about modern shopping that's different for consumers, then?

Sarah: First and foremost, there's the shopper. Fifty years ago, shoppers weren't very informed. They would just come into the shop and browse, not always knowing much about the product they were looking for. Nowadays shoppers know everything about the product they're looking for. Usually, they've already compared the price online from a dozen different stores and often they know the exact specifications of whatever they are buying. And they shop around to get the best bargains. All the information they might need is on their phone, so really they're just as knowledgeable as the assistants in the shop.

Mike: So how have shops adapted to this change?

Sarah: Well, shop assistants now need to receive special training, to make sure that the shopper doesn't contradict them. It would be very embarrassing if the shopper knew more than the assistant!

Mike: I suppose so. Yes, I can imagine that assistants would be placed in a very difficult position if that happened.

Sarah: Exactly. And if customers are paying a lot of money for an item, as can often be the case, they will want to do their research.

Mike: Fair enough. In what other ways has shopping changed?

Sarah: Well, the second thing is there are more options nowadays in terms of how we shop.

Mike: What do you mean, exactly?

Sarah: Well, a lot of shops nowadays let their customers shop online. There's no need for the shopper to leave their house and to queue up for hours on end in a busy store. They can find the product, ask any questions they might have and even order it online. The product will then be delivered a couple of days later. It's a completely different process. In the old days, going to the shops took time and effort, and shoppers were unlikely to go home without buying anything.

Mike: I suppose that one thing that's not so good about internet shopping, especially with clothes or shoes, is that you can't try on anything you might buy.

Sarah: Yes, that's true. But if the clothes are very cheap, some people are happy to try to find a good deal online, knowing that if they don't like what they buy, or it doesn't fit, it can be donated to charity and won't have cost them very much. They haven't really made an investment in these items, or not a big one, at least, so they're happy to give them away.

Mike: And what about paying for items online? How safe is that?

Sarah: Well it's pretty safe, although no system is ever going to be completely free of risk. It's getting better all the time, though and banks and credit card companies are definitely making it harder for thieves to target online shoppers.

Mike: I suppose another feature of online shopping is the review system.

Sarah: Yes, that's actually very important. Reviews from others that have bought products online can be seen and scrutinised, so any seller whose goods are substandard is going to struggle.

Mike: You've talked mainly about advantages for the

customer in the change towards shopping online. Are there any other disadvantages?

Sarah: Well, I think that depends a lot on the individual. Not everyone enjoys online shopping. There's less human contact and it's nice to be able to see what you're getting, for example, if a supermarket decides to sell off food cheaply at the end of the day.

Mike: Do you think that buying from home affects what people buy?

Sarah: I think so. If you're handing over cash, that might be a reminder of what your purchases are really costing you. You might be less tempted to splash out on luxuries and spend money you haven't really got!

Mike: Yes. I remember I used to go to my local market to bargain over the prices of things I wanted to buy. That's something I miss with online shopping! Sending an email isn't really the same …

Sarah: True. Although at least you have fewer wasted journeys, as you can see immediately if an online shop has sold out of the item you want to buy from them.

Mike: Good point. Right, if you were asked to sum up what has changed most in people's shopping habits, what would you say, then?

Sarah: Hmm … Well I think I'd have to say it's to do with customer information levels, shopping around for bargains, no queuing, expectations about convenience and easy access to reviews from other shoppers.

Mike: That's great. Thank you very much, Sarah, for coming on the show. You've given all of us lots to think about.

Sarah: Thank you for asking me, Mike.

KEY

(Clues underlined in Audioscript.)

31 online **32** as much as **33** queue (up) **34** try on
35 donated to charity **36** reviews **37** contact
38 luxuries **39** bargain **40** waste journeys

HOW DID YOU DO?   PAGE 100

- Go through answers with the class and tell students to mark their work.
- Ask the class what went well and what went less well, and how they think they could improve their performance.

VOCABULARY AND GRAMMAR

VOCABULARY ACTIVITY 1   PAGE 101

- This activity revises and reinforces students' understanding of the key vocabulary from the interview about shopping habits.
- Ask students to complete the short texts with the corect forms of the words and phrases from the box.
- Check answers with the class.

KEY

1 browse **2** order **3** find a good deal
made an investment **5** bargain

VOCABULARY ACTIVITY 2   PAGES 101–102

- This activity further consolidates students' understanding of verbs related to shopping from the interview and should help them to gain a clearer idea of meaning.
- Ask students to read the descriptions, and match them with appropriate verbs from Activity 1. Tell students they can use a dictionary if necessary.
- Check answers with the class.

KEY

1 find a good deal **2** bargain
3 make an investment **4** browse **5** order

GRAMMAR ACTIVITY 3   PAGE 102

- Ask students to read through the section on pages 268–269 of the Grammar Reference about separable and inseparable phrasal verbs before attempting this activity.
- Go through the verbs in the box with the students. Check meaning and establish whether each verb is separable or inseparable.
- Ask students to complete the sentences with the correct form of the phrasal verbs from the box. Check answers with the class.

UNIT 3: LISTENING PREPARATION — LISTENING PART 4

KEY

1 shop around **2** queue up **3** try on **4** sell off
5 splash out **6** sold out

GRAMMAR ACTIVITY 4 — PAGE 103

- Ask students to match the phrasal verbs to their definitions. Students should recognise them from the previous activity, but suggest that doing the ones they find easiest first may be helpful.
- Check answers with the class.

KEY

try on	wear clothes or shoes briefly to see if they fit
sell off	reduce stock by lowering prices
queue up	wait in line
splash out (on)	spend lots of money on something; to be extravagant
sell out (of)	no longer have goods for sale
shop around	try to find goods at a range of shops, perhaps to find the cheapest

GRAMMAR ACTIVITY 5 — PAGE 103

- Ask students to complete the diary entry with the correct form of the phrasal verbs from Activity 4.
- Check answers with the class.

KEY

1 sell out **2** sell off **3** try on **4** queueing up
5 shop around **6** splash out

GRAMMAR ACTIVITY 6 — PAGE 103

- These discussions will provide useful preparation for the Speaking paper for the next unit, which is about clothes and fashion.
- Ask students to discuss the questions in pairs. Elicit answers and encourage a class discussion.
- Ask the pairs of students to think of more questions on the topic of shopping. Then put the pairs into groups to discuss their questions.

KEY

Students' own answers.

GRAMMAR ACTIVITY 7 — PAGE 104

- Ask students to read through the section on pages 271–272 of the Grammar Reference about the passive before completing the table with the different forms of the verb *be*.
- Elicit answers from the class. This completed table will be a useful reference point for students' as they do the following activities on the passive.

KEY

	Simple	Continuous	Perfect
Past	was/were	was being	*had been*
Present	*am/are/is*	is being	has been
Future	will be	*will be being*	will have been

GRAMMAR ACTIVITY 8 — PAGE 104

- Ask students when we use the passive rather than active voice (when we don't know who performed the action, or it isn't important). Refer students back to Grammar Reference on pages 271–272 as necessary.
- Draw students' attention to the example answer and ask which word has been removed in the passive sentence (*people*) and why (because who bought the video games is not important information).
- Ask students to transform the remaining sentences in the activity into the passive form and check answers with the class.

LISTENING PART 4 — **UNIT 3: LISTENING PREPARATION**

KEY

1 In New Guinea, more languages are spoken than in any other country.
2 In India, more books are read per year than in any other country.
3 In China, more tea is drunk than in any other country.
4 In Switzerland, more chocolate is eaten than in any other country.
5 In the USA, more television is watched than in any other country.

GRAMMAR ACTIVITY 9 — PAGE 105

- This activity extends practice of passive forms using a range of verb tenses and is slightly more challenging than the previous ones.
- You can suggest students break down the activity by identifying the subjects in each of the sentences (they, Paul, he, she, many people, they, Alia and Gill, they, people) as they are usually not mentioned in the passive form.
- Remind students that the object of the active sentence becomes the subject of the passive sentence.
- Ask students to complete the activity in pairs before you check answers with the class.

KEY

1 The meeting is being held in Room C.
2 The presentation has been given already by Paul.
3 Nothing was known at that time.
4 The chemicals were being mixed.
5 The new album will be heard on the radio tomorrow.
6 The shipment will have been delivered by the end of the month.
7 These reports have already been checked by Alia and Gill.
8 Several languages are spoken in that country.
9 The results of the election will be known next week.

EXTENSION

Research and write ten sentences about inventions and scientific discoveries using the passive voice, e.g.
The iron was invented in America in 1882.
Penicillin was discovered in 1928.
Cut the sentences in half before the verb:
The iron / was invented in America in 1882.
Penicillin / was discovered in 1928.
Students cut the sentences in half, mix them up and give them to another group to match.

SELF-EVALUATION — PAGE 105

Tell students to look at the Self-evaluation table and tick the boxes that are true for them. Ask them if there are any topics they don't feel confident about yet.

UNIT 4: SPEAKING PREPARATION — SPEAKING

SPEAKING

OVERVIEW

Topic: Fashion
Exam skills: Identify intonation and stress, identify ways to improve English pronunciation, identify long and short vowels
Assessment Objectives: 4A, 4B, 4C
Vocabulary: Adjectives: fashion
Grammar: Use past perfect, revise past tenses
Practice text type: Speak about clothes and the role of fashion in your life
Additional resources: audio player, dictionaries, recording devices (optional) (internet access)

PREPARING THE WAY — PAGE 108

- Tell students to read the chapter topic title and ask them what they think about today's common fashions. Elicit vocabulary or types of vocabulary that students think they will need to discuss this topic, e.g. types of clothing, adjectives to describe clothing.
- Ask students to read the questions about fashion and discuss them in pairs. If they are able to sustain a class or small group discussion, you can ask students to discuss each question in detail.
- If they need more support, put some key words and phrases on the board (see Key below). Ask students to produce brief written responses and compare their ideas with a partner or in groups.
- Take feedback from the class and find out how motivated they are by this topic. Ask students to describe what kind of clothes are fashionable for people their age at the moment and what is unfashionable. This will need to be managed sensitively.

KEY

Students' own answers. Suggested sentences for discussion:
I think fashion is important because ...
Judging people by what they wear is ...
I prefer wearing ...
Some celebrities are more fashionable than others, for example ...
At the moment ... are fashionable / it's fashionable to wear ...
Ten years ago, people wore more / less ...
Useful words and phrases:
fashionable / unfashionable, to look ..., style / stylish, comfortable, smart, casual clothes, designer clothes, accessories

EXTENSION

Suggested activities:

- Make list of fashion 'rules' for teenagers. If it is suitable for your classroom, ask students to write (and perhaps illustrate) some dos and don'ts for what teenagers should wear.
- Design and label in detail outfits for a range of people in different contexts, e.g. a child's birthday party, a school celebration or graduation, a formal occasion such as a wedding.
- Have a debate on the topic 'Fashion should be banned'. Explore the arguments for and against in speech and/or in writing.
- Write a story in which an item of clothing is central or significant in some way.
- Write a newspaper report on a fashion show.
- Revise colours and adjectives and names of clothes items by writing words on small slips of paper and playing a game. Create two piles: names of pieces of clothing and names of colours. Students take a word from the clothes pile and a word from the colours pile and draw the piece of clothing in the correct colour.
- Ask students to discuss this quotation from Coco Chanel: *Fashion fades, only style remains the same*. As a follow-up, students could find other quotations on the topic of fashion and explain why they agree/disagree with them, in speech or in writing.

TEACHING TIPS

To help students list the key words they used in the discussion, you can record their conversations. Students can then listen to them several times. Recording the students speaking is a good way to support them in their preparation for the Speaking exam.

SPEAKING UNIT 4: SPEAKING PREPARATION

ACTIVITY 1 — PAGE 108

- Review the vocabulary students used in Preparing the Way.
- After students have listed the words they used under the three headings, ask them to expand their lists to cover other words and phrases that they can think of.
- For *descriptions of clothing*, you can ask students to think of words in the sub-categories of colours, materials (*wool, cotton*), shape (*A-line, flared*) and size. For *opinion words*, ask students to think of phrases for giving opinions.
- Take feedback from the class and list the words and phrases for each category on the board. Ask students whether the words and phrases are nouns, verbs, adjectives or other parts of speech.
- Ask students if they can think of other categories for the topic of fashion. Write the categories on the board and elicit more words and phrases.
- Tell students to choose one of the original three categories and ask them if it's possible to list different parts of speech for that category. Tell them to use a dictionary to find at least three more new words for that category. Elicit the new words and write them on the board.

KEY

Students' own answers.

ACTIVITY 2 — PAGE 109

- Ask students to look at the six photographs and elicit descriptions of them. Elicit or teach the words *necklace* and *jacket* if the students don't produce them naturally in their descriptions.
- For Q1, explain that students are going to listen to six extracts from a fashion show and that they need to match the photos with the extracts. Before you play the recording, elicit or explain the following words: *outfit* (a set of clothes that are worn together), *model* (in this context, a usually good-looking man or woman who wears clothes in a fashion show), *pattern* (a repeated decoration or design), *stunning* (very beautiful or good-looking), *stylish* (the adjective form of *style*), *trendy* (fashionable).
- Play the recording twice for students to number the photos in the order they hear them and check their answers. Confirm answers with the class.

- Tell students to read the words in the box for Q2. Give them some time to match the words in the box with the pictures that illustrate them. Then play the recording again so they can check their answers. They should see if they can hear the words they have picked used in the descriptions. When you check answers with the class, try to elicit at least one sentence for each word.

AUDIOSCRIPT: Student Book page 287

1 Well, first down the runway we can see this rather stunning outfit that would be very suitable for office wear. The <u>checked</u> pattern looks really smart and if you pair it with the right shirt, this is a look that could be a real winner.

2 Checks are popular this year but so are <u>spots</u>, as you can see from these amazing shoes. Wear these to stand out in any crowd! They're guaranteed to turn heads on any occasion.

3 Next, turn your attention to the necklace this model is wearing. It's a heart-shaped delight – a perfect example of <u>bling</u> – and will go well with any look.

4 This trendy <u>denim</u> jacket is a real favourite of mine. Stylish and comfortable – it's a real winner and is the ultimate in looking cool.

5 This collection has a real emphasis on elegance – look at this fantastic hat – it doesn't get much more <u>chic</u> than that!

6 Everyone needs to carry their belongings round with them – this <u>handbag</u> gives us an example of a perfect and stylish way to do it!

KEY

1 a 5 b 6 c 4 d 1 e 3 f 2
2 **checks** d **handbag** b **denim** c **bling** e **chic** a **spotty** f

TEACHING TIPS

- You can point out that the words might be used in slightly different forms in the Audioscript and on the page. The recording has *checks* (noun) and *spotty* (adjective). The words in the box are *checked* (adjective) and *spots* (noun).
- Explain that *bling* means jewellery or accessories that either look very expensive and/or are very bright and shiny and will attract attention.
- It might also be helpful to teach the different types of pattern on fabric that are mentioned: *spots* (*spotty*), *checks* (*checked*). An alternative not included in these photos is *stripes* (*stripy*).

UNIT 4: SPEAKING PREPARATION — SPEAKING

FOCUSING ON THE EXAM — PAGE 109

- This part of the exam is optional. However, speaking practice is important in a language course. The skills and language practised in this unit will help to prepare students for all areas of the exam.
- Ask students to read the text in the box and tell you what they think will be challenging about this part of the exam.
  Assessment Objectives are:
  Assessment Objective 4A: Give information and express opinions on a range of topics at different levels of complexity.
  Assessment Objective 4B: Respond to a range of questions on a variety of topics.
  Assessment Objective 4C: Use a range of vocabulary, grammar and structures appropriately.
- Go through the three different task types with the class. Explain that:
  Part 1 is an introductory interview between an individual candidate and the examiner.
  Part 2 is an extended individual answer or presentation.
  Part 3 is an extended discussion that requires a candidate to sustain a longer conversation.
- Ask students which of these tasks they think they will find the most difficult and why.

EXAM SKILLS: SPEAKING SKILLS PAGE — PAGE 109

- Tell students to read the information in the box about speaking skills or read it together as a class. Then, ask students to cover the text and tell you from memory what skills are mentioned and the advice given for how to demonstrate them to the examiner.
- Elicit that students should:
  a) use a range of different structures and expressions to give their opinions.
  b) avoid giving one-word answers but develop their ideas with more detail and examples.
  c) make sure they listen to the questions that the examiner asks carefully and answer the questions as fully as possibly.
  d) speak clearly and avoid speaking too fast.
  e) respond spontaneously (not by giving answers they have previously learned by heart).
- Draw students' attention to the Watch out! box. Emphasise the importance of staying calm. Students don't need to panic if they don't understand everything. They should focus on what they do know and understand.

ACTIVITY 3 — PAGE 110

- In this activity, students design their own questions. This will help them anticipate the type of questions they might be asked.
- Explain that although they can't predict everything that they will be asked about in the exam, there are many questions that they can predict.
- Direct students to the words and phrases in the box and give them a few minutes to choose two of the words or phrases and write three 'predictable' questions about them.
- Point out to students that the category 'opinion words' is not a topic in the same way as the other phrases. If students choose this phrase, they can write questions that are asking about opinions.
- When they are ready, tell students to work in pairs and take turns to ask and answer each other's questions. Circulate and monitor while students are speaking. Make notes of any recurring errors you hear. Correct these with the class at the end of the activity.

KEY

Suggested questions:
food: *What is your favourite / least favourite food? What do you usually eat for breakfast / lunch / dinner? What kind of foods are healthy/unhealthy?*
pets: *Do you have a pet? What kind of pets do you like? What is your pet's name?*
opinion words: *What is your view on …? Can you give your opinion about …? What do you think of …?*
sports: *Do you play any sports? Do you like sports? What is your favourite sport?*
travel and holiday: *Have you ever been on holiday in a foreign country? What is your ideal type of holiday? Would you like to do a lot of travelling?*

DIFFERENTIATION

Strengthen: Give students written versions of the questions so they can prepare answers in advance and build their confidence before introducing unseen questions.
Challenge: Ask more confident students to take the role of examiner using questions they have devised themselves.

EXAM SKILLS: PRONUNCIATION SKILLS — PAGE 110

- Tell students to read the list of tips and suggestions for improving their pronunciation.
- Elicit which areas of English pronunciation students find the most difficult so that you can work on those together.

SPEAKING UNIT 4: SPEAKING PREPARATION 75

ACTIVITY 4 PAGE 110

- Direct students to the sentence and ask for volunteers (or nominate different students) to try to read it aloud, pronouncing all words correctly. Correct their efforts, eliciting the meaning of the individual words as you do so.
- Play the recording for students to listen and repeat the whole sentence. Do this several times, as necessary. Double-check that students understand the meaning of the different words by eliciting (if appropriate) the translation of the entire sentence into their own language.
- Elicit any other examples of words with similar spelling and pronunciation patterns, e.g.

  tough – rough, enough, stuff

  through – do, you, zoo

  thorough – borough (explain that this word means 'town' in old English)

  thought – bought, brought, ought, sort, court, caught

  though – sew, so, low

KEY

Students' own answers.

EXAM SKILLS: INTONATION AND STRESS
PAGE 110

- Explain to students that intonation is the way a speaker's voice goes up and down when they are speaking. It is important in conveying meaning. Learning to understand what is conveyed by intonation will help students to improve their listening skills.
- To help students distinguish between the four intonation patterns listed, you could write some sentences and phrases on the board and read them aloud, asking students to identify whether you are asking a question, are surprised, unsure, etc. and how they would describe the intonation pattern, e.g.

  He's here already? (Use rising intonation at the start and falling intonation on the final syllable to indicate that you are asking a question.)

  He's here already! (Use rising intonation and place stress on the middle syllable of already and further rising intonation on the final syllable of already to indicate surprise that he is there so soon.)

  He's here already …? (Use wavering intonation to indicate uncertainty.)

  He's brought his clothes, his shoes, his books, his computer, his violin and all his money. (Use rising intonation on each item in the list but not the last one, which has a falling intonation, to show that it is the end of the list.)

- Ask students to repeat each sentence after you to practise producing the intonation patterns themselves.
- Use the example He's here already. to demonstrate how meaning can be inferred or changed by stressing different words, e.g

  He's _here_ already. (You expected him to be in another place.)

  He's here _already_. (You didn't expect him to arrive so early.)

  _He's_ here already. (You are not surprised or not happy that this person is here so early.)

- Ask students to write a short sentence themselves and experiment with changing the meaning by stressing different words.

TEACHING TIPS

Hint: Recording students and listening to the recordings may be helpful in experimenting with intonation.

ACTIVITY 5 PAGE 111

- This activity provides more practice in understanding how stressing certain words in a sentence can change its meaning.
- Give students half a minute to read quickly through the sentences in the tables and then play the recording for students to listen and decide which version they hear.
- Check answers with the class and then ask students to work in pairs to match the different stress patterns with the meanings for each set of sentences.
- Check answers with the class and then ask students to practise reading the sets of sentences to each other in pairs to practise the stress patterns.

KEY

1 1b 2c 3b 4c
2 1a - iii   b - ii   c - i
   2a - iii   b - i   c - ii
   3a - i   b - iii c - ii
   4a - iii   b - i   c - ii

UNIT 4: SPEAKING PREPARATION

PRACTICE TIME: SPEAKING PART 1
PAGE 112

- Students now have the opportunity to practise some exam tasks. They will need individual time slots for this, which may be challenging to organise. However, practising in pairs, recording answers and getting feedback will all be helpful, even if it is not possible to create exam conditions.
- Speaking Part 1 is an individual interview with the examiner. Allow students to prepare by reading the questions and spending some time thinking about what they are going to say.
- Direct students to the Exam Hints for Speaking Part 1 and read them aloud with the class. Emphasise what they say should have variety and interest. Students must avoid giving one-word answers but provide detailed (as long as the detail is relevant) responses using a range of vocabulary and grammatical structures.
- If it is not possible to interview all students in the class individually, ask students to practise in pairs as a role play, taking turns to be examiner and student. The student pretending to be the examiner reads the questions.
- Students can record their dialogues. You could listen to these after the class and provide feedback in the next lesson.

KEY

Students' own answers.

PRACTICE TIME: SPEAKING PART 2
PAGE 112

- Speaking Part 2 of the exam is where students talk at length about the given topic. It is important for students to practise making notes and preparing and structuring their answers as they will be given one minute for this in the exam. Tell students to make sure their notes are key words and phrases rather than sentences.
- Direct students to the Exam Hints for Speaking Part 2 and read them aloud with the class. Stress that the important skills for students to learn here are how to support their answers with details and examples, and how to select details that are pertinent and relevant to their answer.
- Give students time to read carefully through the question and the opportunity to ask you about any words spend phrases they don't understand. Check that they know *peer pressure* (the feeling that one must do the same things as other people of one's age and social group in order to be liked or respected).
- Ask students to try to think of two or three things to say for each bullet point, including supporting examples and details.
- You can put students into groups to practise giving their presentation to the other members of the group. As well as giving their own feedback, the other group members can record the presentation for the teacher to check later. Stress that group feedback should be supportive and students must try to think of at least one positive thing to say about each speaker's performance as well as offering suggestions for improvement.

KEY

Students' own answers.

PRACTICE TIME: SPEAKING PART 3
PAGES 112–113

- Speaking Part 3 of the exam involves discussion and exchange so is arguably the most challenging task. Allow students to prepare by reading the questions and spending some time thinking about the kind of things they could say and the different expressions and structures they could use to give their opinions.
- Direct students to the Exam Hints for Speaking Part 3 and read it aloud with the class. Emphasise that it is important that students must be able to support their opinions and develop them coherently with reasons and arguments.
- When they are ready, put students into groups to discuss the questions. If it is possible, have students record what they say. Encourage students to listen and evaluate their own performance, trying to think of ways in which it could be improved.
- Give students feedback on their performance for all three parts of the exam. Indicate any areas of weakness you have identified and direct student to available resources to work on improving these areas, e.g. pronunciation activities for particular pronunciation issues or extra grammar practice.
- It is important for students to recognise that their speaking and listening may be improving, but they may still find the next Practice Time harder than the first. This could be a result of the different vocabulary required. In the Speaking exam, student knowledge of the specific topic vocabulary will affect performance.

SPEAKING | **UNIT 4: SPEAKING PREPARATION** | **77**

KEY

Students' own answers.

HOW DID YOU DO? PAGE 113

- Ask students to answer the questions and think about what they need to improve for the Speaking paper.
- Ask students to tell you if there are any areas they don't feel confident in yet.

PRONUNCIATION

PRONUNCIATION ACTIVITY 1 PAGE 113

- Go through the table with the class. Say the words in the table aloud and model each of the sounds for the students, having students repeat the word several times. Contrast the long and the short vowels so that students can hear the difference between them.
- Put students into pairs to do the activity and ask them to take turns saying the words aloud to each other in order to help them decide where to put the words in the table.
- Check answers with the class, modelling the sounds for them in each case, and explaining the meaning of any unknown words.

KEY

short *a*: act, map, ran, gas
long *a*: bake, pain, weight, day
short *e*: friend, said, tread, bed
long *e*: peach, gene, sweet, feel
short *i*: pig, fit, ship, kick
long *i*: file, crime, hide, knight
short *o*: not, pot, slot, knot
long *o*: toe, know, slow, no
short *u*: but, shut, nut, rut
long *u*: cube, huge, tomb, cute

DIFFERENTIATION

Strengthen: Model the pronunciation of the words for the students. Say the words aloud so they can choose which column of the table to put them in.

Challenge: Ask students to try to add a new word to each column in the table.

PRONUNCIATION ACTIVITY 2 PAGE 114

- Direct students to the list of words. Ask students if there are any words that they don't understand. Teach the meanings or elicit the meanings from the class.
- Ask students to work in pairs and take turns to say the words aloud to each other and decide which is the silent letter.
- When you check answers with the class, say each word aloud and ask students to repeat it after you.

KEY

1 h~~our 2 do~~ubt 3 rece~~i~~pt 4 nigh~~t 5 cal~~m
6 Wed~~nesday 7 cast~~le 8 ~~psychology 9 sci~~ence
10 k~~nife

VOCABULARY AND GRAMMAR

VOCABULARY ACTIVITY 1 🔊 PAGE 114

- Give students some time to read the questions and underline the key words. Give students the opportunity to ask you about any words they don't know. You could check the meaning of *contemporary* (happening in or belonging to the present/now) and *trend* (fashion).
- Play the recording for students to listen and follow along in their books. Students might need help with some of the vocabulary, e.g. *to fit in with* (to be like other people so that they will accept you), *casual* (relaxed and informal), *scruffy* (the opposite of smart), *drab* (dull without colour or interest), *overrated* (when something is considered better than it is).
- Ask students to answer the questions and encourage them to compare their ideas with a partner before you check answers with the class.

78 UNIT 4: SPEAKING PREPARATION — SPEAKING

AUDIOSCRIPT

Samira: The topic I've chosen to talk about is fashion, as I think it's a very important subject for teenagers like me. Looking stylish does matter to me – not because I'm very interested in clothes, but because it makes me feel like I fit in with my friends. It's funny how it always seems to be teenagers and young people who lead the way with fashion. Maybe that's because they are trying to find an identity, a sense of who they are.

I tend to dress differently around different people, because I try to adapt to the situation I'm in. If I'm going to a good restaurant with my parents, I try to look smart and wear nice shoes and a dress. My mum hates it if I wear old clothes. She says I look untidy and scruffy! But with my friends, I prefer to wear casual clothes like jeans, trainers and a T-shirt.

Casual clothes are really comfortable, but it's important to me and my friends that they're also stylish. I want to look like my friends but not too much like them, if you know what I mean. I want to be a little bit original in the things I wear. It would be really embarrassing if I showed up in exactly the same outfit as my friend! I think it's important know what the latest trends are. No one wants to look old-fashioned. I also like wearing bright colours because I don't want to be drab and boring.

I end up spending about four hours shopping for clothes every month. That's probably less than some people my age, but I try not to let it take over my life. I think contemporary fashion is interesting but a lot of it is overrated and not even that nice! Some people seem to buy it just because they feel they have to.

There's huge pressure on people, especially people my age, to be stylish. Sometimes it feels as if there's a new trend every week and it's no accident. I think the fashion industry makes a lot of money out of the teen market. I guess that's the world we're living in, though.

KEY

Suggested answers:
(Clues underlined in Audioscript.)
1 Looking stylish makes Samira feel she fits in with her friends.
2 They are trying to develop an identity/a sense of who they are.
3 Samira varies her way of dressing around different people because she wants to adapt to different situations.
4 When she is with her friends Samira likes to dress in a way that is comfortable and stylish. She wants to look similar to them but not too similar.
5 Samira spends about four hours clothes shopping every month.
6 Samira thinks contemporary fashion is interesting, but also overrated, and not that nice.
7 Samira thinks the fashion industry makes a lot of money out of young people.

DIFFERENTIATION

Strengthen: Allow students to read the audioscript when you go through the answers.

Challenge: Ask students to write an account of their own views on fashion.

VOCABULARY ACTIVITY 2 — PAGE 115

- Ask students to work individually to match the fashion-related vocabulary from Activity 1 to the definitions.
- Encourage students to compare their ideas with a partner before you check answers with the class.

KEY

1 drab 2 comfortable 3 smart 4 overrated
5 scruffy 6 old-fashioned 7 casual 8 embarrassing
9 original 10 stylish

VOCABULARY ACTIVITY 3 — PAGE 115

- This activity consolidates students' knowledge of the adjectives related to fashion that they have been studying and helps them to gain a clearer idea of meaning.
- Ask students to work independently to choose the correct options and compare their ideas with a partner before checking answers with the class.

KEY

(See highlighted words in the Audioscript.)
1 original 2 Casual 3 scruffy 4 embarrassing
5 comfortable 6 Drab 7 stylish 8 old-fashioned
9 overrated 10 smart

SPEAKING UNIT 4: SPEAKING PREPARATION

VOCABULARY ACTIVITY 4 — PAGE 116

- Ask students to complete the short texts with suitable adjectives related to fashion from Activities 2 and 3.
- Encourage students to work with a partner and take turns to read the texts aloud to each other to practise pronunciation, word stress and intonation. Hearing as well as reading the text may also help students to decide on the missing adjective.
- Check answers with the class.

KEY

1 smart **2** embarrassed **3** overrated **4** old-fashioned **5** original **6** stylish **7** drab **8** comfortable **9** scruffy **10** casual

GRAMMAR ACTIVITY 5 — PAGE 116

- Ask students to revise the formation and use of the past perfect tense on page 265 of the Grammar Reference. Give students some time to read and then elicit that the past perfect is formed with *had* + past participle of the verb. We use the past perfect tense when we are already talking about the past but need to refer to a point or an action further back in time. If appropriate, ask students if a similar tense exists in their own language and how it is formed.
- Tell students to close the Grammar Reference and elicit the answer to Activity 5 from the class.

KEY

c

GRAMMAR ACTIVITY 6 — PAGE 117

Ask the class which two elements from the list we use to make the past perfect.

KEY

f j

GRAMMAR ACTIVITY 7 — PAGE 117

- Elicit from the class the rule for forming the positive, negative and interrogative forms of the past perfect tense as a reminder before students do the activity.
- Ask students to complete the sentences and check answers with the class.

KEY

1 Hadn't he met **2** She had ... woken up **3** They had not ... served **4** I had ... left **5** Had you tried

EXTENSION

Ask students to think of an important moment in their life, e.g. their first day at school, and then make a list of five things they hadn't done before that moment in time, using the past perfect.

I had not met my friend Chris.
I had not studied English.

GRAMMAR ACTIVITY 8 — PAGE 119

- Ask the class to review the formation and use of the past simple and past continuous tenses, the past perfect and the present perfect by looking through pages 263–266 of the Grammar Reference.
- Give students the opportunity to ask you about any aspect of these, and then direct students to the activity. Remind students of the character of the celebrity/singer Rachel Ritz, whom they met in Unit 2, and ask them to choose the best options.
- Check answers with the class.

KEY

1 was **2** was wearing **3** did you wear **4** wanted **5** was **6** have been able to **7** had watched

UNIT 4: SPEAKING PREPARATION — SPEAKING

GRAMMAR ACTIVITY 9 — PAGES 118–119

- Briefly revise the differences in use for the past simple, the past continuous and the past perfect with the class. Explain that the past simple tense is the one that we use the most for finished events in past. We use the past perfect to refer to things that happened before that moment and the past continuous tense is usually for ongoing background events that are often interrupted.
- Ask students to complete the sentences with the appropriate tenses. Explain that sometimes more than one answer is possible.
- Check answers with the class, asking students to give reasons for their choices.

KEY

1. She was sleeping, the alarm went off
2. He went
3. were they doing, the show was taking place
4. The road was, it rained/had rained
5. She was travelling, she got engaged to her husband
6. Kate had, won
7. were you doing/did you do, you heard
8. He didn't have/He hadn't had, he was
9. I got, I hadn't remembered
10. We felt, we hadn't had/didn't have

TEACHING TIPS

Q1: This refers to a longer and shorter simultaneous action. The action of sleeping was continuous and was interrupted by the alarm going off.

Q2: This is a finished action in a finished time frame.

Q3: These actions were both 'happening' at the time of speaking, so both clauses take a continuous form.

Q4: The past perfect is possible, but we are more likely to use past simple for both.

Q5: This refers to a longer and a shorter simultaneous action.

Q6: This refers to one event occurring before another, and is therefore past perfect.

Q7: The meanings here are different – *What were you doing* refers to a simultaneous action, whereas *What did you do* refers to their immediate response to the news.

Q8: Either are possible, depending on how strongly you want to emphasise the causal relationship.

Q10: The usage depends how strongly you wish to emphasise the causal relationship between events.

GRAMMAR GAME: TENSES DUELLING — PAGE 119

- Follow the instructions in the Student Book to play the game. Demonstrate how to play with the whole class by asking the students to line up in two rows facing each other and eliciting a few example sentences from volunteers.
- At the beginning of the game, the teacher decides if the sentences are correct or not. As more students are eliminated, they can start to take over this role and become a jury that votes on whether or not to accept the sentences.

SELF-EVALUATION — PAGE 119

Tell students to look at the Self-evaluation table and tick the boxes that are true for them. Ask them if there are any topics they don't feel confident about yet.

READING PART 1

OVERVIEW

Topic: Travel and holidays
Exam skills: Revise the requirements for Part 1 of the Reading and Writing exam, practise Part 1 sample questions, evaluate your exam practice
Assessment Objectives: 1A
Vocabulary: Compound adjectives
Grammar: Use modals of obligation, advice and permission
Practice text type: Tourist brochure: 'London with Lonsdale Tours', Holiday leaflet: 'Halliday's Holidays'
Additional resources: audio player, travel magazines, dictionaries, small blank cards/slips of paper (internet access)

I have not been abroad yet, but in future I hope to go to …
The idea of living abroad really appeals/doesn't appeal to me because …
In my country, the most interesting city is probably …
It is hard to choose which of my country's cities is most interesting because …
I prefer quiet holidays to active ones because …
Active holidays definitely appeal to me more than quiet ones because …
For me the best thing about travelling is …, the worst is …

PREPARING THE WAY   PAGE 122

- Holidays and travel is a topic that many will find motivating and there are a lot of readily available resources online and elsewhere on this subject which you could use for extension or support activities.
- Tell students to read the chapter topic title and elicit from them the holidays they enjoyed most/least and why.
- Focus students on the questions. Check that they understand the meaning of *abroad* (in or to a country that is not your own country). If students are able to sustain a class or small group discussion, ask them to discuss each question in detail.
- Point out that these discussion tasks are useful practice for the speaking exam, which is revisited in the final unit of the book.
- If students need more support, put some key words and phrases on the board (see Key below). Ask them to produce brief written responses and compare their ideas with a partner or in groups.
- Take feedback from the class and build up a list on the board of the countries in the world students have visited. Find out the class's attitude towards travel and the sort of holidays and holiday destinations students find appealing.

EXTENSION

Suggested activities:

- Students write and/or present a detailed description of their best holiday ever, explaining: where they went, who they went with, what the journey was like, why the holiday was so good.
- Students write a series of postcards home from a holiday that a) started badly and got better or b) started well and got worse.
- Give students access to holiday brochures or web pages and get them to design their own brochure entry for their ideal holiday resort and hotel.
- Ask students to provide a list of instructions for enjoying a successful holiday, e.g. research the location, pack your suitcase, confirm travel arrangements. Cut the list up into separate slips (one per instruction) and have them swap with a partner and try to put the list back in the right order.
- Divide students into two groups. Ask one group to research the damage done by the tourist trade/holiday industry and another to research the benefits (could be in students' own country or a different one). Get them to compare their findings, e.g. in a class debate, through creating display work.
- Ask students to discuss this quotation from Lao Tzu: *A good traveller has no fixed plans, and is not intent on arriving.* As a follow-up, they could find other quotations on the topic of travel and explain why they agree/disagree with them, in speech or in writing.

KEY

Students' own answers.
Suggested sentence structures for discussion:
I have been abroad once, when I visited …

82 UNIT 5: READING PRACTICE — READING PART 1

ACTIVITY 1 🔊 PAGE 122

- Tell the class that they are going to listen to a short radio interview with a tour guide (someone who shows tourists/visitors around tourist sites) and practise their listening skills in a topic-related context.
- Ask students to read the questions and underline key words so they know what information to look out for. Check they understand the meaning of *natural attraction* (natural feature of a landscape that people like to visit/look at), *disappointing* (not living up to or meeting expectations).
- It might also be a good idea to check/pre-teach: *tourist spots* (places that are popular with tourists), *on call* (available to respond to problems and/or requests), *awe-inspiring* (causing you to feel great respect or admiration, 'awe'), *fed up* (annoyed, frustrated, tired of), *most impressive* (grandest, most spectacular).
- Tell them that the order of the questions follows the sequence of the interview.
- Direct students to the photo of the Oriental Pearl Tower. Try to elicit its name, where it is and as much information as the students know about it. (See above in Background Info)

Background information

The building in the photograph which is mentioned by the tour guide is the Oriental Pearl Tower in Shanghai, built in 1994. At 468 metres high, it is the second tallest building in China (after the Shanghai World Financial Center) and has become an important landmark and tourist attraction in the city. It contains a revolving restaurant and history museum and offers a great view over the city. The other famous building mentioned in the recording is the Taj Mahal in Agra in India. It was built between 1631 and 1648 by the Mughal emperor, Shah Jahan, to house the tomb of his favourite wife, Mumtaz Mahal, and is a famous tourist attraction. It is constructed entirely of white marble and is surrounded by gardens.

AUDIOSCRIPT: Student Book pages 287–288

Oscar: So, Zelda, what's it like being a tour guide?
Zelda: Well, I must say it's a fantastic job. I've travelled all around the world, for a start.
Oscar: Really? Which countries have you visited?
Zelda: I was in Japan last week and China just before that. I've also been to Egypt and to India, as well as lots of countries in Europe.
Oscar: I would guess that you've seen lots of well-known tourist spots then?
Zelda: Yes, I have, although my favourite places are often the places that aren't quite so well-known.
Oscar: Oh?

Zelda: Mm. Some of the most awe-inspiring sights are the natural ones, like waterfalls, rather than buildings, although of course there are some 'must-see' buildings too!
Oscar: Yes. I guess you've seen all the world-famous ones?
Zelda: Most, yes. Although I haven't seen the Taj Mahal, yet and I'd really like to. Apparently, it's absolutely amazing. And I'd love to go up the Oriental Pearl Tower and enjoy the all-round, 360-degree view.
Oscar: So, what's it like actually working as a tour guide? Don't you get fed up, feeling that you're on call for twenty-four hours a day if something goes wrong for the travellers you're looking after?
Zelda: I can see how you might think that and I suppose it could be a problem. But usually things are fine. It's quite rare for there to be any big problems and if anything does go wrong, I can usually sort it out quite quickly.
Oscar: What sort of things go wrong?
Zelda: Well, sometimes people don't like the view they have from their hotel, for example. They may expect to be looking out at forest-covered mountains and instead their room overlooks a car park. That doesn't make them happy.
Oscar: No, I can understand that. So, what can you do about it? You can't build a mountain for them!
Zelda: Well, no. But if the hotel has any available rooms with a better view, they can arrange for the guests to be moved. Mainly, I think it's about people having full and accurate information when they book, so that their expectations are realistic.
Oscar: Definitely.
Zelda: After all, if they've paid for a three-star hotel, they can't expect a five-star experience!
Oscar: That's very true ...

KEY

(Clues underlined in Audioscript.)
1. travelling the world
2. Japan, China, Egypt, India, lots of countries in Europe
3. natural places rather than buildings
4. waterfalls
5. the (all-round/360 degree) view
6. People might not like the view from their hotel.
7. The hotel could move them into a different room.
8. get full/accurate information when booking

DIFFERENTIATION

Strengthen: Check that students have underlined or identified appropriate key words in the questions that will direct them towards the answers as they listen, e.g. Q1 *advantage*, Q2 *countries*, Q3 *impressive*, Q4 *attraction*.

Challenge: Ask students to write some further questions for Zelda, and her answers to them.

READING PART 1   **UNIT 5: READING PRACTICE**

EXAM REFRESHER — PAGE 122

- This section revisits the Reading paper and gives students more practice with exam-style materials.
- Ask students to read through the Exam Refresher box and remind themselves of what they have to do in Part 1 of the Reading and Writing exam.
- Give students a minute or so to read the requirements and then ask them to tell you (without looking back at the text) what skills are important in this part of the exam. Try to elicit the following: understanding the overall message, skimming, scanning and matching and sorting information.

ACTIVITY 2 — PAGE 123

- Tell students they are now going to think about exam technique. Ask them to read the statements and decide with a partner whether or not they think each one is correct.
- Give students a minute or so to go through the statements and compare their ideas about them with another pair. Then check answers with the class.

KEY

✗ The first time you read the paragraphs, make sure you understand the all the details.
  Hint: The first time students read they should concentrate on just understanding the main ideas. They will not have enough time to consider every single detail until they have a clearer sense of the information they are looking for.

✓ Use scanning skills: look for synonyms in the questions and text(s) to help you.
  Hint: This should help students locate the relevant information.

✗ If you can't decide between two answers, you should put crosses for both of them.
  Hint: This will get a mark of zero even if one answer is correct.

✗ Don't answer any questions you're not sure about.
  Hint: Unanswered questions will definitely gain zero. Guessing is not ideal, but it does give students a chance of being right.

PRACTICE TIME 1 — PAGES 123–125

- Read the Exam Hints for Reading Part 1 aloud with the class before students start the practice. Elicit from the group when they should use skimming skills (whilst reading the text the first time to get an idea of what it is about and how it is structured), and when their scanning skills will be useful (whilst searching for specific information and key words to answer specific questions).
- Remind students to read the questions first so they know what to look out for even when reading the text for the first time. Advise them to underline the key lexical words in each question. Remind students to think about looking for synonyms of these words as well as the words themselves.
- Check the meaning of some of the more challenging vocabulary items in the text with the class, e.g. *antiques* (very old objects such as furniture, pictures), *stunningly* (amazingly or surprisingly), *put someone off something* (to make someone dislike something or someone, or to discourage someone from doing something), *dummy* (a figure of a person), *flock* (to come in large numbers), *a host of* (a lot of), *exhibits* (the things there are to look at in a museum), *display* (a collection of objects or pictures arranged for people to look at).
- Give students time to complete the activity, working individually under exam conditions, then check answers with the class.

KEY

1 G **2** I **3** D **4** B **5** A **6** J **7** F **8** E **9** C **10** J

84 UNIT 5: READING PRACTICE — READING PART 1

> **REFLECT** — PAGE 125
>
> - Ask the class to work through the Reflect questions with a partner and discuss which of the things listed they did or did not manage to do.
> - Tell students to help their partner evaluate his or her progress and set a target for the next Practice Time test.
> - Encourage students to give each other positive support.

> **PRACTICE TIME 2** — PAGES 125–127
>
> - Ask students to check their outcomes from the first Practice Time, and to pay attention to the areas they need to work on. Is there anything they can learn from the first Practice Time that could help them with this next Practice Time?
> - Before they start the activity, remind students that the questions might focus in more detail on some paragraphs of the text than others.
> - Some expressions you could help students with here could include: *to unwind* (to relax), *a spot of* (a bit of), *complimentary* (free or included as extra at no extra cost), *antics* (funny or silly or strange behaviour), *feast for the eyes* (beautiful to look at), *legendary* (very famous and admired or spoken about), *renowned* (well-known or famous for), *chime* (the sound a clock makes on the hour).
> - As before, give students time to complete the activity, working individually under exam conditions, then check answers with the class.

KEY

1 F 2 C 3 J 4 I 5 B 6 A 7 H 8 D 9 E 10 J

TEACHING TIPS

Hint Q1: The two key words are *wildlife* and *coastline*. Paragraphs C, E and F mention the sea or sea travel (C *leisurely cruise*, E *turquoise sea*, F *cruise ship*) but only F also mentions *wildlife*.

Hint Q2: Several paragraphs mention specific items of food/drink (A *hot chocolate*, I *apple strudel*), but only two mention dining in a more general way (C *restaurant*, H *cuisine*). Of these, H says nothing about free dining, whereas C refers to a *24-hour free on-board restaurant*, so this is clearly the answer.

Hint Q3: Two key words appear in the question: *city* and *night*. Three paragraphs, D, I and J use the word *city*, but it is only J that also has a clear reference to night ('*Moonlight Tour*').

Hint Q4: The key phrase in the question is *photo opportunities*. This is where students need to be familiar with the nature of each different section of the exam and what it is testing. Two paragraphs, F and G, refer to views that are *spectacular* (F) or *amazing* (G). There is an implication here that these views would make good photographs. However, this section tests students' ability to match information, not to use inference (and in any case students should always look for the answer that matches the question most closely). In this case, the answer is clearly I, which refers explicitly to the city of Heidelberg being a *photographer's dream*.

Hint Q5: The key phrase *lively place* to shop should direct students to Paragraph B, which refers to *colourful and busy markets*. A market is a place where people can shop (shopping is not mentioned elsewhere) and the adjectives *colourful* and *busy* match the description *lively place*.

Hint Q6: This question is relatively easy if students recognise the phrase *winter sports*, as this should lead them to Paragraph A, which contains the related vocabulary *Swiss Alps, skiing, log fire* and *snowboarding*. Even if they do not know the word winter, they should recognise sports, and again this should guide them to the correct paragraph, particularly if they recognise skiing and snowboarding as sports.

Hint Q7: Paragraphs A, C, H and I broadly mention food (see Q2) so the word *exceptional* is important here. Two paragraphs, A and I, can be discounted, as before, because they are referring to one specific item (in the case of A this is a drink, not an item of food). This leaves C and H. C was the answer to Q2, but the rubric states that *Paragraphs may be used more than once or not at all*, so that in itself does not rule C out. However, C refers to a *restaurant* whereas H refers directly to *cuisine*, a better match for *food*, suggesting that H is the answer. In addition (as a checking mechanism and/or for students who do not recognise the word *cuisine*), the emphasis in C is that the restaurant is *24-hour, free* and *on-board*, saying nothing about the quality of the food itself, whereas H describes the *cuisine* as *legendary*.

Hint Q8: The words *international* and *sporting* would guide most students directly to the correct answer, D, because of its reference to the *Olympic stadium*. Paragraph A refers directly to sport, so some students might need to guess. Narrowing the possibilities down to two answers does give them a higher chance of guessing correctly than if they chose an answer at random. Matching the words *venue* and *stadium* might also be a clue for some students.

Hint Q9: This could be challenging in that none of the paragraphs refer directly to *swimming*, so students will need to identify other key words associated with swimming to guide them to the answer. Two paragraphs are possibilities, G (*traditional beachside holiday*) and E (*pool ... fabulous turquoise sea*). It should immediately then be clear that E must be the answer, as the question refers explicitly to *different types* of swimming. G suggests only one (*beachside*), whereas E identifies two different options (*pool* and *sea*).

Hint Q10: Again, the answer is not given directly, and students may struggle if they do not know the word *bell*. If they do, in the absence of any explicit reference to bells, they could find the words *chime*, *clock tower* and *listen*. However, even if they do not recognise *bell*, they are likely to recognise *tell the time*, or at least *time*. The word *clock* would then be a clue to the correct answer.

READING PART 1 — UNIT 5: READING PRACTICE

EVALUATE YOUR EXAM PRACTICE
PAGE 127

- Tell the class to work through the exam evaluation questions with a partner.
- Ask students to help their partner evaluate his or her progress and set targets for areas to work on and for the forthcoming exam.
- Encourage students to distinguish between different types of errors they may have made, e.g. missing answers out, not following the exam rubric, not knowing specific vocab, getting confused about the question. Do any patterns emerge?
- Encourage students to give each other positive support.

VOCABULARY AND GRAMMAR

VOCABULARY ACTIVITY 1 — PAGES 127–128

- Write *freshly-baked* on the board and ask the class what kind of word it is. Elicit that it is an adjective and further elicit or tell the class that it is a compound adjective, made of two words joined by hyphen.
- Ask the class if they can give you examples of compound adjectives. Try to find some examples in the class, e.g. *a black-and-white bag, a ten-page essay*.
- Ask students to find compound adjectives in the text to match the meanings given.
- Check answers with the class.

KEY

1 forest-covered (paragraph I line 38)
2 awe-inspiring (paragraph F line 26)
3 24-hour (paragraph C line 13)
4 five-star (paragraph D line 16)
5 on board (paragraph I line 41)
6 world-famous (paragraph D line 19)
7 week-long (paragraph A lines 1–2)

VOCABULARY ACTIVITY 2 — PAGE 128

- Ask students to work in pairs to try to come up with the clearest and best definition for each of these compound adjectives.
- If students are not sure about the meaning, tell them to look at the word in context in the text in which it appears. Using their knowledge of what the individual words in the compound mean will also help.
- Check answers with the class and agree on the group's preferred definition for each word.

KEY

LT = Lonsdale tours, HH = Halliday's Holidays
Suggested answers:
1 must-see (LT line 4, HH line 33): should not be missed; important, impressive
2 open-air (LT line 6): outside, not indoors
3 360-degree (LT line 10): from every direction, all-round
4 well-known (LT line 12): famous, or at least familiar to lots of people

VOCABULARY ACTIVITY 3 — PAGES 128–129

- Ask students to work either individually or in pairs to match the words to make compound adjectives. Explain that there are a few correct alternative pairings (*cold-blooded* and *warm-hearted* which could also be *warm-blooded* and *cold-hearted*).
- Check answers with the class before going on to the second part of the activity and try to elicit examples of each compound adjective used to describe a noun, e.g. *a part-time job*, *a man-eating crocodile*.
- Then ask students to classify the adjectives according to whether they relate to time or physical and emotional characteristics. Note that *full-length* can refer to both time and physical qualities.

KEY

1 part-time, man-eating, full-length, twentieth-century, middle-aged, three-minute, heart-breaking, cold-hearted, warm-blooded

2

Compound adjectives – time	Compound adjectives – characteristics (physical or emotional)
part-time	man-eating
full-length (e.g. film)	full-length (e.g. coat)
twentieth-century	heart-breaking
middle-aged	cold-hearted
three-minute	warm-blooded

VOCABULARY ACTIVITY 4 — PAGE 129

- This gap-fill activity will consolidate students' knowledge and understanding of the compound adjectives they have been working on.
- Ask students to complete the activity and then compare their ideas with a partner before you check answers with the class.

KEY

1 non-stop 2 five-star 3 well-known
4 awe-inspiring 5 mouth-watering 6 freshly-baked
7 360-degree 8 week-long

GRAMMAR ACTIVITY 5 — PAGE 130

- Tell students to revise modal verbs by looking at Grammar Reference page 269.
- Ask students to work in pairs to order the modal verbs of permission from least formal to most formal, and then to complete the sentences using the correct modal verb.
- When you check answers with the class, explain that in modern English *may* is used in formal situations as a polite way of asking permission, *can* is the informal way of doing this and *could* is somewhere between the two. It's more formal than *can* but less formal than *might*.
- For Q2, explain that we use *might* to indicate that something is possible, but we are not completely sure if it will happen or not, e.g. *It might rain tomorrow*. We use *must* to show obligation, e.g. *You must wear your raincoat*.
- *May* can also be used in a similar way to *might* to talk about things we are not sure of. *It may rain.* means the same as *It might rain*. Tell students this if they ask about it or the subject comes up, but this particular usage of *may* is not covered at this point in the Student Book.

KEY

1 c a b
2 a might b may c must

GRAMMAR ACTIVITY 6 — PAGE 130

- Go through the meaning of the modal verbs in the box with the class, referring back to what they have just revised in the Grammar Reference.
- Ask students to fill in the gaps with the most polite option. Point out that they need to decide whether the speaker is asking permission (*may I*, *could I* or *can I*), giving advice or saying that something is a good idea (*should*) or asking someone to do something (*would*, *could*, *can*).
- When students choose a verb which is correct as far as the meaning is concerned but not the most polite option, encourage them to discuss the differences between the different options.

KEY

1 May 2 should 3 Would/Could/Can
4 May/Could/Can 5 Would/Could/Can

GRAMMAR ACTIVITY 7 — PAGE 130

- Remind students of the difference between obligation (related to tasks to be completed) and permission (rules made by another person).
- Ask students to complete the table.
- Some students may be uncomfortable with the idea of *should* and *ought to* as obligation. If this is the case, encourage them to think of these words as expressing the same idea as *must* and *have to*, but in less strong terms.

KEY

Obligation	Permission
should	can
must	could
have to	may
ought to	

EXTENSION

These activities are designed to give students further practice using modals for giving advice, and using modals of obligation and permission.

- In order to practise using the modal verbs *should* and *ought to*, ask students to write down a list of imaginary problems that they (or somebody else) might have. Then, have them ask each other advice and reply using *should* and *ought to*. A typical exchange could be:

    A: I keep losing my pens. What should I do?

    B: You ought to buy a pencil case.

    These problems can be as imaginative and interesting as the students like.

- In order to practise modals of obligation and permission, ask students to create a list of class rules as a group. For example:

    Students must speak in English during the class.

    Students don't have to speak in English during the break.

    Students can ask for help if they do not understand.

    Students mustn't come late to class.

GRAMMAR ACTIVITY 8 — PAGE 131

- Ask students to work in pairs to circle the correct modal verbs for each sentence. Sometimes both options can be correct. They can refer to Grammar Reference page 270 if necessary.
- Remind them to think about whether the situation involves asking permission to do something, asking another person to do something, talking about obligation or giving advice.
- Check answers with the class.

KEY

1 should 2 Could 3 Would 4 mustn't
5 must/ought to 6 Should/Do 7 must 8 can
9 must 10 Can 11 Could 12 don't have to
13 Do 14 may 15 Could

TEACHING TIPS

Hint Q1: Dentists give you advice, but they do not create not an actual rule or law.

Hint Q2: *Would* is used only when making requests of other people, not when making offers.

Hint Q3: *Would* indicates a request to another person; *must* would be asking about obligation.

Hint Q4: *Don't have to* would mean that students can use their mobile phones if they wish to, but actually they are forbidden to.

Hint Q5: Both are possible here depending on the meaning: *must* is obligation whereas *ought to* indicates that it would be preferable. This is a good opportunity to clarify the difference between these two modals of obligation with students.

Hint Q6: We use *should* when requesting advice; *do* would indicate a direct question.

Hint Q7: *Must* is used for emphasis; *have to* would be an actual obligation.

Hint Q8: *Can* indicates permission; *might* would indicate possibility.

Hint Q9: Speed limits are obligations; *should* would be a suggestion.

Hint Q10: *Can* is used for requests; *would* is not used with *I* when making requests.

Hint Q11: *Could* is used for requests; *might* is used for possibility.

Hint Q12: *Don't have to* is used when something is not an obligation; *mustn't* would mean that eating breakfast is forbidden.

Hint Q13: *Have to* is conjugated like a regular verb in the present simple, with *do*.

Hint Q14: *May* is used when making a polite request with *I*.

Hint Q15: *May* is not used when making a polite request with *you*; *could* can be.

GRAMMAR GAME: LOCATION MODALS — PAGE 131

- Follow the instructions in the Student Book to play the game. Depending on how much time is available, you could ask students to write more than one set of sentences.
- You could put some more examples of sentence headers on the board to help students make phrases for their descriptions, e.g. *You can eat ..., You can see ...*

SELF-EVALUATION — PAGE 132

Tell students to look at the Self-evaluation table and tick the boxes that are true for them. Ask them if there are any topics they don't feel confident about yet.

88 UNIT 5: READING PRACTICE — READING PART 2

READING PART 2

OVERVIEW

Topic: Gadgets and technology

Exam skills: Revise the requirements for Part 2 of the Reading and Writing exam, practise Part 2 sample questions, evaluate your exam practice

Assessment Objectives: 1B, 1C, 1D

Vocabulary: Phrasal verbs

Grammar: Use future simple, future continuous and future perfect tenses; use *going to* and other ways of expressing the future

Practice text type: Articles: 'Driverless cars are going to save the world', 'The teaching assistants of the future'

Additional resources: audio player (internet access)

KEY

Students' own answers.

Suggested sentence structures for discussion:
Of all the gadgets I own, my favourite is …
I would love there to be a gadget for …
I used to have a … but …
My … broke some years ago, and …
I think that current technology will …
Some technology may …

Useful words and phrases: *change, transform, useful, to own, to save up for, to become out-dated, obsolete, invention*

PREPARING THE WAY — PAGE 133

- Tell students to read the chapter topic title and elicit from them the gadgets (a small device or machine that helps you in some way) or technology they use most. Also ask them if they feel there are some gadgets or technology that are overused at the present time.

- Ask students to read the questions and discuss them in pairs. If the students are able to sustain a class or small group discussion, you can ask them to discuss each question in detail. For the second question about gadgets and technology in the future, ask them to think about possible different kinds of machines that would help them.

- If students need more support, put some key words and phrases on the board (see Key below) and ask them to produce brief written responses and compare their ideas with a partner or in groups.

- Take feedback from the class and find out what students' favourite gadgets are and what they predict might appear in the future.

- You could ask follow-up questions to extend the discussion. For example, you could ask students' opinions on whether gadgets are important, whether they improve people's lives (and whether these improvements are important) and whether they are a waste of money.

EXTENSION

Suggested activities:

- Ask students to design a new gadget. They could present their ideas to their classmates and/or produce a written version of them.

- Ask students to work in pairs. Student A has to present Student B with a problem (e.g. *I keep losing my keys.*) and Student B has to find a way to solve it by inventing a new technology.

- Research new technologies currently being developed. What changes will they make to a) human life, b) the natural world?

- Ask students to list ten technological advances and to rank order them in order of usefulness, e.g. *smartphone, computer, lightbulb, wheel, telephone, television, internet, Satellite Navigation Systems, radar, bar coding* (that lets shops scan goods electronically, for example), *CCTV* (Closed Circuit Television), *space rockets, helicopters, planes, submarines, cameras.*

- Ask students to discuss the question: Do you think that certain technologies should not be used, even though they are possible?

- Ask students to come up with the storyline for a new science-fiction film and write an outline of the main characters and events, basing it on what they know about the science-fiction genre (i.e. film type).

- Ask students to discuss this quotation from Clive James: *It is only when things go wrong that machines remind you how powerful they are.* As a follow-up, they could find other quotations on the topic of technology or the future and explain why they agree/disagree with them, in speech or in writing.

READING PART 2 UNIT 5: READING PRACTICE 89

ACTIVITY 1 PAGES 133–134

- Direct students to the picture and the questions and check that they know what science fiction is. You can explain that the term covers books, films or cartoons about an imagined future, especially about space travel or other planets.
- Ask students what they think the connection is between the picture and science fiction. Elicit or suggest that the figure could be exploring another planet where the sky is a different colour and there are big rock formations, etc.
- Elicit examples of science-fiction books students have read or films they had seen (for example the *Star Wars* films).
- Explain that students are going to hear a radio interview with a science-fiction writer. Ask what sort of person they think a professional science-fiction writer would be, for example what would he/she be interested in?
- Tell students to read the questions and underline key words so they know what information to listen out for. You could check the meaning of: *relativity*, *nuclear physics* and *atom-splitting* (important scientific theories and discoveries), *Doctor Who* (a popular English television show based on time travel), *inspiration* (source of ideas), *abandoned* (deserted, left behind), *rethink* (to reconsider), historical figures (people from the past), *feedback* (comments, reactions).
- Play the recording, more than once if necessary, and ask students to answer the questions.
- After completing the listening part of the activiity, ask students to work in pairs to list out the books, cartoons, films and television shows that are related to the future or techonolgy. They can draw a table in their notebooks to do this. Once their lists are complete, ask students what the different categories have in common.

AUDIOSCRIPT: Student Book page 288

Farah: Morning, everyone. I'm delighted to be joined today by one of my favourite science-fiction writers, Abdu Karim. Great to have you here, Abdu.
Abdu: Great to be here!
Farah: Thank you so much for coming to talk to our group. First question: What got you interested in science fiction in the first place?
Abdu: Well, <u>as a child I loved reading and I also loved science</u>, so …
Farah: Sounds like science fiction was perfect for you!
Abdu: It was. As a child, I just loved escaping to another world through reading. Reading science fiction was a perfect escape, with so many stories about what could happen in the future.

Farah: And what is it about science that interested you most strongly? What particular area were you most drawn to?
Abdu: I'm really interested in the theory of relativity and in nuclear physics and atom-splitting, but what interests me most is <u>the concept of time and time travel</u>.
Farah: So, I'm assuming that, like me, you're a huge fan of *Doctor Who*, then?
Abdu: Definitely!
Farah: So, what is it about time travel that appeals to you?
Abdu: <u>I think we can learn from the past.</u> If we went back to see earlier times, <u>we could get inspiration from ideas that we may have abandoned before</u> and maybe rethink if they could actually be useful in the present! And there are definitely some historical figures I'd like to track down and talk to! Science fiction lets us imagine a world where all of that is possible.
Farah: It's certainly an interesting idea … If we met them, we might find that certain people would go up in our estimation!
Abdu: Or down!
Farah: Yes, indeed! And is this the basis of your new book, the one that's coming out this week?
Abdu: That's right. <u>I'm going to upload the first chapter to my website on Monday at midnight</u> and then people will have to buy the book if they want to find out what happens next.
Farah: Great. And can they post feedback on your website too?
Abdu: Of course.
Farah: Sounds good. And just before you leave us, Abdu, what, for you, is the main reason we should keep reading and writing science fiction? What makes it important?
Abdu: Ah, that's a good question. For me, <u>it gives us an insight into where technology may be heading</u>. Once the ideas are in place, it's only a matter of time before the science catches up.
Farah: Fascinating. Thank you so much for your time, Abdu. Good luck with the new book!

KEY

(Clues underlined in Audioscript.)
1 A **2** C **3** B **4** D **5** A
2 Students' own answers.

DIFFERENTIATION

Strengthen: Check that students have underlined or identified appropriate key words in the multiple-choice answers that will help them differentiate and pick out the precise information they hear.

Challenge: Ask students to write some further questions for Abdu, and his answers to them.

90 UNIT 5: READING PRACTICE   READING PART 2

EXAM REFRESHER — PAGE 134

- Ask students to read through the Exam Refresher box and remind themselves of what they have to do in Part 2 of the Reading and Writing exam.
- Give students a minute or so to read and then ask them to tell you (without looking back at the text) the main skills they have to use and the main task types that they have to deal with in this part of the exam. Try to elicit the following:
  skills: identifying attitudes and opinions in the text, identifying different types of information, comprehension and analytical skills.
  task types: gap fill, multiple-choice questions.

ACTIVITY 2 — PAGE 134

- Tell students they are now going to think about exam technique. Ask them to read the statements and decide with a partner whether or not they think each one is correct.
- Give students a minute or so to go through the statements and compare their ideas about them with another pair. Then check answers with the class.

KEY

✗ For short-answer questions, you can use your own words, but you must not write more than the specified number of words.
  Hint: Students must use words taken directly from the text.
✗ Try to write a sentence for the three-word answers.
  Hint: This is not necessary/possible.
✓ If you aren't sure of the answers to multiple-choice questions, you should choose one anyway.
  Hint: This will give students a chance of getting a mark.

PRACTICE TIME 1 — PAGES 135–137

- Read the Exam Hints for Reading Part 2 aloud with the class before students start the practice.
- Remind them again that they must follow the requirements for word limits exactly or they will lose marks.

- Remind students to read the questions first so they know what to look out for even when reading the text for the first time. Advise them to underline the key lexical words in each question. Remind students to think about looking for synonyms of these words as well as the words themselves.
- Remind students that the answers follow the sequence of the exam and of the texts. Reading Part 2 begins with Q11 because Reading Part 1 ended with Q10. Within the texts, Q11–20 follow the order of information given in the text about driverless cars, but so do Q21–25. So, when students start looking at the second set of questions, they will need to study the passage about driverless cars from the beginning again.
- You might want to check the meaning of some of the more challenging items in the text, for example: *game changer* (something which completely changes a situation), *power-steering* (a system for changing the direction in which a road vehicle is moving by using power from the engine to help the driver turn the vehicle), *congestion* (being blocked or crowded), *snarled-up* (here, blocked by traffic and difficult to drive through).
- Give students time to read the text and answer Q11–25, working under exam conditions.

KEY

11 (a) game changer   12 sci-fi films   13 power-steering   14 congestion   15 road capacity   16 less pollution   17 road rage   18 (using) social media   19 convenience and ease   20 a joy   21 C   22 A   23 D   24 B   25 C

TEACHING TIPS

Hint Q11: The writer makes a number of statements at the start of the passage about the change to driverless cars; only the correct answer, *a game changer*, fits the three-word requirement.

Hint Q12: These two sentences distinguish between the past and now: *For a long time, driverless cars have been a staple of sci-fi films. However, it now looks as if the future has arrived.* Therefore, the answer is *sci-films*.

Hint Q13: The word *first* gives the clue that the answer here is *power steering*.

Hint Q14: In terms of *cost* and *energy*, *congestion* (the answer) is described as being *massively expensive* and is linked to two different kinds of costs, direct and indirect.

Hint Q15: The answer supplied is very close to a paraphrase of the question: *A University of Texas study suggests that if*

*90 per cent of cars on motorways were **self-driving**, road capacity would be **doubled**.*

Hint Q16: The answer to this is clear: *They'll be driven much more fuel-efficiently too*, which will mean less pollution.

Hint Q17: Remind students that their answers must match the question in terms of their syntax and grammar. This question asks about *negative emotional states*, so *stressful* and *road rage* are both possible answers, but only *road rage* fits grammatically. Students would have to change the wording of the text from *stressful* (adjective) to *stress* (noun), which is not permitted.

Hint Q18: The key is the notion of time use/gain, which links to the reference in the passage to *more hours to use productively*. The writer then explores a range of possibilities: *Perhaps you'll … Perhaps you'll …*, before explaining what he thinks people will actually do with their time, i.e. spend it on social media.

Hint Q19: The writer states that *People love convenience and ease more than they love abstract notions of rights*. The phrase *abstract notions* links with the key word *ideas*, which is used in the question, and the fact that *two advantages* are mentioned in the question is a further clue.

Hint Q20: The key here is the numeric *80s*, which is easily distinguishable in the passage.

Hint Q21: Of the four adjectives supplied, C (*revolutionary*) is the best match, as *change*, a synonym, is repeated throughout the first section.

Hint Q22: The student needs to identify the correct type of benefit from the four options provided. Several are described, but the key word in the question is *first*. This should guide students to the sentence that says: *For a start, the economic upsides are huge*. The answer is *financial* (from the same lexical family as *economic*).

Hint Q23: Three of the options are not directly mentioned in the passage, so the answer is D.

Hint Q24: The key phrase students should look for is *walking and cycling*. They then have to deduce the writer's opinion of these activities as he experiences them currently. His reference *to a soup of burnt hydrocarbons and road rage* rules out A and B as answers. D is possible but only by extension; what he describes may or may not involve noise, but it definitely sounds *unpleasant*, hence the answer is B.

Hint Q25: This question is relatively easy, as the passage refers to the writer's son, which tells students where to find the answer (at the end of the passage). Of the options given, C is the best synonym for *silly*, but even without knowing this word, students could work out the answer through a process of elimination – none of the others fit.

REFLECT — PAGE 137

- Ask the class to work through the Reflect questions with a partner and discuss which of the things listed they did or did not manage to do.
- Tell students to help their partner evaluate his or her progress and set a target for the next Practice Time test.
- Encourage students to give each other positive support.

PRACTICE TIME 2 — PAGE 138–140

- Ask students to check their outcomes from the first Practice Time, and to pay attention to the areas they need to work on. Is there anything they can learn from it that could help them with this Practice Time?
- Draw students' attention to the Exam Hints for Reading Part 2 on the left-hand side of the page before they start the activity and remind them again that they must follow the requirements for word limits exactly or they will lose marks.
- Remind students to read the questions first so they know what to look out for even when reading the text for the first time. Advise them to underline the key lexical words in each question. Remind students to think about looking for synonyms of these words as well as the words themselves.
- You might want to check the meaning of some of the more challenging items in the text, for example: *transform* (change completely), *compulsory* (you have to do it, you can't choose), *to query* (to ask questions about), *to anticipate* (to guess or imagine something before it happens).
- Give students time to read the text and answer Q11–25, working under exam conditions.

KEY

11 computer science **12** 10000 **13** low retention rates **14** 2014 **15** (a) computer code **16** (relevant) reading material **17** (a) hidden forum **18** 26 April **19** Tyson Bailey **20** next term **21** D **22** A **23** C **24** D **25** D

TEACHING TIPS

Hint Q11: The answer is given clearly in the passage: *the Knowledge Based Artificial Intelligence (KBAI) class is a compulsory element of the computer science programme*.

Hint Q12: Keys words are *posts*, *forum* and *each group of students*. The word *posts* does not appear but the synonym *messages* does, and the answer is explicit: *using online forums provided by the college. There are about 10 000 messages for each cohort of students*.

Hint Q13: Relevant information appears in two sentences: *online classes struggle to keep students* and *They have low retention rates compared to face-to-face classes*. Both statements are relevant, so students need to consider the form their answer must take, i.e. it must be three words or less and taken from the passage. This rules out the first option and leaves the second as the correct answer.

Hint Q14: The word *when* suggests the answer relates to a time or date. Because KBAI is the subject being asked about, the answer should be clear from the proximity of KBAI and a date, i.e. *the KBAI course launched in 2014*.

Hint Q15: Following the sequence of information in the passage, the answer should be clear, as a sentence soon after the answer to Q14 refers to *computer code written specifically for Jill*.

Hint Q16: The answer is clear and follows on immediately in the first line of paragraph 5, which states an issue for that students was *where to locate reading material*.

Hint Q17: The next part of the text deals with the errors that Jill made early on, so does not at first sight appear to be relevant to this question. However, the text goes on to explain that these errors were posted in a *hidden forum*, which is the answer.

Hint Q18: The word *reveal*, important in this question, does not appear directly in the passage. However, the word *told* does, followed by the phrase *huge surprise*. These three words together act as a synonym for *reveal*, for students who are struggling to identify the answer from the information as it is given in context.

Hint Q19: The phrase *Which student* should tell students to look for the name of an individual in the relevant section of the text, i.e. towards the end. The answer, *Tyson Bailey*, is then clear, especially as he is introduced as *one student*.

Hint Q20: Assuming they got Q19 correct, students should know to look for a *time* when Jill will return to work. Students who know the word *term* will find it particularly easy to find the answer, *next term*. Even without this, they may be able to work the answer out through the context and detail supplied.

Hint Q21: As always with multiple-choice questions, students should try to eliminate answers that are clearly wrong before comparing answers that are potentially valid. As the question asks why Goel employed a virtual TA for his online course, the answer is likely to be connected to the statement *This is why Jill is so vital*, lines 24–25. Of the four options given, students need to find the closest match to the line before the one quoted, i.e. *This is often because students don't feel sufficiently supported*. This rules out A and C, as these answers are irrelevant. That leaves B and D. B refers to the busy-ness of staff whereas D refers to the volume of questions. The passage does not give information explicitly about how busy staff are, but it does refer explicitly to the volume of questions. The answer, therefore, is D.

Hint Q22: The key words in this question are *students*, *failing* and *complete online*. The key statement in working out the answer is *online classes struggle to keep students … often because students don't feel sufficiently supported*. In terms of the best match here, only A refers to students not getting enough *help* (a synonym for support) so that is the right answer. (It is important to remind students that the answer needs to come from the passage itself, as directed by the question. Some of the other answers may be valid answers to the original question, but they do not appear in the passage, so should not be selected.)

Hint Q23: This question again requires students to locate the relevant information, and in this case it appears in brackets. (Students should remember that text appearing in brackets is still part of the text and is still important.) In this case the passage says *when online courses attract more students, the volume of questions increases, but the range of questions doesn't*. The question identifies a mathematical enquiry: *If the number of students in an online class increases, what happens to the questions asked?* Looking at the options, it is clear that the answer is C, because A (*decreases*) and B (*remains exactly the same*) do not match the key word *increases*. D refers to a *much bigger variety of questions*, but the passage explicitly states that the range of questions does not increase. Therefore, the answer is C.

Hint Q24: For this question, students needed to understand the process that the passage describes: students asked for help; Jill produced answers but made some mistakes; she was given a hidden forum in which to practise; when her accuracy scores were high enough, she was allowed to interact with students herself. It was TAs who made the decision about her readiness, and although this is not stated directly, it is implied, and all of the other options are incorrect, so D is the answer.

Hint Q25: This question is relatively easy, as the passage states that students *were excited to hear the news* about Jill's real identity. They need to look, therefore, for the closest match to the adjective *excited*. Out of the four options, this is clearly the adverb *positively*, so the answer is D.

READING PART 2 | **UNIT 5: READING PRACTICE** 93

EVALUATE YOUR EXAM PRACTICE
PAGE 141

- Tell the class to work through the exam evaluation questions with a partner.
- Ask students to help their partner evaluate his or her progress and set targets for areas to work on and for the forthcoming exam.
- Encourage students to distinguish between different types of errors they may have made, e.g. missing answers out, not following the exam rubric, not knowing specific vocab, getting confused about the question. Do any patterns emerge?
- Encourage students to give each other positive support.

VOCABULARY AND GRAMMAR

VOCABULARY ACTIVITY 1   PAGE 141

- Ask the students to match the phrasal verbs to the correct definitions. Encourage the students to view the phrasal verbs in context in the second article (teaching assistants) in order to help them discern meaning.
- Then, for Q2, ask students to try and think of any other meanings for the phrasal verbs in Q1.
- If students are unable to think of any other phrasal verbs with *come*, you can ask them to look on the following pages for examples: page 32 (*come across*), page 60 (*come up with*), page 156 (*come back*), page 231 (*come round*). Then have students deduce their meaning from context.

KEY

1. get stuck on (line 38): find it impossible to progress beyond a certain point
   come out (line 37): appear, emerge
   go over (line 40): revise or revisit
   go up (line 32): increase or improve
   track down (line 29): search for and find
2. Suggested answers:
   get stuck on has the literal meaning to be physically stuck to (*The tape got stuck on his top.*)
   come out also means to disappear when it refers to dirt or a stain
   go up also means to build a building (*There's a new building going up on the corner.*)
3. Students' answers will vary. Alternative phrasal verbs with *come* include: *come across* (find), *come along* (join an outing), *come back* (return somewhere, or become popular again), *come by* (visit someone for a short time), *come down with* (become ill with a disease), *come into* (inherit), *come out with* (launch a new product or say something unexpected), *come over* (visit somebody, usually at home), *come round* (visit somebody, or regain consciousness), *come through* (succeed when people might not expect you to), *come up with* (invent a new idea or produce something new).

EXTENSION

Suggested activities:
- Write or dictate the following two columns, and ask students to connect the verbs with *go* to their definitions. Ask them to share their ideas in small groups and to use dictionaries as necessary.

1 go along with	a leave
2 go ahead	b activate or explode (a clock, a bomb, etc.)
3 go away	c match (clothes, colours)
4 go by	d pass (time)
5 go off	e study something in detail
6 go on	f experience something difficult
7 go out	g stop working (something electrical)
8 go over	h agree with what somebody says
9 go through	i start something
10 go up	j increase (a number)
11 go with	k continue

Go through the answers with the class and check understanding.

KEY
1 h 2 i 3 a 4 d 5 b 6 k
7 g 8 e 9 f 10 j 11 c

- Ask students to write example sentences for some or all of the verbs. Some examples are given below.
Paulie went along with my idea for the party.
Go ahead and begin the exercise.
I wish this bad weather would go away.
Several hours went by while we waited.
My alarm went off at six this morning, although I set it for seven.
If there is a fire alarm, people should not go on working.
The lights in my building have gone out.
Let's go over the plan for the concert again.
David went through a hard time when his parents were sick, but they are better now.
The price of petrol has gone up lately. What are you wearing? That shirt doesn't go with those trousers.

UNIT 5: READING PRACTICE — READING PART 2

VOCABULARY ACTIVITY 2 — PAGE 141

- Ask students to circle the correct phrasal verb for each sentence. They can refer back to the definitions in Activity 1 if necessary.
- Ask students to compare their answers with a partner before you check answers with the class.

KEY

1 been over 2 come out 3 track down 4 went up
5 get stuck on

VOCABULARY ACTIVITY 3 — PAGE 142

- This activity encourages students to actively produce the vocabulary from Activity 1.
- Ask students to use the five phrasal verbs from Activity 1 to complete the sentences.
- Let students know that they should be careful to put the verb in the correct tense while doing the activity.

KEY

1 get stuck on 2 going over 3 came out
4 track down 5 go up

GRAMMAR ACTIVITY 4 — PAGE 142

- Tell students to revise the formation and use of *will* and *going to* on pages 265–267 of the Grammar Reference before attempting the activity.
- Ask students to work independently but to compare their answers with a partner before you check answers with the class.
- Discuss why each answer is correct.

KEY

1 a 2 a 3 b 4 a

TEACHING TIPS

Hint Q1 and Q3: We use *will* for recently made plans.

Hint Q2: We use *will* for decisions made at the time of speaking.

Hint Q4: We use *going to* for plans that we have had for a while.

GRAMMAR ACTIVITY 5 — PAGES 142–143

- Ask students to explain the difference between the future simple and the future continuous. Elicit that the future continuous emphasises that an action is ongoing. We often use it to talk about a future event that will be going on around a certain time in the future, e.g. *This time tomorrow I will be sitting in the sun by the swimming pool.*
- If you think it would be helpful, tell students to see pages 265–266 of the Grammar Reference again before attempting the activity.

KEY

1 Raul won't disappoint 2 will you be doing
3 They will make 4 Will you sleep / Will you be sleeping 5 will you be wearing 6 I will be waiting

---

TEACHING TIPS

Hint Q1: We use the future simple for promises. This is a good opportunity to stress that *won't* is more common than *will not*.

Hint Q2: We use the future continuous with an action continuing during a specific moment in the future.

Hint Q3: We use the future simple for promises.

Hint Q4: Both are possible, but the meaning changes. *Will you sleep* asks if the listener will begin sleeping at ten, while *Will you be sleeping* asks if they will have already begun sleeping before ten. This is a good opportunity to stress this difference.

Hint Q5: We use the future continuous for continuing actions in the future, as is the case with *during the interview*.

Hint Q6: We use the future continuous with an action continuing during a specific moment in the future.

EXTENSION

- For more practice with future forms, play the grammar game *What Will Go Wrong?* Put the students into groups of three or four and choose one student to be the planner. The others are the problem-makers.
- One student has to state a plan that they have for the future using *going to*, e.g. *I'm going to play football on Saturday*.
- The other students have to invent reasons why that plan won't work using *will*, e.g. *the referee will forget to bring the ball*.
- The first player then has to solve the problem using *will*, e.g. *I'll bring a spare ball with me* or change the plan, e.g. *Then I'll go to the cinema instead*.
- The other students must continue to invent reasons why the new plan won't work.
- If the original student can't think of a new plan in four seconds, then a different student takes a turn to be the planner.

GRAMMAR ACTIVITY 6 — PAGE 143

- Tell students they need to imagine their lives in 50 years' time and write a paragraph about it. Tell them to consider the bullet points given and to start their paragraph as suggested in the example.
- Remind students to use the future continuous throughout the activity.
- After you have checked answers with the class, tell students to ask each other some more questions about their future lives.

KEY

See sample answer below.

SAMPLE ANSWER FOR ACTIVITY 6:

In 50 years' time, I will be living in the Bahamas in a big villa. I will be relaxing by the pool on a deck chair, reading a book. I will be wearing a T-shirt and shorts. My friends will be swimming in the pool near me.

GRAMMAR ACTIVITY 7 — PAGE 143

- Ask students to think about how technology will have changed in 50 years' time. Elicit some ideas from the class. You can direct them to the example and ideas listed in the activity.
- Ask students to write eight predictions about how technology will have changed in 50 years' time. They can use ideas elicited above or their own ideas. If necessary, you could write verbs that are commonly used with the future perfect ont the board, e.g. *change, stop, begin, end, forget, improve, get worse, start*.
- Compare answers as a class and make sure that students have used the future perfect correctly throughout.

KEY

Students' own answers.

GRAMMAR ACTIVITY 8 — PAGES 143–144

- Direct students to page 267 of the Grammar Reference to revise other structures for talking about the future.
- Tell students to match the sentences to the definitions. They should work independently but compare their ideas with a partner before you check answers with the class.
- Then ask students to look at the sentences in Q1 again and say what verb form follows the modals verbs in bold (the infinitive or base form).
- Ask students to write four sentences using *should, due to, likely to* and *about to*.

KEY

1 a ii b iv c i d iii
2 the infinitive or base form – Students' own answers.

UNIT 5: READING PRACTICE — READING PART 2

GRAMMAR ACTIVITY 9 — PAGE 144

- Ask students to work in pairs to circle the correct options. You might want to double-check their understanding of the difference between *about to* (to talk about something that is imminent and will happen any moment now), *due to* (to talk about something which should happen according to a schedule or a plan), and *likely to* (to talk about something that has a high probability of happening) before you start the activity.
- For all the sentences, tell students to think about whether the emphasis is on the continuation of the activity around a certain time in the future, or on the finished event.
- Check answers with the class.

KEY

1 should be arriving   2 is about to do
3 due to hand in   4 likely to   5 should be landing
6 likely to finish

TEACHING TIPS

Hints Q1, Q3, Q4: *About to* is used for something which will happen shortly, not at a planned later date.

Hint Q2: *Should be doing* is possible colloquially, if you suspect Haley is doing something else, but would not refer to the future.

Hint Q5: *Is likely to* is not followed by the *-ing* form of the verb.

Hint Q6: *Due to* is not followed by the *-ing* form of the verb.

GRAMMAR ACTIVITY 10 — PAGE 144

Ask students to work independently to locate and correct the mistakes in the email. They can then compare their ideas with a partner before you check answers with the class.

KEY

See annotated email below. Note some small variations may be possible.

To whom it may concern,

I am *about to* ~~being~~ be in a lot of trouble at school. I need to finish an essay which ~~will~~ should be completed by tomorrow. However, my computer isn't working, so tomorrow my teacher is ~~due~~ *likely* to be furious with me. Each time I press spellcheck, my essay turns into a series of random letters. I am about to cry~~ing~~. It ~~will~~ might be OK, if you could write me an email explaining that my computer is not working and so I won't be ~~being~~ able to complete my essay. I go to school at 7 o'clock, so please *can* you ~~will~~ write the email before then.

Best wishes,

Daphne

GRAMMAR GAME: FUTURE ACTION MIME — PAGE 145

- Follow the instructions in the Student Book.
- Demonstrate the activity by miming some actions yourself in front of the class, allowing students to continue in their groups once you are sure they have understood what they are supposed to be doing.
- Ensure that students use the future continuous throughout.

SELF-EVALUATION — PAGE 145

Tell students to look at the Self-evaluation table and tick the boxes that are true for them. Ask them if there are any topics they don't feel confident about yet.

READING PART 3 | **UNIT 5: READING PRACTICE** 97

READING PART 3

OVERVIEW

Topic: Houses and other buildings
Exam skills: Revise the requirements for Part 3 of the Reading and Writing exam, practise Part 3 sample questions, evaluate your exam practice
Assessment Objectives: 1B, 1C, 1D
Vocabulary: Nouns and verbs: buildings
Grammar: Use conditionals
Practice text type: Website: 'Pyramids', Magazine article: 'Learning about the Leaning Tower!'
Additional resources: audio player, dictionaries, small blank cards/slips of paper (internet access)

KEY

Students' own answers.
Suggested sentence structures for discussion:
The most famous building in … is …
I think the most attractive building I've seen in real life is …
I prefer modern houses to old-fashioned ones because …
The buildings I like best are inside / outside cities; this is because …
Useful words and phrases: *well-known, popular, tourists, pleasant to look at, ancient, modern*

PREPARING THE WAY   PAGE 146

- Tell students to read the chapter topic title and elicit from them all the names of all the different types of buildings the class can think of and write them on the board, e.g. *skyscraper, office block, castle, palace, tower, church, temple.*
- Ask students to read the questions and discuss them in pairs. If they are able to sustain a class or small group discussion, you can ask them to discuss each one in detail.
- If they need more support, put some key words and phrases on the board (see Key below), and ask them to produce brief written responses and compare their ideas with a partner or in groups.
- Take feedback from the group and find out what kind of buildings they admire and whether they prefer modern architecture and living spaces or historic buildings. Ask students to explain their answers and give reasons.

EXTENSION

Suggested activities:
- Ask students to find images of unusual buildings from different parts of the world. Imagine standing very close to them. Write the script for a phone conversation in which they describe to a friend or family member what they can see, in as much detail as possible.
- Ask students to discuss and/or write about one or more of the following topics:
  Would you prefer to live in a rural or an urban area?
  What are the types of things you should consider when buying a house?
  Which country do you think has the most beautiful architecture?
  Which is more important: the house's interior or the house's exterior?
  Is eco-friendly housing popular in your country?
- Ask students to work in pairs to do a mini-project on a famous building of their choice. For example, they could find out about its history, its architect, what it is made from, what purpose it has and whether this has changed, when it was built and why, what is likely to happen to it in the future.
- Ask students to collect images of famous buildings and then make them into a display, adding a description of each one.
- Ask students to discuss this quotation from Philip Johnson: *Architecture is the art of how to waste space.* As a follow-up, they could find other quotations on the topic of houses and other buildings and explain why they agree/disagree with them, in speech or in writing.

UNIT 5: READING PRACTICE — READING PART 3

ACTIVITY 1 PAGES 146–147

- Focus the class on the photos and ask students to describe what they see, e.g. *The first building has a round top and it has a rectangular strip of water in front of it. This shows a reflection of the building.*
- Write students' descriptions on the board and elicit any necessary words that they don't know for these types of buildings (and didn't produce in the first discussion activity), such as temple, palace, monument, etc.
- Put students into pairs to do the matching activity and check answers with the class. Then ask students to tell you what they know about each building and which two they would like to visit.

KEY

1 a Taj Mahal: India **b** Burj Khalifa: United Arab Emirates **c** Himeji Castle: Japan **d** Great Sphinx of Giza: Egypt **e** Angkor Thom: Cambodia **f** Leaning Tower of Pisa: Italy

2 Students' own answers.

Background information

Taj Mahal: This is a white marble mausoleum in Agra in India which was built between 1631 and 1648 by the Mughal emperor, Shah Jahan to house the tomb of his favourite wife.

Burj Khalifa: This is a very tall tower in Dubai in the United Arab Emirates. It was finished in 2010 and, at 828 metres tall, is currently the tallest structure in the world.

Himeji Castle: This is in an ancient castle dating from 1333 which stands on top of a hill near the city of Himeji in Japan. It was originally built by the Samurai warrior Akamatsu Norimura.

Great Sphinx of Giza: This famous limestone monument is in the desert in Egypt near Giza. It has the head of a human and the body of a lion and is thought to date from 2,500 BCE.

Angkor Thom: This is the ruins of an ancient city in Cambodia built in in the 12th century. It used to be the capital city of the Khmer empire and the ruins today cover an area of 9 km^2.

Leaning Tower of Pisa: This is the bell tower of the cathedral in the Italian city of Pisa. It was built between the 12th and the 14th centuries. Construction stopped for 200 years when the tower started to lean to one side because its foundations were not deep enough. Today it still leans to one side but is stable.

ACTIVITY 2 PAGE 147

- Elicit from students what an *architect* is (a person whose job it is to design buildings).
- Ask the class what the picture shows and elicit that it is an architect's plan of a building, probably drawn to scale using special equipment.
- Explain that students are going to hear an interview with an architect and ask them to read the questions and underline the key words.
- Ask them to think about what kind of information they will be listening for in each case, e.g. an object for Q5.
- You might want to check some of the vocabulary used in the recording before students hear it, e.g. *studio* (room where radio/television interviews are held), *fascinating* (really interesting), *observe* (notice, look at closely and remember), *take for granted* (be so used to something that you no longer notice it), *freshness* (sense of newness, not familiar), *originality* (quality of being unusual, not copied, one-of-a-kind), *functional* (designed mainly for usefulness rather than beauty), *blend in* (merge, look like part of the same thing, not stand out), *steel* (strong metal that is silver in colour), *concrete* (strong material, made of cement), *tower* (very tall building, typically narrow as well as high), *impose* (include/create in a way that's unpleasant), *drawing pad* (book in which to sketch pictures). Note that the Taj Mahal, the Leaning Tower of Pisa, and Angkor Thom were all included in the previous activity, so students can be reminded of their name/appearance if necessary.
- Play the recording twice for students to listen and answer the questions. Check answers with the class. Ask them if anything that Gabriela said surprised them and if they think that being an architect would be an interesting job.

AUDIOSCRIPT: Student Book page 288

Piers: Hello Gabriela, it's good to have you in the studio. You've worked as an architect for over twenty years and have had a fascinating career. I'd love to start by asking you: If a young person came to you asking for advice about how to get into the business, what would you say to them?

Gabriela: Hello. I think it's important that they get in the habit of <u>observing the buildings</u> around them carefully. Try to notice the <u>detail</u>. People see the buildings in their area but <u>they often take them for granted</u> – try to <u>look at how they work as buildings and whether they're successful</u>.

READING PART 3   **UNIT 5: READING PRACTICE**   99

Piers: You mean, when people see a building every day, they might not pay so much attention to it?

Gabriela: Yes, exactly. If you go abroad and look at a building like the Taj Mahal or the Leaning Tower of Pisa, you will tend to study it, because it's new; it's different. Try to look at the buildings in your own area with that same sense of freshness.

Piers: I see. And what about originality? Should architects all be trying to design the next Angkor Thom?

Gabriela: Well, originality is certainly important. But a building needs to be functional too. And it also needs to blend in with the landscape. If it can't do those two things, then it's not a success.

Piers: You mean they should match what is already there?

Gabriela: Well, not necessarily. But you wouldn't want to build a steel and concrete tower in a village that's made of brick and wood. You need to have a sense of place and not to impose something that doesn't fit.

Piers: I see. And finally, as an architect, what's the most important item to carry with you at all times?

Gabriela: That's easy – my drawing pad – I'd never be without it! I don't know what I'd do if I lost it!

Piers: Brilliant! Thank you, Gabriela, for joining us in the studio today.

Gabriela: Thank you for inviting me.

KEY

(Clues underlined in Audioscript.)
1 the detail of the buildings around (in areas well known to them)
2 They take them for granted, i.e. they don't really notice or appreciate them because they are so familiar.
3 when they go abroad (because the buildings are new to them)
4 They should be functional and blend in with the landscape.
5 her drawing pad

DIFFERENTIATION

Challenge: Ask students to write a short paragraph about which buildings they would most like to visit and why.

EXAM REFRESHER   PAGE 147

- Ask students to read through the Exam Refresher box and remind themselves of what they have to do in Part 3 of the Reading and Writing exam.

- Give students a minute or so to read and then ask them to tell you, without looking back at the text, what the main skills that they have to use are and the main task types that they have to deal with in Part 2 of the exam. Try to elicit the following:
  skills: identifying attitudes and opinions in the text, identifying different types of information, comprehension and analytical skills.
  task types: true/false or not evidenced, gap fill, choosing correct words from list to complete a summary.

ACTIVITY 3   PAGE 147

- Tell students they are now going to think about exam technique. Explain that it is useful if they can understand as much as possible about the marking process, so they should read this additional explanation carefully.
- Ask them to read the statements and decide with a partner whether or not they think each one is correct.
- Give students a minute or so to go through the statements and compare their ideas about them with another pair. Then check answers with the class.

KEY

✗ If some information suggested in the question is not given in the text, the information is probably false.
  Hint: If information is not supplied, it counts as *not given*. *False* should be used only where wrong information is provided.

✓ Make sure you do not use more than the number of words specified in the question.
  Hint: Students will not get a mark for any question where they use more than the number of words specified.

✓ In gap-fill activities, it is important to check that your answers fit grammatically.
  Hint: This answer is correct. It is also important not to alter the words chosen to make them fit grammatically, e.g. by adding -s.

✗ When you have to choose a word from a word box, there may be more than one possible answer.
  Hint: The word box tasks Q41–45 are designed to ensure there is only one correct response, although for Q31–40 there is occasionally more than one valid answer. For example, Q37 could be *several deep pits* or just *deep pits*. Both would gain marks.

100 UNIT 5: READING PRACTICE — READING PART 3

PRACTICE TIME 1 — PAGES 148–150

- Remind students that this part of the exam tends to be based on a longer passage.
- Remind the class to look at and follow the Exam Hint for Reading Part 3.
- Explain that sometimes the text will include specialist vocabulary that students are not expected to know, but they should be able to guess the key words from context. In this case, an explanation of the word *stele,* meaning stone slab, is provided.
- For any passage, some students may have their own knowledge about the topic. Remind them that even where they do, their answers must be based on the text alone.
- As before, the answers for each section follow the passage separately, so students will need to return to the beginning of the passage once they get to Q31.

KEY

26 F 27 NG 28 T 29 T 30 NG 31 ancient Egypt 32 theories 33 house of eternity 34 farmers 35 the flood season 36 20 years 37 (several) deep pits 38 special temple 39 legends 40 young prince 41 ancient 42 origin 43 tombs 44 levels 45 statue

TEACHING TIPS

Hints Q26–30: These questions require students to pay attention to whether ideas that are mentioned are true or are just theories. For example, the information for Q27 is mentioned as an idea/possible explanation. It is not given as a definite fact. Similarly, the passage mentions a young prince clearing the Great Sphinx of sand (Q30), but says this was in a dream, which means the rest of the story is not known.

Hints Q41–45: These questions often test students' understanding of the contexts in which we use words. For example, here, *elderly* and *ancient* have similar meanings, but we would use *elderly* to describe a person rather than a building, hence the correct answer here is *ancient*.

Hint Q43: Sometimes the clue to the correct answer is grammatical. For example, in terms of meaning, the answer to *Pyramids are actually the* (blank) *of early pharaohs,* could potentially be *grave* or *tomb*. However, in the word box, *grave* appears in singular form, whereas *tombs* is plural. The answer must be the plural (*tombs*) to fit grammatically into the sentence.

REFLECT — PAGE 151

- Ask the class to work through the Reflect questions with a partner and discuss which of the things listed they did or did not manage to do.
- Tell students to help their partner evaluate his or her progress and set a target for the next Practice Time test.
- Encourage students to give each other positive support.

PRACTICE TIME 2 — PAGES 151–154

- Ask students to check their outcomes from the first Practice Time, and to pay attention to the areas they need to work on. Is there anything students can learn from it that could help with this Practice Time?
- Remind students of the importance of reading the questions first and of underlining key points.
- Reading the text aloud to students will help them understand it more readily, but it will prevent them from experiencing it in the way they would in an exam.
- When you check answers with the class, draw students' attention to the fact the answer to Q36 is slightly unusual because the text says *about the architect's identity* instead of *about the identity of the architect,* a difference in wording which is unlikely in the exam.

KEY

26 T 27 F 28 T 29 NG 30 F 31 tourist attraction 32 Italian Renaissance 33 bell tower 34 foundation 35 more stable 36 about the identity 37 signature 38 (some) neighbouring regions 39 notorious curve 40 (major) restoration 41 delayed 42 unevenly 43 uncertainty 44 shrouded 45 attraction

TEACHING TIPS

Hint Q41–45: Sometimes the correct word appears in the passage, as is the case for Q41. At other times, as for Q42, the answer has to be deduced. Even though students may not know the meaning of the word *unevenly,* the phrasing of the question requires an adverb, and it is the only adverb that appears as an option. (The word *even* and its relation to *leaning* may also provide a clue.)

Grammatical knowledge may support students in other ways. For example, the answer to Q44 has to be a verb that is used with the preposition *in,* so only *shrouded* fits.

EVALUATE YOUR EXAM PRACTICE
PAGE 154

- Tell the class to work through the exam evaluation questions with a partner.
- Ask students to help their partner evaluate his or her progress and set targets for areas to work on and for the forthcoming exam.
- Encourage students to distinguish between different types of errors they may have made, e.g. missing answers out, not following the exam rubric, not knowing specific vocab, getting confused about the question and so on. Do any patterns emerge?
- Encourage students to give each other positive support.

VOCABULARY AND GRAMMAR

VOCABULARY ACTIVITY 1 — PAGE 155

- If you think it will help your students, point out that many of these words are of Latin origin.
- Ask students to read the article about the Leaning Tower of Pisa again and complete the table with the correct verbs and nouns. As they do so, ask them to underline the verbs and nouns elated to the ones in the table.
- Remind students that *-tion* generally indicates a noun.

KEY

Verbs	Nouns
(to) found	foundation (line 25)
(to) restore	restoration (line 64)
(to) construct	construction (line 52)
(to) locate	location (line 3)
(to) speculate (line 34)	speculation
(to) complete (line 48)	completion
(to) destroy (line 40)	destruction
(to) contribute (line 47)	contribution
(to) continue (line 63)	continuation

VOCABULARY ACTIVITY 2 — PAGE 155

- Ask students to match the verbs and nouns from Activity 1 to the definitions.
- Tell students that the beginnings of the definitions will help them. For example, if the description starts with *To*, this indicates an infinitive, and so the answer will be a verb.

KEY

1 destroy 2 foundation 3 completion 4 locate
5 found 6 construct 7 contribution 8 restoration
9 location 10 speculation 11 continuation

TEACHING TIPS
Hint Q5: Remind students that words can act in different ways depending on the context. *To found* is an infinitive here, however *found* is also the past simple form of *find*, e.g. *The dog found its biscuit.*

VOCABULARY ACTIVITY 3 — PAGE 156

- Ask students to read the article and circle the correct options.
- Pre-teach some of the vocabulary used in the article if desired: *scheduled* (planned for), *initially* (at first), *remaining* (those left), *prime location* (well-placed in a good spot), *campaigned* (fought, worked for), *community* (a network of local people), *vital* (extremely important), *committed to* (dedicated to), *go from strength to strength* (grow in energy and power).
- Students could follow this activity up by writing an article of their own using the same key words, individually or in pairs.

KEY

1 destroyed 2 foundations 3 restoration
4 completion 5 speculation 6 continues
7 construction

VOCABULARY ACTIVITY 4 — PAGE 156

- Ask students to look at the nouns from Activity 1 on page 155. Ask them to use the correct form of those nouns to complete the sentences.
- This activity requires students to think carefully about the form of the word they choose, i.e. noun or verb. This activity is similar to the gap-fill activities in the exam, where a grammatical match is important.

KEY

1 location 2 destruction 3 founded 4 constructed
5 speculate 6 complete 7 contribute 8 restore
9 continuation

TEACHING TIPS

Hint Q3: Draw attention to the difference between the verb *to found* (to establish) and the verb *to find* (to locate). Students may find these confusing, particularly because the past tense of *to find* is *found* (*She found a ball in the grass.*). The past tense of *to found* is *founded* (*He founded a new youth movement.*).

Advise students that some verbs can be used physically or as metaphors, for example we construct houses but also theories.

VOCABULARY ACTIVITY 5 — PAGE 157

- Ask to look at the nouns from Activity 4 and elicit what they have in common (they all end with *-tion*).
- Ask students to work in pairs to think of other nouns that end in *-tion* and to note the verbs they are formed from.
- They could look through books to help them remember the vocabulary they are already familiar with (using the internet would make the activity too easy).

KEY

Suggested answers:
correction: to correct
imagination: to imagine
medication: to medicate
meditation: to meditate
organisation: to organise
pollution: to pollute
relation: to relate (to)
situation: to situate translation: to translate

GRAMMAR ACTIVITY 6 — PAGE 157

- Encourage students to refer to Grammar Reference page 273 to revise the zero conditional before attempting the activity.
- Ask students to form sentences from the words.
- Make sure students conjugate the verbs in both clauses correctly.
- Make sure students use *if*, not *when* with any hypothetical sentences, e.g. *If a dog sings, we shout.*
- Check answers with the class.

KEY

Students' own answers. Suggested answers:
When the sun shines, we are happy.
If a dog sees a cat, it barks.

GRAMMAR ACTIVITY 7 — PAGE 157

- Encourage students to again refer to Grammar Reference page 273 before attempting the activity.
- Clarify the two different elements of first conditional sentences with students: *if* + present simple, *future simple*.
- Ask students to write in the missing halves of the sentences and then compare answers with the class.

KEY

Students' own answers. Suggested answers:
1 *If I do not know the answer,* I will ask the teacher.
2 If I argue with my friend, *I will be unhappy.*
3 *If my computer breaks,* I will try to fix it.
4 If my school finishes early today, *I will go to the park.*
5 *If I get too cold,* I get sick.
6 If it rains tomorrow, *I will take an umbrella to school.*

GRAMMAR ACTIVITY 8 — PAGE 158

- Encourage students to refer to Grammar Reference pages 273–274 to revise the second conditional before attempting the activity.
- Clarify the two different elements of second conditional sentences with students: *if* + past simple, *would* + verb.
- Ask students to imagine their ideal home and write five sentences using the second conditional. They can use the list of questions to help them if necessary.
- Compare answers as a class.

KEY

Students' own answers. Suggested answers:
If I had my own home, I would have a pool.
If I could choose where to live, it would be in the countryside.

EXTENSION

This activity is designed to give students practice using first conditional sentences and *unless*.

- Tell students to imagine that they have built their ideal home and are going to throw a house-warming party. Give them the following list of things that might go wrong at the party: the neighbours might complain about the noise; the food might go cold; people might not like the music; people might not come to the party; too many people might come to the party; the house might get damaged; the family cat might be scared.
- Tell students to write down a plan to deal with all of the above scenarios, using first conditional sentences and *unless*, e.g. *Unless we invite them to the party as well, the neighbours might complain about the noise.*

EXTENSION

This activity is designed to help students feel more comfortable using the second conditional.

- Each student makes a list of ten things they have never done, using the present perfect, e.g. *I have never gone sky-diving.*
- Five of the sentences should be things that the student has never done but which they would do if they had the chance, and five of the sentences should also be things that the student has never done but which they wouldn't do if they had the chance.
- The sentences should be listed in random order and make sure students write false sentences that are not obviously false, e.g. *I have not eaten rocks*.
- Students should exchange lists with a partner.
- Students now have two minutes to decide which are the five things on their list which they would never do.
- Students guess which things their partner would never do, e.g. *I think you would never ...*
- Whoever gets the most guesses right wins and their partner is eliminated from the tournament.
- The winners form new pairs and play again in the same way (the losers should compete for runner-up positions).
- Play continues until only one pair remains, and one winner!

GRAMMAR ACTIVITY 9 — PAGE 158

- Ask students to work in pairs to place the situations into the different columns.
- Ask students to form conditional sentences individually, using the situations. They do not need to use the example sentence *If I won the lottery*.
- First conditional sentences should be used for possible situations. Second conditional sentences should be used for unlikely or impossible situations.

KEY

1

Possible	Unlikely or impossible
the weather is rainy this week	you win the lottery
you wake up early tomorrow	the dog eats your homework
you improve your English	you are able to turn invisible
you make a mistake while speaking English	aliens invade Earth
someone steals your pen today	nobody steals your pen today

2 Students' own answers. Suggested answers:
If the weather is rainy this week, I will stay home.
If the dog ate my homework, I would be very sad.

UNIT 5: READING PRACTICE — READING PART 3

GRAMMAR ACTIVITY 10 — PAGE 159

- Encourage students to refer to Grammar Reference page 274 to revise the third conditional before attempting the activity.
- Clarify the two different elements of third conditional sentences with students: *if* + past perfect, *would* + present perfect.
- Ask students to write third conditional sentences using the past simple sentences for inspiration.

KEY

Suggested answers:

1 *If there hadn't been a traffic jam, we would have taken our usual route.*
If we had taken our usual route, we would have been in a traffic jam.

2 *If my friend hadn't missed his bus, he wouldn't have missed the film.*
If my friend had caught his bus, he would have seen the film.

3 *If Yoko had eaten less at lunch, she could have finished her dinner.*
If Yoko hadn't eaten so much at lunch, she would have been hungry at dinner.

4 *If we had known it was your birthday, we would have bought a present.*
If we hadn't forgotten it was your birthday, we wouldn't have forgotten a present.

5 *If it had been cold this morning, I wouldn't have left my jacket at home.*
If it hadn't been warm this morning, I would have worn warmer clothes.

6 *If my watch hadn't broken, I wouldn't have had to fix it.*
If my watch had kept working, I would have been happier.

EXTENSION

This activity is designed to further familiarise students with the third conditional and revise the past simple.

- Ask students to write a paragraph in the past simple describing the previous day, e.g. *I woke up at seven. I had breakfast at home with my family.*
- Ask students to swap the paragraph they have just written with a partner.
- Tell students to read their partner's paragraph and make a list of five problems at the bottom that could have arisen during their day (but didn't), e.g. *The food could have given you food poisoning.*
- Tell students to swap paragraphs again, so that they now have a paragraph describing their previous day, as well as a list of five problems that could have arisen.
- Tell students to decide how they would have dealt with the problems, if they had arisen, using the third conditional, e.g. *If the food had given me food poisoning, I would have gone to the emergency room.*

EXTENSION

This activity is designed to give students further practice using the first, second and third conditionals.

- Students write six complete conditional sentences about themselves (two in the first conditional, two in the second conditional and two in the third conditional).
- The sentences must all be true, e.g. *If I lost my homework, my teacher would be very upset.*
- Students take it in turns to tell their partner the second half of one of their conditional sentences. Their partner has three attempts to guess the first half of the sentence. If they guess correctly with one of their three guesses, they get a point.
- Whoever has the most points at the end of the six guesses, wins!

SELF-EVALUATION — PAGE 159

Tell students to look at the Self-evaluation table and tick the boxes that are true for them. Ask them if there are any topics they don't feel confident about yet.

WRITING PART 4

OVERVIEW

Topic: Work and jobs
Exam skills: Revise the requirements for Part 4 of the Reading and Writing exam, evaluate sample exam answers, practise two Part 4 sample questions, evaluate your exam practice
Assessment Objectives: 2A, 2B, 2C
Vocabulary: Phrasal verbs: work
Grammar: Use perfect continuous
Practice text type: Informal emails: part-time jobs
Additional resources: audio player, dictionaries, blank cards (internet access)

PREPARING THE WAY   PAGE 162

- Tell the class to read the chapter topic and ask students if they remember any work-related vocabulary from Unit 3 when they studied the topic of work and work experience. Write these categories on the board and ask students to suggest words:
people, e.g. *staff, employer, manager, boss, worker, trainee.*
getting a job, e.g. *interview, candidate, application, apply for.*
pay and conditions, e.g. *salary, earn, uniform, training.*
- Accept any relevant words related to the topic category and write them on the board.
- Focus students on the questions. If they are able to sustain a class or small group discussion, ask them to discuss each question in detail.
- If students need more support, put some key words and phrases on the board (see Key below). Ask them to produce brief written responses and compare their ideas with a partner or in groups.
- Take feedback from the class and find out students' ideas about this topic.

KEY

Suggested sentence structures for discussion:
People work because …
I believe that the main reason people work is …
Some people are motivated by …
I think that work involving … should be paid best.
Ideally, … should be paid the most because …
My ideal job would be …
… would be my ideal job because …
Key words and phrases: *motivation, ambition, security, income, family responsibilities, lifestyle, leisure pursuits, holidays*

EXTENSION

This discussion activity gets students to think about what different types of jobs involve.

- Divide students into groups and list the features of different jobs/professions on a set of blank cards for each group of students, one per card.
- Examples of features are: regular hours, full-time, part-time, working outdoors/indoors, travelling to get to work, working at home, travelling as part of the job (short distances, nationally, internationally), speaking more than one language, working with people, working with animals, working with those who are unwell, working with children, selling goods, being persuasive, being creative, being responsible for the safety of others, helping others, having job security, being a manager, using IT a lot, using artistic skills, working with numbers, flexibility, routine, providing a service, earning a lot of money.
- Invite individual students to pick the job features that appeal to them, and then use their shared knowledge of their group, with teacher input if necessary, to match them to existing careers.
- Follow up by asking students to discuss this quotation from Thomas Edison: *There is no substitute for hard work.* You could ask them to find other quotations on the topic of work and jobs and explain why they agree/disagree with them, in speech or in writing.

UNIT 6: WRITING PRACTICE — WRITING PART 4

ACTIVITY 1 — PAGE 163

- Tell the class that they are going to listen to a *careers advisor* (a person whose job it is to give people advice about work and jobs) talking about getting a job.
- Ask if anyone in the class has already talked to a careers advisor and what kind of useful help and advice they think careers advisors can give young people.
- Ask students to read the questions and underline key words so they know what information to listen for. Check they understand the meaning of *applicant* (a person who is 'applying for' a particular job), *skills* (things you know how to do), *motivated* (enthusiastic and determined because you really want something), *to recruit* (to search for people to work in your company or be part of your organisation).
- Play the recording twice for students to listen and answer the questions.
- Check answers with the class before giving students some time to discuss the questions in Q2 in pairs.
- Ask for feedback on the discussion and find out what sort of work students think is available for young people and what they would choose as their first job.

AUDIOSCRIPT: Student Book page 289

Steven: Breaking into the job market isn't easy for anyone, whatever their age. Getting your first job, though, can be particularly difficult. Unlike older applicants, you have no previous work experience and you may have a smaller range of skills to offer. As a younger person, you are likely to have less life experience. For example, you may have travelled less than someone who is ten years older.

So far, the picture doesn't look too positive for the would-be employee. However, it's not all bad news! Younger workers are often a very appealing option for employers. For one thing, they are often keen to learn and to get a job. This can mean they are very well-motivated. It may also cost less to employ them.

If you are a young person looking for a part-time job, there are several things you can do.

First of all, watch out for job adverts in the local papers and on the internet. Many shops and restaurants put cards up in their windows and recruit staff that way. Friends and family members may also know of job openings. If you are very lucky, they might even own a business where you can work! It is also important to look out for training schemes and work experience opportunities. Who knows, they may be the pathway to your ideal job!

KEY

(Clues underlined in Audioscript.)

1 a A younger person may have no previous work experience, a smaller range of skills, less life experience, e.g. being less well-travelled than an older person.
   b Younger workers are often keen to learn, keen to get a job, well-motivated, and it may cost less to employ them.
   c Younger people can: look for job adverts in local papers and on the internet; look for cards in the windows of shops and restaurants; ask friends and family members; work in family business; look out for training schemes and work experience opportunities.
2 Students' own answers.

EXAM REFRESHER — PAGE 163

- Ask students to read through the Exam Refresher box and remind themselves of what they have to do in Part 4 of the Reading and Writing exam.
- Give students a minute or so to read and then ask them to tell you (without looking back at the text) what they have to write for this part of the exam and what the assessment criteria are.
- Elicit that for Writing Part 4, the students have to write a short informal text and the assessment criteria are: communication, content and organisation (5 marks) and range and accuracy (5 marks).
- Check that students are clear about what these criteria mean. The first 5 marks relate to whether the text transmits the information asked for and whether the writer uses an appropriate tone, register and layout for the type of text it is. The second 5 marks relate to the language the writer uses, the range of sentence structures, spelling and use of vocabulary.

ACTIVITY 2 — PAGE 163

- Tell students they are now going to think about exam technique. Ask them to read the statements about the Writing Part 4 exam tasks and decide with a partner whether or not they think each one is correct.
- Give students a minute or so to go through the statements and compare their ideas about them with another pair. Then check answers with the class.

WRITING PART 4 — UNIT 6: WRITING PRACTICE

KEY

- ✓ Cover all three points fairly evenly.

  Hint: Note the word *fairly*. Coverage should be as even as possible, but occasionally one bullet point is designed to elicit a response that is more or less detailed than the others.

- ✗ Use as many complex words as possible to show off your vocabulary.

  Hint: The register should be informal. Too many complex words are likely to make the text sound too formal and/or unnatural.

- ✗ Make your writing very formal.

  Hint: Not appropriate for this task. Over-reliance on the wording of the task or bullet points can lead to a register that is too formal.

- ✓ Begin and end your writing in a way that is appropriate to the text type.

  Hint: Remember to close your text. Students often forget to do this.

ACTIVITY 3 — PAGES 164–165

- Tell students that they are going to read three opening paragraphs from sample answers, only one of which meets the criteria of the exam task.
- Give the class some time to read the exam task question and the three samples. Also remind students to look at the Exam Hints for Part 4 and Watch out! box.
- Ask students to discuss with a partner which of the three is the best answer and what mistakes the writers of the other two samples have made.
- Discuss the answers with the class.

KEY

Student A uses an appropriate register but takes too long to address the first bullet point. Too many words are spent on irrelevant material.

Student B addresses the task quickly but uses a register that is far too formal. Expressions such as *secured this position* are too formal for an email to a friend.

Student C has written the best answer. His/her response meets the criteria of the task in terms of content and register.

PRACTICE TIME 1 — PAGE 165

- Tell students that the next two tasks will give them the opportunity to practise their writing skills and to build on their initial exam practice for this task.
- Revise again the key points to remember for the Writing Part 4 task. Put these prompts on the board and try to elicit the remainder of the phrase from the students:

  The tone and register of your language should be … (informal)

  Make sure you cover ALL … (bullet points, the information asked for)

  All the information you include must be … (relevant)

  Try not to use the same … (words as the question / bullet points)

- Also remind students to use the appropriate opening and closing phrases for an email or a letter.
- Give students the appropriate period of time, under exam conditions, to read the task instructions carefully and write their answers.

KEY

See the sample answer below. Note it is a sample only. Students can also refer to the Writing Guide in the Student Book for further hints about assessment criteria. Draw students' attention to the consistent (informal) register and the relevance of the information provided in all parts of the response.

SAMPLE ANSWER FOR PRACTICE TIME 1:

Dear Kim,

Hope you're well.

I've just had a really good idea. I'm going to apply for a part-time job! It would give me more spending money, plus I can put it on my CV when I'm older. There aren't many jobs near here, as you know, but a leisure centre just opened a few streets away from my house, so I thought I'd try there and see what happens.

As you've got a part-time job already, have you got any tips for me on how to make a good impression, especially in the interview?

See you soon!

Fai

(99 words)

108 UNIT 6: WRITING PRACTICE — WRITING PART 4

TEACHING TIPS

- When students have finished writing, ask them to exchange their texts with a partner and evaluate their partner's work according to the exam criteria given in the Exam Refresher box on page 163. They should award a mark out of 10 (there are 5 marks for communication, content and organisation and 5 marks for range and accuracy).
- Encourage them to give supportive feedback and find something positive to say when they return their partner's text.
- This activity should increase students' awareness of the marking criteria and how to write a successful answer.

KEY

See the sample answer below. Note it is a sample only. Students can also refer to the Writing Guide in the Student Book for further hints about assessment criteria.

SAMPLE ANSWER FOR PRACTICE TIME 2:

Dear Darcy,

I hope all is well at your end.

I need your advice because I've got a really tricky problem. Do you remember I started that new job a few weeks ago? I hate it! Even though they hired me as a waiter, and that aspect of the work is fine, I have to wash up non-stop for six hours at a time after the restaurant closes. Do you think I should ask them to make me do less washing up? Or should I just leave?

Please write back and tell me what you think!

All the best,

Wolfgang

(*100 words*)

REFLECT — PAGE 165

- Ask the class to work through the Reflect questions with a partner and discuss which of the things listed they did or did not manage to do.
- Tell students to help their partner evaluate his or her progress and set a target for the next Practice Time test.
- Encourage students to give each other positive support.

PRACTICE TIME 2 — PAGE 166

- There are definitions in the Glossary on page 244 for words used in this section:
  metaphor a way of describing something by referring to it as something different and suggesting that it has similar qualities to that thing
  simile an expression that describes something by comparing it with something else, using the words *as* or *like*, e.g. *as white as snow*
- Tell the class to review their results from the first Practice Time by working through the Reflect questions. Is there anything students can learn from having done the first activity that could help them this Practice Time?
- Ask students to set themselves a target to aim for in this task and tell their partner what it is, e.g. *I will check spelling thoroughly so I don't lose marks for spelling mistakes.*
- Give the class the appropriate period of time, under exam conditions, to read the instructions carefully and write their answers.
- As before, ask students to evaluate each other's texts and award a mark out of 10, being careful to give some positive oral feedback when they return the paper.

EVALUATE YOUR EXAM PRACTICE — PAGE 166

- Tell the class to work through the exam evaluation questions with a partner.
- Ask students to help their partner evaluate his or her progress and set targets for areas to work on for the forthcoming exam.
- Encourage students to distinguish between different types of errors they may have made, e.g. missing information out, not following the exam rubric, not knowing specific vocab, getting confused about the question. Do any patterns emerge?
- Encourage students to give each other positive support.

WRITING PART 4 **UNIT 6: WRITING PRACTICE** 109

VOCABULARY AND GRAMMAR

VOCABULARY ACTIVITY 1 — PAGE 166

- This activity introduces students to a number of phrasal verbs in context.
- Read the rubric with the class and elicit or explain the meaning of *workload* (the amount of work that a person has to do).
- Tell students that they are going to listen to a meeting in which people who work together are talking about how to manage all the work they have to do.
- Give them some time to read through the questions and underline key words. Check the meaning of *agenda* (the list of things you are going to talk about in a meeting), *to be snowed under* (have too much to do), *to touch base about something* (to talk briefly about), *evaluation* (here, a report or document which says how good or successful something is).
- Play the recording, twice if necessary, for students to listen and answer the questions.
- Check answers with the class.

AUDIOSCRIPT

Baljit: Right, well, thank you for coming, everyone. I didn't have time to draw up a proper agenda, but I think most of you are aware that I called this meeting to discuss how heavy our workload is at the moment and to try to decide what we can do about it. I thought it might be really useful if we could all meet up. Ralph, can you take notes? I've told David that we'll report back to him after our discussion, so it would be good to have something in writing.

Ralph: Sure. No problem. Do you want me to make a summary of the notes as well, though? I'm a bit snowed under at the moment.

Baljit: Yes please, Ralph. A summary would be great. We'll all appreciate that. Now the first thing I wanted to touch base about was these extra evaluations we've been asked to complete. You know, the ones on yellow paper, where we have to record how we think the phone calls with our clients have gone.

Ralph: Um.

Baljit: Yes, Ralph?

Ralph: I was just going to say, I've come up with a system that lets me get ahead with filling in those evaluations. Perhaps I could run it by everyone?

Baljit: I see. And what system is that, then?

Ralph: Well, I normally write the same thing on every report. Spoke to client, it went well, client happy, the usual stuff.

Baljit: Yes. And?

Ralph: Well, so what I do now is, I fill one in and then photocopy it. That way I just have to put in the date and the client's name, rather than writing it all out in full every time. It's much faster.

Baljit: Hmm ... Yes, I can see that would be faster. I'm not sure how David would feel about it, though.

Ralph: Oh, he likes the idea. I told him all about it when the lift broke last week and we got stuck in between floors. I talked to him about that and about my idea for reorganising the filing system and about the scheme that I figured out to let us use the car-park spaces more effectively. I could tell he was impressed with my ideas. He'll probably ask me to fill in for one of the managers next time they go on holiday. I made lots of suggestions to David. After twenty minutes, he just said 'do whatever you like'. It was a bit annoying, though, because the lift was mended before I could tell him about my idea for redesigning the staff canteen.

Baljit: Right.

Ralph: Yes. I talked to you about my idea for the canteen on Friday, if you remember?

Baljit: Friday. Oh. Yes. It was at going-home time, if I recall correctly.

Ralph: Five o'clock, yes.

Baljit: Well, it was five o'clock when you started. I seem to remember it was after six by the time you'd finished.

Ralph: Yes, well, that's me! I'm not afraid of hard work. I'll probably burn out by the time I'm thirty!

Baljit: Yes, Ralph. That would be a shame, wouldn't it?

KEY

(Clues are underlined in the Audioscript.)

1 to discuss (heavy) workload
2 because he is already snowed under / overworked
3 filling in the new evaluation forms after each phone call with a client
4 He fills in parts of one copy of the form and photocopies it.
5 when they got stuck in the lift the previous week
6 redesigning the (staff) canteen

EXTENSION

- Ralph, in the recording, could be seen as quite annoying (although some of his ideas may be helpful). Ask students to produce a script with a similarly annoying colleague in a work setting of their choice, using the phrasal verbs.
- To support them, the class could discuss the clues that show Ralph is annoying: he talks about himself a lot (*whole audio*); he has a high opinion of himself (*I could tell he was impressed with my ideas. He'll probably ask me to fill in for one of the managers next time they go on holiday.*); he does not recognise the needs of other people (*Well, it was five o'clock when you started [talking]. I seem to remember it was after six by the time you'd finished.*).
- Ideas about annoying workplace behaviour could then be shared centrally to give students a starting point. For example, moving other people's belongings without permission, listening to loud music, arriving late, not preparing for meetings, sending unnecessary emails, gossiping (talking about others behind their backs), spreading false rumours.

VOCABULARY ACTIVITY 2 — PAGE 167

- Tell students that the conversation they have just listened to included a lot of phrasal verbs.
- If necessary, revise that a phrasal verb is a verb combined with a preposition or adverb (or both) that means something different to the verb on its own. The preposition/adverb can sometimes be separated from the verb and be placed after the object of the sentence. Elicit or give some examples, e.g. *I took off my coat. I took my coat off.*
- Play the recording again. Ask the class to tell you if they hear any phrasal verbs and write them on the board.
- Direct students to the transcript of the conversation in their books and ask them to use it to complete the phrasal verbs table.
- Ask students to notice that some phrasal verbs can have more than one meaning.
- Check answers with the class.

KEY

(Phrasal verbs highlighted in the Audioscript.)

Verb	Expression in text/phrasal verb	Definition
run	*run it by everyone run (something) by*	explain or suggest an idea or proposal to someone
meet	*if we could all meet up*	get together
figure	*the scheme that I figured out*	resolve, discover
get	*that lets me get ahead*	progress to a higher/better position
burn	*I'll probably burn out by the time I'm 30.*	be exhausted by work, usually over a longer period of time
draw	*draw up a proper agenda*	give new information in a slightly formal way, in speech or in writing
fill	*fill one in and then photocopy it*	complete a form with missing information
fill	*fill in for one of the managers*	act as a substitute for someone
report	*We'll report back to him*	plan and produce

VOCABULARY ACTIVITY 3 — PAGE 168

- Ask students to circle the correct option to indicate their understanding of the phrasal verbs.
- Encourage them to compare their ideas with a partner before you check answers with the class.

KEY

1 report back **2** fill in **3** burned out **4** meet up
5 run something by you

VOCABULARY ACTIVITY 4 — PAGE 168

- This activity gives students the opportunity to practise the phrasal verbs in use.
- Ask them to complete the sentences with appropriate phrasal verbs from Activities 2 and 3 in the correct tense and form.
- Check answers by reading the dialogue aloud with the class.

WRITING PART 4 — UNIT 6: WRITING PRACTICE

KEY

1 get ahead 2 fill in 3 report back 4 figured out
5 meet up 6 draw up 7 run by 8 burnt out

GRAMMAR ACTIVITY 5 — PAGE 169

- Review the basics of the past tenses with students before attempting this activity. Remind them that:
  finished time periods use past tenses, such as the past simple or past continuous.
  unfinished time periods use perfect tenses, such as the present perfect (finished actions or with stative verbs) or the present perfect continuous (unfinished actions or actions that still have a tangible consequence in the present).
- You can refer students to pages 263, 265 and 267 of the Grammar Reference.
- Ask students to read the sentences and circle the ones that are the clearest.
- Check answers with the class. Ask students to explain their reasons for choosing each answer.

KEY

1 a I've had a job for ten years.
2 a How long have you known him?
3 a Tim's eaten three burgers today.
4 b We've been decorating, so the walls still have wet paint on them.
5 b What have you been doing all day?
6 b Sorry I'm so late. Have you been waiting long?
7 a I was working all of yesterday; I'm very tired.
8 a Has Anusha arrived yet?
9 b Abasi has been cooking for five hours and he's still not finished.
10 a I've been in Georgia for five years now.
11 a I've written four pages already and I'm still writing.
12 a What did you do last summer?

TEACHING TIPS

Hint Q1: *have* in the sense of possession is a stative verb (see Grammar Reference pages 258–259) and has no continuous form.

Hint Q2: *know* is a stative verb, and has no continuous form.

Hint Q3: We use the present perfect when concrete numbers are used with the objects of verbs, such as *three burgers*.

Hint Q4: We use the present perfect continuous to emphasise that this recently completed action still has a tangible consequence in the present.

Hint Q5: *all day* is a lengthy period of time, so the present perfect continuous feels more natural than the present perfect in most contexts.

Hint Q6: We use the present perfect continuous to emphasise that this recently completed action (*waiting*) still has a tangible consequence in the present.

Hint Q7: *yesterday* is a finished time period, so a past tense is more natural than a perfect tense.

Hint Q8: *to arrive* is a momentary action, not a continuous action, so we use the present perfect and not the continuous form.

Hint Q9: This is an unfinished action, so we use the continuous.

Hint Q10: *to be* is a stative verb here in the sense of occupying a physical location, so we use the present perfect.

Hint Q11: *although* this is a continuous action, we use the present perfect when concrete numbers are used with the objects of verbs, such as *four pages*.

Hint Q12: *yesterday* is a finished time period, so it feels more natural to use a past tense than a perfect tense.

GRAMMAR GAME: SENTENCE RACE — PAGE 169

- Follow the instructions in the Student Book, asking questions first to one team, then the other. If the students find the activity too easy, you can open the question to both teams. The student who answers correctly first can return to his or her seat.
- Suggested questions:
  How long have you been living in (town name)?
  What have you been doing this week?
  How long have you been going to school here?
  What have you been learning today?
  How long have you been studying (English / another subject)?
  What have you been eating for lunch recently?
  How long have you been speaking in English today?
  What have you been doing for fun lately?
  How long have you been playing this game?
  What have you been studying in school lately?
  How much homework have your teachers been giving you lately?
  What have you been watching on TV lately?
  What music have you been listening to lately?

UNIT 6: WRITING PRACTICE

WRITING PART 4

GRAMMAR ACTIVITY 6 — PAGE 170

- The focus here is on continuous actions. Ask students to think of reference points in the past and the future before attempting the activity, e.g. *by 2015*, *next Monday*. Direct them to pages 265, 266 and 267 of the Grammar Reference if necessary.
- Ask students to work independently to form their sentences. They can then compare their ideas with a partner before you check answers with the class.

KEY

Students' own answers.

GRAMMAR ACTIVITY 7 — PAGE 170

- Ask students to complete the sentences using the correct tense and verb form. Check answers with the class.
- While checking answers, draw students' attention to the change in word order when forming questions (Q2) and the use of *has* rather than *have* for *he/she/it* (Q5).

KEY

1 I have been living **2** have you been working **3** they will have been building **4** I hadn't been planning **5** He has been acting

TEACHING TIPS

Encourage students to note the point of reference in each sentence when choosing the tense.

Hint Q1: *now* shows that the point of reference is the present, so we use present perfect continuous.

Hint Q2: *here* implies that this question also refers to the present.

Hint Q3: *next month* shows that the point of reference is in the future.

Hint Q4: *then* + past tense (*I found out*) shows that this sentence is talking about the past.

Hint Q5: *lately* means *recently* and is more closely connected to the present than the past.

GRAMMAR GAME: WHAT HAVE YOU BEEN DOING TODAY? — PAGE 171

- Follow the instructions in the Student Book. Select the most interesting cards. Correct any errors before giving them to the student whose turn it is.
- Make sure students do not use the job title when describing what they have done during the day, including any words in the title, e.g. a *gardener*: *I have been planting flowers and watering them.* ✓ *I have been working in the garden.* ✗
- If there are not enough job cards, you can add from the following: *builder, cleaner, dentist, doctor, electrician, flight attendant, gardener, hairdresser, librarian, mechanic, nurse, optician, teacher, pianist, pilot, scientist, secretary, shopkeeper, singer, student, vet, waiter, zookeeper.*

SELF-EVALUATION — PAGE 171

Tell students to look at the Self-evaluation table and tick the boxes that are true for them. Ask them if there are any topics they don't feel confident about yet.

WRITING PART 5   UNIT 6: WRITING PRACTICE   113

WRITING PART 5

OVERVIEW

Topic: Transport and travel
Exam skills: Revise the requirements for Part 5 Reading and Writing exam, evaluate sample exam answers, practise Part 5 sample questions, evaluate your exam practice
Assessment Objectives: 2A, 2B, 2C
Vocabulary: Idioms and expressions: travel
Grammar: Use possessives
Practice text type: Report: transport, Article 'My favourite journey'
Additional resources: audio player, dictionaries (internet access)

PREPARING THE WAY   PAGE 172

- Tell the class to read the chapter topic title and think of as many words as they can for different types of transport and write them on the board (see the Key below for ideas).
- Focus students on the questions. If students are able to sustain a discussion, ask them to discuss the remaining questions in detail in pairs or small groups.
- If students need more support, put some key words and phrases on the board (see Key below). Ask them to produce brief written responses and compare their ideas with a partner or in groups.
- Take feedback from the class and find out students' ideas about this topic.

KEY

Suggested sentence structures for discussion:
My favourite form of transport is ...
I like travelling by ... because ...
My least favourite form of transport is ...
I dislike travelling by ... because ...
I think we need a form of ...
It would use ... for fuel.
Suggested vocabulary:
Land: *car, bus, coach, train, truck, van, taxi, lorry, juggernaut, caravan, trailer, camel, horse, donkey, pony, cart, racing car, jeep, tram*
Air: *helicopter, plane, sea-plane, parachute, hot-air balloon, glider, rocket*
Sea: *ship, boat, submarine, ocean liner, canoe, yacht, inflatable dinghy, cruise ship*

EXTENSION

Suggested activities:

- Students produce detailed written/illustrated/labelled designs for a new type of transport (based on the final question for Preparing the Way).
- Ask students to read English books or stories based on journeys, or retell stories about journeys from their own culture in English.
- Ask students to look at samples of travel writing online and create their own piece of travel writing.
- Ask students to write a set of instructions for using a form of transport safely, e.g. a hot-air balloon. Allow them to research online if needed.
- Set up a mini-project, involving research, on the topic of space travel.
- Ask students to discuss this anonymous quotation: *It's not where you go; it's how you get there*. As a follow-up, they could find other quotations on the topic of journeys and explain why they agree/disagree with them, in speech or in writing.

ACTIVITY 1   PAGE 173

- Explain to students that they are going to hear Frank talking about his new car.
- Elicit from the students or explain the meaning of: *power steering* (a system for changing the direction in which a road vehicle is moving by using power from the engine to help the driver turn the vehicle), *seat warmers* (heating for the seats in a car), *tinted windows* (windows made with darkened glass to protect the eyes from the sun), *navigation system* (a computer system which gives instructions to the driver to tell them how to get to their destination).
- Ask the class if they can think of any other special features that modern cars might have.
- Direct students to read the questions and underline key words so they know what information to listen for.
- Play the recording twice for students to listen and answer the questions.

114 UNIT 6: WRITING PRACTICE — WRITING PART 5

AUDIOSCRIPT: Student Book page 289

Frank: Hi Nina, have you seen my new car? It's parked just here.

Nina: Oh, is that car yours, Frank? <u>It's very big.</u>

Frank: Yes. It's not just big, though. It's <u>also very advanced in terms of technology</u>.

Nina: Really?

Frank: Absolutely. Look at this! <u>Power steering!</u>

Nina: Hmm. Don't most cars have that nowadays? <u>Mine does</u>.

Frank: Ah, but that's not all it's got. I really love the seat warmers too.

Nina: Yes, but lots of people's cars have those. Mine does. So does Raul's. So does Michael's.

Frank: Michael's doesn't! I travelled to Manchester with him last week and the <u>seats were freezing</u>. I'd have been warmer as a pedestrian! I was seriously thinking it would be better to get out and hitchhike my way to Manchester. Or to use public transport. I nearly froze.

Nina: Well he doesn't always use the seat warmers, but his car definitely has them. He mentioned it to me the other day.

Frank: If you say so.

Nina: And Michael's car has a really great navigation system too.

Frank: Well, we got stuck in lots of really bad traffic on the way to Manchester. Some of the time we were <u>travelling at walking pace</u>. And <u>the sun was in our eyes</u> for most of the journey too. Luckily, <u>my own car's windows are tinted, so I don't have that problem</u>.

Nina: Hmm. OK.

TEACHING TIPS

When you check answers with students, you can ask what they think 'specific details' means in the question. It refers to examples of the car's high-tech features, e.g. *seat warmers*.

KEY

(Clues underlined in Audioscript.)

2 a big, has advanced technology
  b Frank's and Nina's
  c cold seats, slow, sun in his eyes
  d tinted
  e protects the eyes from direct sunlight

EXAM REFRESHER — PAGE 173

- Ask students to read through the Exam Refresher box and remind themselves of what they have to do in Part 5 of the Reading and Writing exam.
- Give students a minute or so to read and then ask them to tell you (without looking back at the text) what exactly they have to write for this part of the exam and what the assessment criteria are.
- Elicit that for Writing Part 5, the students have to write a semi-formal text and the assessment criteria are: content and communication (5 marks), use of vocabulary (5 marks), use of grammar (5 marks), organisation of ideas (5 marks).

ACTIVITY 2 — PAGE 173

- Tell students they are now going to think about exam technique. Ask them to read the statements about the Writing Part 5 exam tasks and decide with a partner whether or not they think each one is correct.
- Give students a minute or so to go through the statements and compare their ideas about them with another pair. Then check answers with the class.

KEY

✓ Cover all three points fairly evenly.
  Hint: Note the word *fairly*. Coverage should be as even as possible, but occasionally one bullet point will elicit a response that is more or less detailed than the others.

✗ Make your writing informal.
  Hint: Not appropriate for this task.

✗ Write a long introduction and conclusion.
  Hint: Not appropriate. The focus needs to be on the bullet points – do not provide a conclusion unless explicitly requested to.

✓ Begin and end your writing in a way that is appropriate to the text type.
  Hint: Make sure the beginning and end are right for the genre. For example, an article should not start *Dear –*.

✓ Make your writing semi-formal.
  Hint: Appropriate. Try to keep the register as even as possible throughout the task.

WRITING PART 5 — UNIT 6: WRITING PRACTICE

ACTIVITY 3 — PAGE 174

- Tell students that they are going to read four opening paragraphs from sample answers, only one of which meets the criteria of a Writing Part 5 exam task successfully.
- Give the class some time to read the exam task question and the four sample answers.
- Ask students to discuss with a partner which of the four is the best answer and what mistakes the writers of the other three samples have made.
- Discuss the answers with the class.

KEY

Student A's answer is too informal and reads more like a personal account. There are also two punctuation errors (*load's* and *let's*) and there is some informal vocabulary, e.g. *awesome, cool*.

Student B provides a lengthy and unnecessary introduction which relies very heavily on the wording of the bullet points. This would reduce the marks for grammar and lexis because the student is not using their own words. It is also repetitive.

Student C has written the best answer. His/Her response meets the criteria of the task in terms of content and register.

Student D is too much of a personal account and is also persuasive – not appropriate for a neutral report. This would reduce the mark for content and communication.

EXTENSION

- For extra practice, ask students to complete Student C's report by adding another two paragraphs, one about walking safely and the other about the health benefits of walking.
- A sample answer for these two paragraphs is below:

Sensible footwear is vital for walking safely. This reduces the risk of tripping and falling over. It is a good idea to wear a hat and sun glasses when the weather is hot. Precautions should also be taken to avoid over-exposing the skin.

Despite these risks, walking is generally a very healthy pastime. It helps reduce the risk of many health-threatening conditions, including obesity, and is good for general fitness levels. Walking a few minutes a day can improve people's health, and can even make them feel happier.

PRACTICE TIME 1 — PAGE 175

- Tell students that the next two tasks will give them the opportunity to practise their writing skills and to build on their initial exam practice for this task.
- Elicit what they remember about good and bad practice, based on the previous activity. Revise again the key points to remember for the Writing Part 5 task. Put these prompts on the board and try to elicit the remainder of the phrase from the students:

  The tone and register of your language should be ... (semi-formal)
  Make sure you cover ALL ... (bullet points/the information asked for)
  All the information you include must be ... (relevant)
  Try not to use the same ... (words as the question/bullet points)

- Give students the appropriate period of time, under exam conditions, to read the task instructions carefully and write their answers.

KEY

See the sample answer below. Note it is a sample only. Students can also refer to the Writing Guide in the Student Book for further hints about assessment criteria.

SAMPLE ANSWER FOR PRACTICE TIME 1:

Report on Local Transport

Currently people in this area use a range of different transport methods, although the most popular form of travel is definitely by road. This is not always by car, though, as buses are very popular, especially in the city centre where they are most frequent.

A few people walk or cycle, but the busy roads put cyclists off as some of the traffic goes very fast and they might feel they are in danger. Walkers and cyclists may also be put off by the traffic fumes as the air is quite polluted and the problem is getting worse.

If more people changed to walking or cycling, there would be fewer cars on the road, so there would be a reduction in fumes and the air would be cleaner. Also, walking and cycling would keep people much fitter and healthier.

(143 words)

UNIT 6: WRITING PRACTICE
WRITING PART 5

TEACHING TIPS

- When students have finished writing, ask them to exchange their texts with a partner and evaluate their partner's work according to the exam criteria given in the Exam Refresher box. They should award a mark out of twenty.
- There are 5 marks for communication and content, 5 marks for good use of vocabulary (taking into account range and accuracy), 5 marks for good use of grammar (again, assessing range and accuracy), and 5 marks for good organisation of ideas (including paragraphing and punctuation).
- Encourage them to give supportive feedback and find something positive to say when they return their partner's text.
- Encourage students to reflect on which improvements they could have managed themselves (for example misspelling words used in the wording of the question, or words they know well) and which they needed help with.
- This activity should increase students' awareness of the marking criteria and how to write a successful answer.

REFLECT — PAGE 175

- Ask the class to work through the Reflect questions with a partner and discuss which of the things listed they did or did not manage to do.
- Tell students to help their partner evaluate his or her progress and set a target for the next Practice Time test.
- Encourage students to give each other positive support.

PRACTICE TIME 2 — PAGE 175

- Tell the class to review their results from the first Practice Time by working through the Reflect questions. Is there anything students can learn from doing the first activity that could help them with this next one?
- Ask students to set themselves a target to aim for in this task and tell their partner what it is, e.g. *I will write at least 120 words*.
- Give the class the appropriate period of time, under exam conditions, to read the instructions carefully and write their answers.
- As before, ask students to evaluate each other's texts and award a mark out of 20, being careful to give some positive oral feedback when they return the paper.

KEY

See the sample answer below. Note it is a sample only. Students can also refer to the Writing Guide in the Student Book for further hints about assessment criteria.

SAMPLE ANSWER FOR PRACTICE TIME 2:

Journey of a lifetime!

My favourite journey ever was also my worst. Allow me to explain.

I was travelling with my parents from England to Lefkas, a small Greek island in the Ionian Sea. We were flying from Gatwick Airport, but on the car journey there, a lorry overturned three miles ahead of us, completely blocking the motorway. No one was injured, luckily, but we missed our flight.

Disaster! Or so we thought ... However, by racing around the airport, we managed to find a flight to Corfu with just three seats available. We booked them and landed in Corfu late at night. We then caught a ferry – just! – to Lefkas, and the feeling of happiness and relief when we reached our hotel and woke up there the next morning was amazing. Managing to finish our journey even after missing our original flight was the best thing ever – definitely a trip to remember!

(153 words)

EVALUATE YOUR EXAM PRACTICE — PAGE 176

- Tell the class to work through the exam evaluation questions with a partner.
- Ask students to help their partner evaluate his or her progress and set targets for areas to work on for the forthcoming exam.
- Encourage students to reflect on which improvements they could have managed themselves, e.g. misspelling words they know well or were used in the question, getting confused about the question. Do any patterns emerge?
- Encourage students to give each other positive support.

WRITING PART 5 — UNIT 6: WRITING PRACTICE

VOCABULARY AND GRAMMAR

VOCABULARY ACTIVITY 1 — PAGE 176

- This activity introduces a number of travel-related idioms and allows students to hear them in context.
- Explain to students that they are going to hear an interview with a travel-writer called Jack, who specialises in travelling *on a shoestring* (as cheaply as possible).
- Ask the class to read the questions and underline key words so they know what information to listen for. Check the meaning of *jet-lag* (feeling very tired after a long flight in which you have travelled across time zones), *hitchhiking* (travelling by getting free rides in other people's vehicles), *culture shock* (a feeling of confusion felt by someone visiting a country or place that they do not know and which has a very different culture from where they come from).
- Play the recording twice for students to listen and answer the questions. Then check answers with the class.

AUDIOSCRIPT

Sophia: So, with me here in the studio today is Jack Green, a well-known travel writer who is famous not just for travelling, but for travelling on a shoestring. Welcome to the studio, Jack.

Jack: Thank you very much, Sophia.

Sophia: I'd like to start by asking you why travel appeals to you so much.

Jack: I think it's the variety of countries I see and the range of people I meet. International food too! And also, I'm a culture vulture!

Sophia: You've travelled to a huge range of destinations, often in a short space of time. Aren't you constantly jet-lagged?

Jack: You might expect that, but no.

Sophia: How do you avoid it?

Jack: It's simple. I rarely fly.

Sophia: Ah, I see. And that must cut down costs.

Jack: Definitely. Also, I like to travel light. That means I can hitchhike. I couldn't really do that if I was carrying three huge suitcases!

Sophia: Good point. So, what motivated you to start travelling in the first place?

Jack: I guess I just got itchy feet. I was so sick of staying in one place.

Sophia: Mm, I know the feeling …

Jack: I wanted to visit other places, to experience the way that other people live at first hand. Of course, I got a real culture shock at first.

Sophia: I can imagine. How did you get past that?

Jack: One word: cafés! I just used to sit in the local café, wherever I was, and watch the world go by.

Sophia: Really? And how did that help you?

Jack: I'm not sure, to be honest. I think it just gave me a sense of being connected. It let me feel at home, somehow … like less of a tourist. Often I'd get chatting to people at other tables, so it allowed me to spend time with local people.

Sophia: Sounds great!

Jack: Yes; it's a fantastic lifestyle. I just go where I like; see how the mood takes me and I get to write about it afterwards. That gives me the income that I need to pay for my next trip.

Sophia: What a brilliant way to make a living! Thanks for stopping by and telling us about it, Jack, and good luck with your next adventure!

Jack: Thank you Sophia. It's been fun.

KEY

(Clues underlined in Audioscript.)

1. He enjoys travel because he:
   gets to see a variety of countries,
   meet a range of people,
   gets to eat international food,
   is a culture vulture, i.e. enjoys different cultures.
2. He rarely flies.
3. He travels light.
4. He was sick of staying in one place. / He got itchy feet.
5. by spending time in cafés and watching the world go by
6. by writing about his travels

VOCABULARY ACTIVITY 2 — PAGES 176–177

- Tell students that the conversation they have just listened to included some idioms and other expressions related to travel. Ask the class if they remember any and write them on the board.
- Direct students to the transcript of the conversation in their books and ask them to use it to match the idioms with their meaning
- Check answers with the class.

118 UNIT 6: WRITING PRACTICE — WRITING PART 5

KEY

get itchy feet: become restless and want to visit lots of different places

be a culture vulture: enjoy visiting attractions such as museums, galleries and theatres. (You can explain that a vulture is a bird which eats a lot so the term indicates someone who is interested in any and all types of culture).

travel on a shoestring: spend very little money on a trip or holiday

have/get culture shock: feel confused and challenged by being in a very different country or place

feel at home: be comfortable in a place

travel light: take very few possessions with you when you go abroad

have jet lag: feel tired and confused after flying a very long distance because of the difference between time zones

see how the mood takes you: decide to do something because you suddenly feel like it

watch the world go by: relax by just looking at the people around you

VOCABULARY ACTIVITY 3 — PAGES 177–178

- This activity gives students more practice with using the travel idioms in context.
- Ask them to work individually to complete the sentences with appropriate travel idioms from Activities 1 and 2 in the correct tense and form.
- Check answers by reading the sentences aloud with the class.

KEY

1 is jet-lagged/has jet-lag
2 watching the world go by
3 culture shock
4 gets itchy feet
5 travel light
6 culture vulture
7 travel on a shoestring
8 see how the mood takes
9 feel at home

VOCABULARY ACTIVITY 4 — PAGE 178

- This activity gives students the chance to practise the travel idioms they have just studied.
- Put the students into pairs to discuss the questions.
- Take feedback by asking each pair to share with the class the most interesting things they have learned about the travel experiences of their partner.

KEY

Students' own answers.

GRAMMAR ACTIVITY 5 — PAGE 178

- Ask students to complete the table with the correct possessive adjectives and pronouns. They should know most of the words already, but it may help to give an example for the second and third column, e.g. *I am Paul. This is MY pen. The pen is MINE. You are Rachel. This is … pen. The pen is …*
- Help the students if they struggle to complete the table, and drill examples with the class until you are happy that they have mastered the structures.

KEY

Pronoun	Possessive adjective	Possessive pronoun
I	*my*	*mine*
you	your	yours
he	his	his
she	her	hers
it	its	its
we	our	ours
they	their	theirs

GRAMMAR ACTIVITY 6 — PAGE 179

- Ask students to read and tick the correct sentences. They should compare their ideas with a partner before checking answers with the class.
- When checking answers against the key, discuss with students the reason for each answer.

WRITING PART 5
UNIT 6: WRITING PRACTICE

KEY

1. **b** Is that pen yours? No, it's hers.
2. **a** My sister's house is in Spain.
3. **b** He's a friend of ours.
4. **a** This is the boys' room. They're not home right now, though.
5. **a** Is that his book or her book?
6. **a** That's the entrance of the hospital.
7. **a** Have you seen the dog? I have its food.
8. **a** Well, this is our house.
9. **b** This part of the store is the men's section.
10. **a** Can you see the leg of the table?
11. **b** This is a traditional delicacy of Portugal.
12. **a** That's Paul's mum's friend's car.

TEACHING TIPS

Hint Q4: This is a good opportunity to discuss the importance of correct apostrophe placement to signal a plural possessive rather than a singular.

Hints Q6, Q10 and Q11: These questions are good opportunities to alert students to the fact that *of* is commonly used instead of a possessive apostrophe when we are not discussing humans (in this case, the *hospital* owns the roof, not a person; the leg is part of the table, not a person. *Portugal* owns the delicacy, not a person).

Hint Q7: This is a good opportunity to alert students to the fact that there is no apostrophe in the possessive *its*.

GRAMMAR ACTIVITY 7 — PAGE 180

- This activity gives students the chance to check their understanding of possessives. The errors they have to correct in this passage are ones that occur frequently.
- Ask students to read the passage and find and correct the errors and then compare their ideas with a partner.
- When checking answers with the class, write the correct versions on the board (they are given in brackets in the key below). Ask students to justify and explain their answers.

KEY

See annotations below:

WELCOME TO LONSDALE TOURS

Hello, and congratulation*'s* (*congratulations*) on choosing Lonsdale buses! Our bus*'* (*bus*) company operates in the heart of the centre of London*'s* (*London*). Enjoy you*'re* (*your*) tour through the capital cit*ies* (*city's*) beautiful streets and waterways in a traditional bright red London*'s* (*London*) bus, from which you'll be able to see world-renowned landmarks, famous peopl*es'* (*people's*) houses and spectacular views of the River Thames. Our knowledgeable tour guides can point out tourist*'s* (*tourist*) attractions in 11 different languages.

Thanks for booking, and don't forget to bring your's (*your*) ticket to the meeting point at 11a.m. on the 17th.

TEACHING TIPS

Congratulation's is plural but not possessive so does not need an apostrophe.

Bus' company – *bus* is part of a noun phrase, not a possessive.

London's – *London* is a place name, not a possessive.

You're tour – this should be a possessive adjective rather than a contraction short for *you are*, so the correct spelling is *your*.

This should be the possessive singular *city's* not the plural *cities*.

London's bus – *London* is part of a noun phrase and not possessive.

Peoples' – apostrophe goes before the *-s*.

Tourist's attractions – *tourist* is part of a noun phrase, not a possessive.

The possessive adjective *your* does not need an apostrophe or an *-s*.

EXTENSION

- Students can write a description of a place they know well (the classroom, a room in their house, their house). While writing, they should focus on using as many possessives as possible correctly.
- A typical answer might begin like this:
  The largest <u>room in my house</u> is the lounge. There is a big table in the centre of the room. The <u>legs of the table</u> are very tall. At the moment, <u>my sister's books</u> are on the table, and <u>my cup</u> is too.
- This sample text can serve as another example for students of how we use possessive apostrophes and possessive pronouns for people, and *of* for objects and places.

SELF-EVALUATION — PAGE 180

Tell students to look at the Self-evaluation table and tick the boxes that are true for them. Ask them if there are any topics they don't feel confident about yet.

UNIT 6: WRITING PRACTICE

WRITING PART 6

OVERVIEW

Topic: Health
Exam skills: Revise the requirements for Part 6 Reading and Writing exam, evaluate sample exam answers, practise Part 6 sample questions, evaluate your exam practice
Assessment Objectives: 2A, 2B, 2C
Vocabulary: Collocations: mind and body
Grammar: Use linking words and phrases, use discourse markers
Practice text type: Summaries (Journal articles: 'Adolescence – a time of challenges', 'Maintaining emotional health')
Additional resources: audio player, dictionaries (internet access)

PREPARING THE WAY   PAGE 181

- Tell the class to read the chapter topic title and ask them what they do to stay healthy, physically and metally.
- Focus students on the questions. Check that students understand what is meant by *physical health* (the body and the internal organs being healthy) and *mental health* (the mind and emotions being healthy).
- If students are able to sustain a discussion, ask them to discuss the remaining questions in detail in pairs or small groups.
- If students need more support, put some key words and phrases on the board (see Key below). Ask them to produce brief written responses and compare their ideas with a partner or in groups.
- Take feedback from the class and find out students' ideas about this topic.

KEY

Suggested sentence structures for discussion:
It is important to stay healthy because (if we don't) …
You can stay physically / mentally healthy by …
You can only be physically / mentally healthy if …
I think / don't think that your thoughts can affect your body because …
Key words and phrases: *fitness, keep fit, active, exercise, diet, fruit, vegetables, fat, sugar, manage, stress, relax, relaxation, sense of humour, connect, stress, anxiety, happiness*

EXTENSION

Suggested activities:
- Ask students to design a leaflet informing people about a minor illness and how to treat it at home.
- Ask students to write some guidance explaining how to eat healthily to a teenage audience.
- Ask students to create an illustrated leaflet reassuring young children about their first visit to the dentist.
- Ask students to make a list of ten healthy foods and ten unhealthy ones. Rank order all 20 in order of preference, i.e. favourite is number one. Compare with others in the class.
- Ask students to create a recipe for a nutritious meal Either you or or the students can decide how many courses it should have.
- Ask students to discuss this quotation from John F. Kennedy: *Physical fitness is not only one of the most important keys to a healthy body; it is the basis of dynamic and creative intellectual activity.* As a follow-up, they could find other quotations on the topic of health or mind/body and explain why they agree/disagree with them, in speech or in writing.

ACTIVITY 1   PAGE 182

- Tell the class that they are going to listen to an interview with a doctor talking about a new book that she has just written about how to stay healthy.
- Explain that this activity builds on the introduction and also lets students practise locating and interpreting information, which will help them in the Practice Time tasks.
- Ask students to read the questions and underline key words so they know what information to listen for. Tell them to read questions carefully, particularly noticing whose views are being elicited. For example, the last question asks about the interviewer's opinion, not Dr Gupta's.
- Check students understand the meaning of: *immune system* (the ways that the body has to protect itself against infection and illness), *nutritious* (good for you because it contains many of the substances needed for life and growth), *sociable* (liking to meet other people and spend time with them), *social interaction*

WRITING PART 6

UNIT 6: WRITING PRACTICE

(communicating with and reacting to people), *identity* (who you are, or the qualities that make you unique and different from other people), *peers* (people who are the same age as you or are in the same social group), *peer pressure* (the strong influence of a group, especially of children, on members of that group to behave as everyone else does).

- Play the recording twice for students to listen and answer the questions.

AUDIOSCRIPT: Student Book page 289

Michael: Today we have a very special guest on the show. Dr Janaki Gupta has just written a book on a fascinating area of science: how it can play a role in keeping us healthy in the future. Interestingly, Janaki has been looking into <u>people's emotional health, as well as their physical health</u>. Welcome to the show, Janaki.

Dr Gupta: Thank you.

Michael: So, I've tried to give our viewers a brief outline, but can you tell us a bit more about your book and the research that you did for it?

Dr Gupta: Certainly. As you say, the book isn't just about science and the body – I was also very interested in looking at issues such as <u>emotional development, particularly in teenagers</u>, and also at health conditions where emotional problems might lead to physical problems, <u>such as a weakened immune system, for example. We all know that we are more likely to catch colds and other illnesses when we're feeling stressed</u>. Some scientists are trying to develop technology that enables us to identify those times, so that we can do something about it.

Michael: Interesting. Although I suppose people already know when they're feeling stressed …

Dr Gupta: Well, yes. But this would be a more scientific way of measuring it.

Michael: Right. And are scientists also suggesting changes in the way we approach diet in the future?

Dr Gupta: Definitely. Experts are looking at ways of identifying really nutritious food and they are designing devices that analyse meals accordingly. So you sit down to dinner, type in what you're having and a score will appear on your screen based on how nutritious the meal is.

Michael: Hmm. That sounds … well … It might make people a bit less sociable at mealtimes.

Dr Gupta: Ah, funny you should say that. Social interaction was another big topic that we looked at. A lot of young people nowadays have difficulties with their sense of self. They don't really have a very clear idea of who they are and that is another area that scientists are looking into.

Michael: And what causes people to have these problems?

Dr Gupta: Well, it's a mix of things. <u>A lot of it is to do with peer pressure – social pressure created by people in the same age group.</u>

Michael: I suppose that whereas peer pressure used to come from people in your immediate environment, <u>nowadays it comes from people you meet online too</u>.

Dr Gupta: Absolutely. Scientists are trying to develop the technology to deal with that and to give people a more positive outlook.

Michael: Although you could argue that <u>it's technology that's caused the problem in the first place</u>.

Dr Gupta: Well, yes …

KEY

(Clues underlined in Audioscript.)
1 emotional health and physical health **2** teenagers' emotional development **3** It becomes weakened.
4 peer pressure/social pressure **5** technology

EXAM REFRESHER — PAGE 182

- Ask students to read through the Exam Refresher box and remind themselves of what they have to do in Part 6 of the Reading and Writing exam.
- Give students a minute or so to read. Then ask them to tell you, without looking back at the text, what exactly they have to write for this part of the exam, what register they should use and what the assessment criteria are.
- Elicit that for Writing Part 6, the students have to write a summary of a text in formal or semi-formal register and the assessment criteria are: content and communication (5 marks), use of vocabulary (5 marks), use of grammar (5 marks), organisation of ideas (5 marks). There are also 5 separate marks for reading and information retrieval.

ACTIVITY 2 — PAGE 182

- Tell students they are now going to think about exam technique. Ask them to read the statements about the Writing Part 6 exam tasks and decide with a partner whether or not they think each one is correct.
- Give students a minute or so to go through the statements and compare their ideas about them with another pair. Then check answers with the class.

UNIT 6: WRITING PRACTICE

WRITING PART 6

KEY

- ✓ Cover all three points fairly evenly.
  Hint: Note the word *fairly*. Coverage should be as even as possible, but occasionally one bullet point may elicit a response that is more or less detailed than the others. Some ask explicitly for two or three reasons, for example.
- ✗ Copy words and phrases from the text.
  Hint: Although 5 marks are allocated for reading, this is primarily a test of students' writing skills. Copying the wording of the task and/or bullet points still counts as copying.
- ✗ Write a long introduction and conclusion.
  Hint: Not appropriate. The focus needs to be on the bullet points, so students should not provide a conclusion unless explicitly requested to.
- ✗ Include any extra information that you know about the topic.
  Hint: Not appropriate for this task, which is a test of students' ability to summarise material from an existing passage, not to create it. They need to reword the information but not to introduce new information. This is an important distinction, especially if the topic is interesting or familiar to students.
- ✓ Organise your ideas effectively.
  Hint: The bullet points should help students organise their writing, ideally into paragraphs. Clear and accurate punctuation is an important aspect of organisation, as is cohesion, e.g. the effective use of well-chosen discourse markers and linking words. These are examined in detail in the vocabulary and grammar sections of this chapter.

PRACTICE TIME 1 — PAGES 183–184

- Tell students that the next two tasks will give them the opportunity to practise their writing skills and to build on their initial exam practice for this task.
- Direct students to the Exam Hints for Writing Part 6 on the left-hand side of the page.
- Elicit what they remember about good and bad practice, based on the previous activity. Revise again the key points to remember for the Writing Part 6 task. Put these prompts on the board and try to elicit the remainder of the phrase from the students:

The tone and register of your language should be … (formal or semi-formal)

Make sure you cover ALL … (bullet points/parts of bullet points/the information asked for)

All the information you include must be … (relevant)

Try not to use the same … (words as the question/bullet points)

- Give students the appropriate period of time, under exam conditions, to read the task instructions carefully and write their answers.

KEY

See the sample answer below. Note it is a sample only. Students can also refer to the Writing Guide in the Student Book for further hints about assessment criteria.

SAMPLE ANSWER FOR PRACTICE TIME 1:

Teenagers' moods might seem to alter suddenly, without warning for several reasons. To begin with, hormone levels are rising and falling, and this can affect moods. Secondly, this is the time of life when people may begin to form romantic attachments. Again, this can cause unstable moods. Finally, there may be arguments with friends, and pressures from school – all these factors can cause teenagers' moods to be changeable.

Identity during these years is also changing. Sometimes the teenager acts differently at home and at school. On top of this, relationships can cause problems, especially because of all the other changes going on.

Given all these changes and confusion, it isn't surprising that some teenagers can be difficult to live with. They often want to challenge parents and other rule-makers, but at the same time they need guidance, as they are not fully ready for an independent adult life.

(148 words)

WRITING PART 6 — UNIT 6: WRITING PRACTICE

TEACHING TIPS

- When students have finished writing, ask them to exchange their texts with a partner and evaluate their partner's work using the exam criteria given in the Exam Refresher box. They should award a mark out of 25. (There are 5 marks for reading and including the correct information, 5 marks for communication and content, 5 marks for lexical range and accuracy, 5 marks for grammatical range and accuracy, and 5 marks for effective organisation).

- Ask students to underline any text, particularly whole phrases and/or sentences, that was copied directly from the passage. Remind them that this will be eligible only for the Reading mark out of five. To get marks for vocabulary and spelling they need to use their own words.

- Encourage them to give supportive feedback and find something positive to say when they return their partner's text.

- This activity should increase students' awareness of the marking criteria and how to write a successful answer.

REFLECT — PAGES 184

- Ask the class to work through the Reflect questions with a partner and discuss which of the things listed they did or did not manage to do.
- Tell students to help their partner evaluate his or her progress and set a target for the next Practice Time test.
- Encourage students to give each other positive support.

ACTIVITY 3 — PAGES 184–185

- Tell students that they are going to read three paragraphs from sample answers, only one of which meets the criteria of a Writing Part 6 exam task.
- Give the class some time to read the exam task question and the three different samples.
- Ask students to discuss with a partner which of the three is the best answer and what mistakes the writers of the other two samples have made.
- Discuss the answers with the class.

KEY

These responses show some of the common types of weakness that appear with this task type: **A** = copying, **B** = good practice, **C** = irrelevance.

Student A's response shows the most common weakness, copying. The response is too reliant on the text and contains too much of the original phrasing. Although this answer would score well for content in terms of identifying the correct information, for which an answer can score up to 5 marks, it does not make use of candidates' own vocabulary and grammatical structures, so cannot score good or even mid-range marks for lexical and grammatical range and accuracy. The task requires candidates to put the relevant information from the text into their own words. The response is also slightly long – the student may struggle to cover the other bullet points fully in the words they have remaining.

Student B has produced the best response to the first bullet point. The answer summarises the information in the passage using different vocabulary and different grammatical structures. For example, instead of *hormone levels are likely to affect mood*, the student has changed it to *Hormones have an impact on mood*, and instead of *the pressures of school life may also cause uncertainty during this period,* there is *not forgetting all of the pressure sometimes caused by school*. Sometimes the candidate has only changed tense/pluralisation, but he/she has often substituted vocabulary and used different grammatical structures.

Student C demonstrates another common weakness, irrelevance. They have written an answer based not just on the passage but partly on the candidate's own knowledge. New information is introduced. The new information is not necessarily incorrect but the task does not require it. This mistake is common when the topic of the text is familiar to candidates. Even though candidates may know about a topic, they need to remember that the task is to summarise only the given information.

124 UNIT 6: WRITING PRACTICE **WRITING PART 6**

PRACTICE TIME 2   PAGES 185–186

- Tell the class to review their results from the first Practice Time by working through the Reflect questions. Is there anything students can learn from doing the first activity that could help them with this Practice Time?
- Ask students to set themselves a target to aim for in this task and tell their partner what it is, e.g. *I will use my own words and find synonyms or ways of explaining all the key lexical words in the original text.*
- Give the class the appropriate period of time, under exam conditions, to read the instructions carefully and write their summary.
- As before, ask students to evaluate each other's texts and award a mark out of 25, being careful to give some positive oral feedback when they return the paper.

KEY

See the sample answer below. Note it is a sample only. Students can also refer to the Writing Guide in the Student Book for further hints about assessment criteria.

Note that other sample answers in this Teacher's Book have tended to be at the top end of the word limit. However, students can get full marks for a short answer at the lower end of the word limit too.

SAMPLE ANSWER FOR PRACTICE TIME 2:

Because the mind and body are so closely linked, negative feelings can have a negative impact on a person's health. For example, the immune system suffers, so people are more likely to catch infections. Secondly, people might stop exercising, or eat unhealthy food, or they might even develop an ulcer or some other illness.

To avoid these problems, people need to look after themselves emotionally. One way of doing this is by understanding the feelings that are causing problems. Doing so can help significantly. Another strategy is to talk things through. Many people find that therapists and other professionals can help when friends and family cannot.

In future, I think young people will be taught to be more open about their emotional health problems. They might be encouraged to use online resources to find information or support.

(137 words)

DIFFERENTIATION

Strengthen: Check that students have provided the correct number of points for each answer, for instance where the bullet point specifies two or three different reasons. Also check that they have written their response in the correct person, i.e. third person.

Challenge: Ask students to reorganise the syntax/sentence structure of their writing where their answer is structured in the same way as the original text. For instance, the original passage says: *As long as the body is developing, hormone levels are likely to affect mood.* If a student had written: *While the body is changing, hormone levels might have an impact on mood*, encourage them to change it for: *Hormone levels might have an impact on mood while the body is changing.*

EVALUATE YOUR EXAM PRACTICE
PAGE 186

- Tell the class to work through the exam evaluation questions with a partner.
- Ask students to check whether the extent of copying (if any appeared before) has been reduced or has stayed the same. Assuming the first, what strategies has the student used to achieve this?
- Ask students to help their partner evaluate his or her progress and set targets for areas to work on in the future.
- Encourage students to give each other positive support.

VOCABULARY AND GRAMMAR

VOCABULARY ACTIVITY 1   PAGE 187

- This activity requires students to reread the article on pages 185–186 so it may be useful for them to have access to a version they can write on/annotate.
- Ask students to match the collocations (Q1) and then to classify them according to whether they apply mainly to mental health or physical health (Q3).
- Ask student to compare their answers with a partner and discuss Q3.
- Check answers with the class.

WRITING PART 6 — UNIT 6: WRITING PRACTICE

KEY

1 emotional health, healthy relationship, immune system, nutritious food, physical problems, negative feelings, positive outlook, quality of life, regular routine, social support

2

Mental health	Physical health
emotional health	immune system
healthy relationship	nutritous food
negative feeloings	physical problems
positive outlook	regular routine
quality of life	
social support	
regular routine	

3 Students' own answers.

VOCABULARY ACTIVITY 2 — PAGE 188

- Ask students to complete the sentences with appropriate collocations from Activity 1.
- They should compare their ideas with a partner before you check answers with the class.

KEY

1 nutritious food 2 healthy relationship 3 positive outlook 4 physical problems 5 emotional health 6 quality of life 7 immune system 8 negative feelings 9 regular routine 10 social support

VOCABULARY ACTIVITY 3 — PAGE 188

- Ask students to work in pairs to discuss the questions.
- Ask them to produce lists of the ways in which they look after their physical and mental health. They should then try and think of more things they could do to look after themselves better in each respect to improve their health.
- Encourage students to use the collocations introduced within this chapter by writing them on the board.

KEY

Students' own answers.

GRAMMAR ACTIVITY 4 — PAGE 189

- Ask students to sort the linking words and phrases into the two columns, making sure they understand the difference between addition and contrast.
- Ask the students to think of further words that would fit in either category.
- Ask the students if all of the words in the original table are followed by verbs, or if any are followed by a noun phrase (*in spite of*).
- Ask the students to complete the final three sentences with words from the Contrast colunm.

KEY

1

Addition	Contrast
	although (+ vp)
consequently (+ vp)	whereas (+ vp)
furthermore (+ vp)	in spite of (+ np)
in conclusion (+ vp)	as long as

2 Students' own answers.
3 Answers are in brackets in table above.
4 a although   b whereas   c in spite of

GRAMMAR ACTIVITY 5 — PAGE 189

- Ask students to complete the text with the appropriate linking words and phrases from the box.
- Tell them to consider the relationship between the phrases on either side of the gaps to help them make their choices. For example, does the second phrase build on or contrast with the one before?
- Encourage students to compare their ideas with a partner before you check answers with the class.

KEY

1 although   2 Consequently   3 As long as
4 in spite of   5 Furthermore   6 In conclusion

GRAMMAR ACTIVITY 6 — PAGE 190

- Ask students to read the sentences carefully, noting in particular the function and use of the linking words and correcting any mistakes that they notice.
- Let students know that not every sentence has an error in it. To give extra help, you could tell them that only two sentences need corrections.
- Encourage students to compare their ideas with a partner before you check answers with the class.

KEY

1 correct
2 Despite ~~of~~ the weather, we had a great time.
3 correct
4 correct
5 I will finish my English homework, as long as ~~if~~ nobody distracts me.

TEACHING TIPS

Hint Q2: We know there is a mistake in this sentence because *despite* should be followed by a noun phrase, not by *of*.

Hint Q5: We know that there is a mistake in this sentence because *as long as* should never be followed by *if*, but by a subject and verb.

GRAMMAR ACTIVITY 7 — PAGE 190

- Ask students to complete the sentences with their own ideas.
- Check answers with the class by nominating individuals or asking for volunteers to read out their answer for each item. Ask students who had a similar answer to raise their hands and get a sample of the alternatives by asking some of the remaining students for their answers.

KEY

Suggested answers:
1 the results were surprising 2 I forgot the cake and nobody came 3 she held her breath
4 We scored a couple of goals 5 Albert Einstein
6 I feel tired 7 I love it 8 it can be quite helpful
9 the computer crashed and we lost half our work
10 The heating is being repaired,

GRAMMAR GAME: LINKING WORDS — PAGE 190

- Create sets of cards for the game, or have the students do so for you, with these words: as long as, although, whereas, in spite of, consequently, furthermore, in conclusion, despite.
- Divide the class into two teams and follow the instructions in the Student Book on how to play the game.
- Start by giving an example. Pick up a card yourself, show it to the class, give a phrase that contains the linking word on the card and elicit possible ways in which the sentence could be continued, e.g.

Whereas my friend likes Italian food ... I like Spanish food.

I missed my bus and consequently ... I arrived late to school.

- When you are satisfied students understand what to do, ask them to continue with the game and play until all the linking word cards have been used.

GRAMMAR ACTIVITY 8 — PAGE 191

- Make sure students have the correct answers for Activity 5 on page 189 before starting this activity. Ask students to match the discourse markers to their functions. Encourage them to look in the text in Activity 5 on page 189 to find examples of how they are used in context.
- Ask students to compare their ideas with a partner before you check answers with the class.
- Ask students to scan the text in Activity 5 on page 189 to see how many discourse markers they can find.

KEY

1 for instance: to introduce an example
so/therefore: to introduce a consequence
firstly, secondly, thirdly: to organise an argument into points
because: to introduce a reason
likewise: to introduce a similar point
significantly: to introduce an important point
but/however: to introduce a contrasting idea
finally: to introduce the last point

2 One: *significantly* (*so* can function as a discourse marker, but in Activity 5 it is introducing a result.

TEACHING TIPS

Here are some examples for each of the discourse markers:

for instance: *Many birds can fly, for instance, the hawk.*

so: *We will be hungry after the journey, so we should make sure there is food waiting for us.*

therefore: *He is slow and therefore will not be able to play as a winger.*

firstly, secondly, thirdly: *Firstly, we must be creative; secondly, we must be persistent; thirdly, we must be lucky.*

because: *He is cold because of the weather.*

likewise: *Paul is very happy at his job. Likewise, Maria and Ahmed said they were very satisfied as well.*

significantly: *Significantly, 90% of the negative results of the survey were from people living in London.*

but / however: *I don't like vegetables, but I eat a lot of them.*

finally: *Finally, I would like to thank you all for coming.*

EXTENSION

- After Q1: Ask students to give oral examples for use of each discourse marker to check understanding, e.g. *Many birds can fly, for instance, the hawk.*
- After Q2: Ask students to work in pairs and decide where they might introduce discourse markers into the text for Activity 5. Discuss what effect this has on the text.

SELF-EVALUATION   PAGE 191

Tell students to look at the Self-evaluation table and tick the boxes that are true for them. Ask them if there are any topics they don't feel confident about yet.

UNIT 7: LISTENING PRACTICE

LISTENING PART 1

OVERVIEW

Topic: Sport and fitness

Exam skills: Revise the requirements for Part 1 of the Listening exam, practise two Part 1 sample questions, evaluate your exam practice

Assessment Objectives: 3A, 3B

Vocabulary: Phrasal verbs: sport and fitness

Grammar: Use modals in the past tense, use modals of deduction and speculation

Practice text type: Short extracts: people talking about sports venues and extreme sports

Additional resources: audio player, dictionaries, blank cards (internet access)

For me, 'a sport' is …
I believe that … is a sport whereas … is not.
I do not believe that … is a sport, because …
The most famous sportsperson in our country's history is …

Useful words and phrases: *sporty, competitions, rules, equipment, referee, fitness levels, entertainment, participation, involvement, excitement, result, score, luck, skill, practice (noun), to practise (verb)*

PREPARING THE WAY — PAGE 194

- Tell students to read the chapter topic title and ask them how many different types of sports (competitive ball sports and other types of sporting activity) they can think of and write them on the board.
- Focus students on the questions. If they are able to sustain a class or small group discussion, you can ask them to discuss each question in detail.
- If students need more support, put some key words and phrases on the board (see Key below). Ask students to produce brief written responses and compare their ideas with a partner or in groups.
- Take feedback from the class and find out how motivated they are by this topic. Ask students to describe what kind of sports they enjoy, as spectators and/or players. How much does sport feature in their school's curriculum? What extra-curricular sports are available? How much of an interest do they take in international sporting competitions like the Olympics? Why?

EXTENSION

Suggested activities:

- Ask students to write an article reporting on a sporting match that they have watched either live, online or on television.
- Ask students to invent a new sport and write out the rules for players to follow.
- Get students to discuss the advantages and disadvantages of having more compulsory sports lessons at school. Which sports would they like to see added to the school curriculum?
- Get students to write a description of a time when a sporting event went very well for them or very badly.
- Ask students to write a story in which sport or a sporting event is central or significant in some way.
- Ask students to research the origins of some well-known and less familiar sports, as well as some that have disappeared or have become less popular over time.
- Ask students to discuss this quotation from Yevgeny Yevtushenko: *I love sport because I love life, and sport is one of the basic joys of life.* As a follow-up, they could find other quotations on the topic of sport and explain why they agree/disagree with them, in speech or in writing.

KEY

Students' own answers.
Suggested sentence structures for discussion:
My favourite sport to play is …
My favourite sport to watch …
This is because …
The reason I like watching/playing … is …

LISTENING PART 1 | **UNIT 7: LISTENING PRACTICE**

ACTIVITY 1 — PAGES 194–195

- Direct students to the photos and elicit descriptions of what is happening in each, reviewing vocabulary from Preparing the Way as necessary.
- Ask students to match each picture with one of the words in the box and confirm the answers with the class.
- For Q2, ask students to discuss the questions in pairs and elicit answers from the class. Elicit or teach the relevant vocabulary for the equipment and facilities needed for each sport as you go through them, and write it on the board.
- By the end of the activity, you will have built a big vocabulary bank of useful words and phrases related to the topic that students will be able to use in future activities.
- Take feedback from the class about the students' experience of doing each type of sport. Then for Q3, find out which of the sporting activities shown students would most and least like to try.

KEY

1. **a** skateboarding **b** cycling **c** windsurfing **d** climbing **e** skiing **f** gymnastics
2. Students' own answers. Suggested answers: **skateboarding:** helmet, kneepads, elbow pads, skateboard park; **cycling:** bicycle, clothing as for skateboarding, cycle paths, anywhere; **windsurfing:** windsurf board, wetsuit, lakes, the sea; **climbing:** ropes, harness, helmet, crampons, mountains, rock faces; **skiing:** skis, ski poles, boots, goggles, snow (real or artificial); **gymnastics:** ropes, mats, bars, vault beam, gym or sports centre
3. Students' own answers.

EXAM REFRESHER — PAGE 195

- Ask students to read through the Exam Refresher box and remind themselves of what they have to do in Part 1 of the Listening exam.
- Give students half a minute to read and then ask them to tell you (without looking back at the text) how many marks they can score this part of the exam. Also elicit what three activity types they might have to do.
- Elicit that this part of the exam is worth 10 marks. The three possible activity types are matching spoken information with written statements, multiple-choice questions and completing or writing an answer with up to three words.

ACTIVITY 2 — PAGE 195

- Tell students they are now going to think about exam technique. Ask them to read the statements about the Listening Part 1 exam tasks and decide with a partner whether or not they think each one is correct.
- Take feedback from the class and elicit from the students the reasons why the incorrect statements are wrong and what the consequences would be if they did these things in the exam (see Key below).

KEY

✗ If you can't decide between two answers, mark crosses for both of them.
  Hint: This will automatically get a mark of zero.

✗ Miss out any questions you find difficult.
  Hint: Questions missed out will definitely get zero. An attempt may earn a mark.

✓ Keep to the specified word limit.
  Hint: The exam rubric cannot be ignored without losing marks. It is there to ensure the exam is fair to everyone.

✗ Don't worry about grammar. Concentrate only on vocabulary.
  Hint: Grammar is important and needs to be correct.

PRACTICE TIME 1: Section A 🔊 — PAGES 195–196

- It is possible to offer extra support, for example, by pre-teaching some key vocabulary. However, it is advisable to try and minimise this support as students need to move towards a point where they can tackle the exam independently.
- Remind the class to look at and follow the Exam Hints for Listening Part 1. Depending on how much extra help you want to give them, you could read the list of places aloud with the class and elicit what sort of sport you might do in each.
- You could also briefly come up with words related to each sport to give the students some extra ideas of related vocabulary to listen out for.
- Play the recording twice for students to listen and answer the questions.
- Check answers with the class. Ask students to tell you any key words or phrases they can remember which helped them to identify each place. These are underlined in the Audioscript below.

UNIT 7: LISTENING PRACTICE

LISTENING PART 1

Audioscript

1 I love watching my <u>team</u> play here. It's a great place to be. The moment the first <u>player</u> <u>kicks off</u> is really exciting, as the <u>match</u> could go either way. The result could be brilliant, or it could be disastrous – what if the best player <u>gets sent off</u>? Either way it'll be worth watching.

2 I like the fact that there's such a range of things to do here. Once you've <u>warmed up</u> you can really do anything you like. Some days I just <u>work out</u> for half an hour or so, but even that helps to <u>keep me fit</u>.

3 This is a great place to visit with friends and family. No one takes it too seriously and there's a really good atmosphere, although it can be noisy. You can get some <u>snacks and have a drink while you play</u>. My best friend Sasha is great at <u>getting strikes</u>! She always knows where to direct the <u>ball</u>.

4 What's nice is that people of all ages can come here. Even small children are safe, as long as they're accompanied by a responsible adult. And it can help with getting fit as well as relaxing – depending how hard you want to push yourself. Sometimes I just do a couple of <u>lengths</u> and then give up, but it all helps! At least the <u>water</u> is warm!

5 I wasn't at all sure about coming here at first, but I'm really pleased I did. I've started trying to beat my own record and I prefer that to competing against others. I love being outside too. I just put my <u>trainers</u> on and <u>whiz round</u> for fun – it all helps me to stay fit.

KEY

(Clues underlined in Audioscript.)
1 E 2 G 3 F 4 B 5 H

DIFFERENTIATION

Strengthen: Pre-teach some of the key vocabulary from the Audioscript and write it on the board: *team* (group of players on the same side), *match* (competition), *seriously* (seen as important), *atmosphere* (feeling, sense of a place or event), *getting strikes* (knocking all ten 'pins' down), *accompanied by* (with), *responsible adult* (grown-up who can look after a young person), *beat my … record* (improve on own highest score), *whiz* (move very quickly).

Note that there are various phrasal verbs in the text that are not included in this list as they are target words in later vocabulary activities.

Challenge: Ask students to write paragraphs about other sports venues/events and to get their partner to match them to brief descriptions of them, for example, a cricket or rugby match; a gymnastics, skiing or skating competition.

PRACTICE TIME 1: Section B
PAGE 196

- Again, you could choose to give students minimal support for this activity to get them used to working under exam conditions. However, if necessary, allow students to listen to the recording an additional time to make the task easier.
- Ask the class to read the rubric and remind students that whereas they listened to several separate descriptions for Section A, Section B has a longer single section of speech to listen to.
- Point out that 'no more than three words' means that one-, two- and three-word answers are acceptable as long as they contain the information required. However, if students write more than three words, they will lose marks.
- Tell students to read the questions and underline the key words. Ask them to think about what kind of information they will be listening for in each case.
- Remind students to look at and follow the Exam Hints.
- Play the recording twice for students to listen and answer the questions, and then check answers with the class. Find out if any of the students have experience of skiing and ask them if they know how to do the snow plough.

Audioscript: Student Book page 286

Kim: Hello, everyone! My name is Kim and I'm going to be your ski instructor for today's lesson. First of all, I'd like to welcome you to this lovely resort. This is probably your first time skiing and hopefully you'll love it so much that you'll soon come back for more! As this is your first lesson, we won't be attempting anything too difficult. I won't expect you to perform <u>jumps or tricks</u> straightaway, that wouldn't be at all fair!

Goal number one for today is for you to have <u>an enjoyable lesson</u>. But for that to happen, you need to be safe. We can build up your skills later in the week.

First of all, then, I want to teach you about <u>slowing down</u>. That's very important, as you may find that your skis start moving faster than you want and once you're moving down the slope at speed, anything can happen. So, the first technique I need to teach you is called 'the snow plough'. Let me explain it to you.

The aim of the snow plough is to slow ourselves down when skiing – at least, it is if you're a beginner. As you become more skilled, you will learn <u>alternative techniques</u>, but I'm going to teach you to snow plough today so that you'll be able to keep yourselves safe on the slopes.

LISTENING PART 1

Now, if you think about the way you skied over here to the beginners' slope, you'll remember that some of you travelled faster than others. If you managed to slow yourself down, it's likely you snow ploughed without even realising it. Yes, that's right! You probably stood like this and turned the tips of your skis in towards each other.

You might have noticed that this caused a decrease in your speed. The further apart the backs of your skis were, the slower you'll have moved. Some of you didn't use the snow plough and kept your skis parallel to each other. Those were the people who <u>fell over</u> …

KEY

(Clues underlined in Audioscript.)

6 jumps or tricks   **7** an enjoyable lesson   **8** slowing down   **9** alternative techniques   **10** they fell over

DIFFERENTIATION

Strengthen: Pre-teach some of the key vocabulary from the Audioscript and write it on the board: *ski instructor* (someone who teaches skiing), *resort* (holiday destination), *straightaway* (immediately), *technique* (strategy; way of doing something), *snow plough* (a ski technique where the toes are close together and the backs of the skis far apart), *beginners' slope* (gentle hill; place for new skiers to practise), *parallel* (side by side at same angle).

Challenge: Ask students to write an instructional speech for a different sport to be delivered to a) a group of beginners b) a group of experts.

REFLECT   PAGE 197

- Ask the class to work through the Reflect questions with a partner and discuss which of the things listed they did or did not manage to do.
- Tell students to help their partner evaluate his or her progress and set a target for the next Practice Time test.
- Encourage students to give each other positive support.

PRACTICE TIME 2: Section A
PAGES 197–198

- Tell the class to review their results from the first Practice Time and the answers to the Reflect questions. Is there anything students can learn from doing the first practice sessions that could help them with the next one?
- Give the class the appropriate amount of time, under exam conditions, to read the instructions carefully. As this is the final practice for this part of the exam, students should ideally attempt it with a minimum of teacher support.
- Play the recording twice for students to listen and choose the correct answers.
- Check answers with the class. Ask students to tell you any key words or phrases they can remember which helped them to identify each sport.

UNIT 7: LISTENING PRACTICE — LISTENING PART 1

Audioscript

1 This is a great sport as long as you don't mind getting too wet and cold. Actually, if you <u>fall out</u>, it can be a bit miserable. But the <u>speed</u> and <u>excitement</u> make up for it, although sometimes the <u>water's</u> a bit <u>rougher</u> than you expect, especially if you hit a branch or two by mistake. For me, though, that's all part of the fun.

2 It takes a lot of skill to get there, but what I enjoy most is the feeling of satisfaction when you reach the <u>top</u> – it's like nothing on Earth. Often the <u>views</u> on the <u>way up</u> are just spectacular, especially if you're next to the sea. I also enjoy the challenge of working out the <u>route</u>.

3 You actually travel much faster than people realise and that's why it's important to wear the right protection and to avoid this sport if it's snowy or icy. If you <u>fall</u>, you can really hurt yourself. On the other hand, there's nothing like working hard to perfect a certain <u>technique</u>. Just don't let the <u>ground</u> take you by surprise on those <u>tricky</u> jumps!

4 Some people find the idea terrifying, but I find it really peaceful. I think it's the feeling of <u>looking down</u> over the landscape below that I enjoy most. The pace is quite gentle too. Having said that, you need to know what you're doing. Personally, I love it, but it's definitely not everybody's thing, especially if you can't stand <u>heights</u> …

5 I still feel nervous when I put the <u>suit</u> on and check that my <u>breathing apparatus</u> works. That soon goes, though, once I'm <u>underwater</u>. It's amazing how much you can see and it's a world that most people never even glimpse. I've been to some amazing locations. I don't think anything else in life ever makes me feel so happy.

KEY

(Clues underlined in Audioscript.)
1 F **2** C **3** G **4** A **5** D

DIFFERENTIATION

Strengthen: Pre-teach some of the key vocabulary from the Audioscript and write it on the board: *miserable* (unhappy), *landscape* (scenery/setting), *route* (path, way to go), *breathing apparatus* (device that lets people breathe underwater).

Note that there are various phrasal verbs in the text that are not included in this list as they are target words in later vocabulary activities.

Challenge: Ask students to use appropriate words or combinations of words to invent names (Musclemaxi can be used as an example) for a range of other sporting venues, e.g. a skating rink, a football training organisation, a swimming pool, gymnastics centre, a boxing ring, weight-lifting arena, a karate centre.

PRACTICE TIME 2: Section B 🔊 PAGE 198

- Remind students that this is their last opportunity to practise this type of Listening Part 1 question.
- Ask students what the first thing they should do when approaching this kind of Listening Part 1 question is and elicit that they should read the questions and underline the key words.
- Remind students to look at and follow the Exam Hint.
- Play the recording twice for students to listen and answer the questions. Then check answers with the class.

Audioscript

Chad: Hey there. I'm Chad, your trainer for today. So, let me get started by saying that Musclemaxi isn't your average gym. We don't leave you to work out by yourself. We will design a specific exercise routine for you, with your body goals in mind. You have to <u>use your Musclemaxi Electronic Card to log into the machines</u>, which will keep track of how many calories you burn and <u>print out a report</u> at the end of the day so you can track your progress.

And the most important thing: we're here to make sure you never give up. Your healthy future starts here.

So, we'll start with a warm-up, which is really important. Football players wouldn't just kick off for a big match without getting their muscles warmed up first. There's no way they would perform well – they'd probably lose and get knocked out of the competition or, worse still, injure themselves …

Now it's time to get started with <u>some light exercises</u>. Today we're going to do a full body workout, starting off with some work on your biceps and triceps, your arm muscles. First, we'll lift some weights. We'll do ten repetitions with each arm and then gradually increase the weight. Is that too heavy for you? No? Great. Just curl your arm up and down. Try not to lift above the shoulder. The rest of you, join in when you're ready.

Now, you may have <u>felt a sort of pleasant burning sensation</u> in your arm, but it shouldn't have caused you any pain – is that what's happened? Ok, good. You must have done this before.

Anyone who has fallen behind and needs to move at a slower pace, you can catch up when you're ready. I think most of you are ready to move up to <u>lift more weight</u> and then we'll move onto the next exercise. Let's just take a minute's rest and catch our breath. You'll soon find you'll be able to live up to your expectations, once you start coming here regularly. OK …

KEY

(Clues underlined in Audioscript.)
6 the machines **7** a report **8** light exercises
9 burning sensation **10** more weight

LISTENING PART 1 — **UNIT 7: LISTENING PRACTICE**

TEACHING TIPS

Sometimes several answers appear to be valid and students then have to choose between them. For example, the answer to Q8 could either have been *warm-up* or *light exercises*. The fact that Q9 refers back to the *first exercise* confirms that the second option must be the right one.

EVALUATE YOUR EXAM PRACTICE
PAGE 198

- Tell the class to work through the Practice Time questions with a partner.
- Ask students to discuss and compare their results for the two practice tests and identify areas where they improved.
- Take feedback from the class regarding which of the question types students find more difficult and elicit ideas for strategies for overcoming those difficulties.

DIFFERENTIATION

Strengthen: Pre-teach some of the key vocabulary from the Audioscript and write it on the board: *Musclemaxi* (name of the gym the passage is based on), *exercise routine* (pattern of movements designed to improve fitness), *electronic card* (that can be used in/read by a machine), *calories* (units of energy), *injure* (hurt).
Note that there are various phrasal verbs in the text that are not included in this list as they are target words in later vocabulary activities. Also, answers to the questions have been omitted.
Challenge: Conduct the activity entirely under exam conditions including setting a time limit. Put the students into pairs and then ask them to work in groups of four to correct and review the other pair's answers.

VOCABULARY AND GRAMMAR

VOCABULARY ACTIVITY 1 — PAGE 199

- This section aims to familiarise students with some more phrasal verbs. It includes phrasal verbs that the students may already be familiar with and others that they may be able to deduce from context.
- Focus students on the list of phrasal verbs and explain that they all come from the recording the class has just listened to of the trainer talking to gym users. Ask them to work with a partner to match as many phrasal verbs as they can with the definitions.

- You can play the recording again for students to hear the phrasal verbs in context (the phrasal verbs are highlighted in the Audioscript above). Alternatively, you can make copies of the Audioscript available for students to read.
- Confirm answers with the class.

KEY

(Clues highlighted in Audioscript.)
catch up: do enough or move fast enough to keep up with others
give up: stop trying, accept defeat
join in: participate
kick off: start a football match
knock out: eliminate from a contest
live up (to): do as well as expected
warm up: do exercises to loosen the muscles
work out: exercise

TEACHING TIPS

- Remind students that some phrasal verbs are separable and others or not. Unfortunately, there are no rules for this so students just have to learn whether the verb is separable or not when they learn it.
- Most of the verbs here are not separable except for:
knock out (always separable): *Venus Williams **knocked** Serena Williams **out** of the tennis tournament.*
warm up (can be separable or inseparable): *This exercise is designed to **warm up** your stomach muscles. / This exercise is designed to **warm** your stomach muscles **up**.*
give up (can be separable or inseparable): *I am trying to **give up** chocolate. / I am trying to **give** chocolate **up**.*

VOCABULARY ACTIVITY 2 — PAGE 199

- This activity aims to contextualise the vocabulary of the previous activity, and give students further practice using phrasal verbs.
- Ask students to read the sentences and circle the best option. Encourage them to try to complete the activity without looking back at the definitions in the previous activity.
- When they have completed the activity, you can encourage students to compare their ideas with a partner and to check against the definitions in Activity 1.
- Confirm answers with the class.

KEY

1 warm up 2 kicked off 3 knocked out 4 give up
5 live up to 6 working out 7 caught up 8 join in

UNIT 7: LISTENING PRACTICE — LISTENING PART 1

VOCABULARY ACTIVITY 3 — PAGE 200

- Ask students to read the email and complete it with the phrasal verbs in the box in the correct form.
- Ask students to try to complete the activity without referring back to the previous two activities.
- Check answers with the class by asking different students to read the sentences in the email and supply the phrasal verb in the correct form.

KEY

1 work out **2** warm up **3** join in **4** giving up **5** caught up **6** live up

TEACHING TIPS

Hint Q4: *Giving up* is in the *-ing* form because it comes after *feel like*, one of the verbs that is always followed by the *-ing* form.

Hint Q5: *Caught up* is in the simple past because it refers to a finished event in the past, i.e. *When I got behind, he made everyone stop while I caught up.*

EXTENSION

- Ask students to look back at Activity 2 and write five more similar items. Each one should be a full sentence and should propose one correct and one incorrect phrasal verb option.
- Tell the class they can use a mixture of both phrasal verbs from Activities 1 and 2 and other phrasal verbs that they know.
- If students find it difficult think of enough phrasal verbs, you can elicit some of the following: *switch on, switch off, fill in, look for, look after, try on.*
- When students have written their sentences, they should swap with a partner and try to complete each other's activities.
- After they have completed the activity, students can swap back, and correct the activity that they created.

GRAMMAR ACTIVITY 4 — PAGES 200–201

- Direct the class to Grammar Reference pages 269–271 to revise the past form of modals.
- Ask students to complete the activity by rewriting the sentences in the past tense.
- Encourage them to compare their ideas with a partner before you check the answers with the class.

KEY

1 She should have played football more. **2** Xavier had to study for eight hours every day. **3** Juana couldn't swim very well. **4** Malek didn't have to work very hard. **5** Pauline couldn't stay out after ten o'clock. **6** Hans might have been sick. **7** Danielle could sing well. **8** Samira worked/was working until seven, so she must have been at the office.

EXTENSION

- Read out some sentences and ask students to write their guesses about what *must/might/could/couldn't have* happened. Give an example to start with, e.g. *Raul feels very sick*. Then ask students to speculate about the reasons for this with the sentence stems *He must/might/could/couldn't have*, e.g. *He must have eaten too much. He might have stayed out in the sun too long. He could have caught a stomach bug.*
- Continue by giving students the following prompts and asking them to write their ideas:

  Daniel feels very cold. (Possible answer: He must have left his jacket at home.)

  Claire is very tired. (Possible answer: She must have worked a lot.)

  Jack is very hungry. (Possible answer: He might have missed breakfast.)

  Rebecca can't find her keys. (Possible answer: She could have left her keys at home.)

  Selina failed the test. (Possible answer: She can't have revised.)

  Gamze isn't in class. (Possible answer: He might have overslept.)

  Mario cannot find the princess. (Possible answer: The princess could have left the castle.)

GRAMMAR ACTIVITY 5 — PAGE 201

- Ask students to work with a partner to put the sentences in order from the least to the most certain.
- Encourage them to check their ideas in the Grammar Reference on pages 269–271 before you confirm the answers with the class.
- Confirm also that all the sentences relate to the past and elicit that the past form of most modal verbs is *have* + modal verb + past participle of main verb. Explain that the exception is *have to*, for which the past form is *had to/didn't have to* + infinitive form of the main verb.
- If students find it strange that *He must have stayed* is less certain than *He stayed*, explain that we use *must have* when we personally believe that something has happened, but we don't have any proof. We use *He stayed* to talk about a fact, something that definitely happened.

KEY

1 d c a b
2 Yes, all of these sentences are making a deduction/statement about the past.

GRAMMAR ACTIVITY 6 — PAGE 201

- This activity focuses on the meaning of different the modal verbs. You might like to remind students of the meaning of *should/shouldn't* for giving advice and talking about whether things are a good idea or not.
- Ask students to work individually to complete the text using appropriate modals in the word box. Warn them that, in many cases, there is more than one possible answer, indicating different shades of meaning.
- Allow students to refer to Grammar Reference pages 269–271 and to compare their ideas with a partner before you check answers as a class.
- Where more than one answer is possible, elicit the differences in meaning between the various options.

KEY

1 can/should **2** mustn't/can't/shouldn't
3 shouldn't **4** might/could **5** should/might
6 mightn't **7** could/might
8 can't/mustn't/shouldn't

GRAMMAR GAME: *SHOULD HAVE* AND *SHOULDN'T HAVE* — PAGE 202

- Divide the class into groups of four or five and ask all the students in each group to write one or two pieces of advice in the past tense on separate cards.
- Each group should then put all their cards together in a pile in the middle of the table and mix them up.
- Students then take it in turns to take a card at random and talk about when and in what circumstances this advice would be useful. The rest of the group have to guess what the advice is.
- Demonstrate the activity yourself using one of the examples in the Student Book and elicit the appropriate piece of advice. When you are sure students understand the activity, let them continue playing the game in groups.
- If possible, make sure the sentences written on the cards are correct before playing. While students play, listen carefully, correcting any errors during or after the activity depending on which is more helpful for the students' fluency.

GRAMMAR ACTIVITY 7 — PAGE 202

- Ask students to work with a partner to put the sentences in order from the most to the least certain by numbering them 1 to 5.
- Encourage them to check Grammar Reference pages 269–271 before you confirm the answers with the class.

KEY

1 Paul **2** Reyna **3** Kurt **4** Daniel **5** Erica

UNIT 7: LISTENING PRACTICE

LISTENING PART 1

GRAMMAR ACTIVITY 8 — PAGES 202–203

- Ask students to read the sentences and circle the best option.
- Check answers as a class.

KEY

1 will **2** can't **3** may **4** might **5** must **6** can't **7** may **8** won't

---

TEACHING TIPS

Hint Q1: We use *will* for a prediction about the future.

Hint Q2: We use *can't* for a deduction about the present.

Hint Q3: We use *may* for a possible future action.

Hint Q4: We use *might* for a deduction about the present in which we are not certain.

Hint Q5: We use *must* for a deduction about the present in which we are almost certain.

Hint Q6: We use *can't* for a deduction about the present. *Mustn't* would signify an obligation, and is also possible, but given the context of *He has work until two.* we are probably speculating.

Hint Q7: We use *may* for a possible future action.

Hint Q8: We use *won't* for a prediction about the future.

GRAMMAR ACTIVITY 9 — PAGE 203

- This activity should help students understand how modal verbs add meaning to a sentence. Ask them to complete the sentences using appropriate modals.
- Make students aware that, in many cases, there is more than one possible answer, indicating different shades of meaning.
- Discuss answers as a class, including the implications of the different possibilities.

KEY

1 must/might **2** must/should **3** can't **4** must **5** shouldn't/can't **6** should/must

SELF-EVALUATION — PAGE 203

Tell students to look at the Self-evaluation table and tick the boxes that are true for them. Ask them if there are any topics they don't feel confident about yet.

LISTENING PART 2

OVERVIEW

Topic: Science
Exam skills: Revise the requirements for Part 2 of the Listening exam, practise two Part 2 sample questions, evaluate your exam practice
Assessment Objectives: 3B, 3D
Vocabulary: Phrasal verbs: separable and non-separable
Grammar: Use gerunds and infinitives
Practice text type: School lesson: a teacher talking about moles to a biology class, Class talk: a man talking about gemstones
Additional resources: audio player, dictionaries (internet access)

PREPARING THE WAY   PAGE 204

- Tell students to read the chapter topic title and elicit the names of any different different branches (types) of science that students might know and write them on the board, e.g. *biology, chemistry, physics, astronomy, botany, zoology, meteorology, information technology, geology, psychology*.
- Focus students on the questions. If they are able to sustain a class or small group discussion, you can ask them to discuss each question in detail.
- If they need more support, put some key words and phrases on the board (see Key below). Ask students to produce brief written responses and compare their ideas with a partner or in groups.
- Take feedback from the class and find out which aspects of science seem to interest them the most. Since it is not easy to analyse and define a field as broad as science, the background information given below may be helpful.

KEY

Students' own answers.
Suggested sentence structures for discussion:
Science is the study of ...
There are different branches/types of science ...
Science has helped people by ...
I think that science will change the world in the next 50 years by/through ...
My favourite science subject is ...
I think Biology/Geology/Astronomy is important because ...
Useful words and phrases: *experiment, cure, measure, explore, theory, replace, be replaced by, discover, developments, test, hypothesis, apparatus*

Background information

Science can be understood as a body of knowledge and also as a process. It is both the process of the systematically studying the world around us through observation and experiment and the knowledge gained from this. The different branches of science are defined by which area of the natural and physical world is being studied. For example, the science of *biology* is related to life forms and can be subdivided into various sub-categories such as *zoology*, the study of animals (of which *human biology* is one branch), and *botany*, the study of plants. Scientific activity is defined by the fact that it focuses on the natural, physical world and aims to explain and understand it. Scientific activity is also based on testable ideas, and relies on evidence and proof.

EXTENSION

Suggested activities:
- Ask students to choose and research a well-known scientist and/or a well-known scientific discovery. Their findings could be presented in speech or writing and could be the basis of a mini-project.
- Set students the task of researching a famous scientific law, e.g. gravity, and then list the changes that would have to be made if it didn't exist.
- Ask students to consider what personality/character traits are needed to be a good scientist. What traits or behaviours would not make someone a good scientist? They could then write a job advertisement for a scientist.
- Write this quotation from Edwin Powell Hubble on the board and ask students to discuss: *Equipped with his five senses, man explores the universe around him and calls the adventure science.* As a follow-up, they could find other quotations on the topic of science and explain why they agree/disagree with them, in speech or in writing.

138 UNIT 7: LISTENING PRACTICE   LISTENING PART 2

ACTIVITY 1   PAGES 204–205

- Ask students to look at the six photographs and elicit descriptions of them. They will probably need some of the following vocabulary, e.g. *mole, underground, earth, diamonds, gemstones, shiny, valuable, coal, molten lava, volcano, earthworm, amethyst, crystal, rock*.
- Feedback in class, confirm what each picture shows and elicit what these things have in common.
- For Q2, go through the table and check student understanding of the headings. Ask the class to compete the table with the properties of each of the items in the photos. If students are not allowed to write in their textbooks, they could write the relevant words after each item, e.g. *a mole – living, soft, dry to touch, moves*.
- Explain that in some categories, more than one answer is possible, e.g. *coal* may be seen as valuable by some people and not by others.
- For Q3, give students some time to write their sentences to describe each picture. The table headings could help them. Then ask them to take turns with a partner to read their sentences and guess which picture they refer to.
- Take feedback from the class by asking for volunteers to read their sentences aloud for the whole class to guess.
- The pictures will also be referred to in the next activity.

Background information

- A mole is a small underground mammal that digs holes and tunnels, and eats worms. Moles are the subject of a Practice Time in this chapter.
- Diamonds are valuable gemstones. They are formed under conditions of extreme heat and pressure underground and as a result are extremely hard. Because of this and other unique properties, they have a wide range of applications in industry and medicine. They are also decorative and are a traditional symbol of wealth because they are so expensive.
- Coal is a type of black or dark brown rock formed from the remains of prehistoric vegetation. Coal is combustible and burns slowly, giving off heat, so has been used as fuel for many centuries.
- Underground volcanic activity. The picture shows lava, which is molten rock (rock so hot it is in liquid form).
- Worms, or earthworms, live underground. They eat decaying leaves and plants and other vegetable material. They provide food for birds and moles, among other animals.
- Amethysts are purple. Like diamonds they are a form of gemstone, often made into jewellery, but they are less expensive and valuable.

KEY

1 The images show different creatures or substances that are found underground.
2 a mole: living, soft, dry to touch, moves
  b diamonds: non-living, valuable, dry to touch
  c coal: non-living, valuable (up to a point), dry to touch, hot to touch (only if lit)
  d lava: non-living, hot to touch, dangerous, moves
  e worm: living, moves
  f amethyst: non-living, valuable, dry to touch
3 Students' own answers.

ACTIVITY 2   PAGE 205

- Tell students they are going to listen to three scientists talking about their work. Review the names of the different branches of science students produced in Preparing the Way and add any more they can think of.
- Ask which branches of science students think the pictures in Activity 1 relate to, e.g. the picture of the mole would relate to biology, zoology, natural history. The scientists' specialisations are underlined in the Audioscript. Elicit students' ideas but don't say whether they are right or wrong yet.
- Elicit answers from the class before playing the recording a second time and asking students to note which pictures from Activity 1 relate to each speaker. Tell them that some pictures might match with more than one.
- Encourage students to compare their ideas with a partner before checking answers with the class.

LISTENING PART 2   **UNIT 7: LISTENING PRACTICE** 139

Audioscript: Student Book page 290

1 Jemma: My branch of science is Geology. Geology is known as an earth science. It looks at the way that rocks are formed and the history of the Earth itself, so it's very exciting. We look at how gems like diamonds form and at the chemicals that make up the Earth itself. We're used to looking at natural landscapes. Geology is the study of how these are formed and much more. It's fascinating!

2 Karl: Like my Geologist colleague, my interest is also in the materials that make up the Earth, but I approach them from a slightly different perspective.

Chemistry is the science I have chosen to specialise in and it is interesting – in my opinion, at least – because it looks in detail at the chemical formation of, potentially, every single substance on the planet. It also examines the reactions between different chemicals and explores what happens to them at different temperatures. Why the lava inside volcanoes, for example, is liquid and how and why it hardens as its temperature cools. To me, Chemistry is vital, as it looks at the building blocks of the world we live in. Where would we be without it?

3 Ricky: Rather than studying the Earth, I study Natural History, so that means looking at the creatures and plants that live on our planet. There is an amazing range of creatures and vegetation on this planet. Even a single species can vary tremendously. Natural History also looks at the way that animals have evolved over centuries to live in specific environments. Take moles as an example. They spend almost all of their lives underground, in almost total darkness and their bodies are really well adapted to this.

KEY

(Clues underlined in Audioscript.)
Speaker 1 and **Speaker 2** b, c, d, f **Speaker 3** a, e

EXTENSION

Ask students to write a similar paragraph for someone working in a branch of science of their own choosing. They could record their paragraphs to help practise their speaking skills.

EXAM REFRESHER   PAGE 205

- Ask students to read through the Exam Refresher box and remind themselves of what they have to do in Part 2 of the Listening exam.
- Give students half a minute to read and then ask them to tell you (without looking back at the text) how many marks they can score in this part of the exam. Also elicit what three things are mentioned that they have to do.
- Elicit that this part of the exam is worth 10 marks. The three activities mentioned are listening to a longer text, completing a range of tasks and identifying implicit and explicit information.

ACTIVITY 3   PAGE 205

- Tell students they are now going to think about exam technique. Ask them to read the statements about the Listening Part 2 exam tasks and decide with a partner whether or not they think each one is correct.
- Give students a minute or so to go through the statements and compare their ideas about them with another pair. Then check answers with the class.

KEY

✗ Don't answer difficult questions.
Hint: It is always worth attempting every question.

✗ Don't worry about grammar. Concentrate only on vocabulary.
Hint: The correct answer will always be grammatically correct within the sentence.

✓ You should listen for implicit information, such as the writer's opinion.
Hint: This is one aspect of what is being tested.

✗ If you can't decide between two answers in a multiple-choice question, you should mark crosses for both of them.
Hint: Avoid this – you will get no marks.

PRACTICE TIME 1   PAGES 206–207

- Remind students to spend time reading the two tasks carefully and check that they understand what they have to do. Direct them to read and follow the information in the Exam Hints box.
- Point out the instructions given for writing no more than three words for the first task and for what students should do if they change their mind about which box to cross in the second task.
- When students are ready, play the recording twice for them to listen, complete and check each task. (The key information is underlined in the Audioscript below.)

Audioscript

Mrs Hill: OK everyone, settle down now please. So in today's class I want to continue our work on animals and their environments. There's an animal called the mole. You've heard of it, haven't you? So to start, we're going to look at some facts about these amazing underground creatures. Please can you listen and make some notes about them.

Did you know that worldwide, there are approximately 20 species of mole and that they live in parts of the globe ranging from Asia to Europe to North America? These small mammals (the European mole, for example, is about 12–15 cm long, with the females being slightly smaller than the males) are pretty tough creatures! If they run out of space or food they simply dig more tunnels. They can move huge quantities of earth in a very short space of time.

So, moles are pretty small, but they come in different shapes and sizes, the smallest one being the American shrew mole, about five centimetres and the largest being the Russian desman. Whatever their size, though, they have a lot in common! As you know, they generally travel underground, spending their relatively short lifespan (on average three to four years in the wild, longer in captivity where they are protected from predators) in a network of tunnels that they dig with their powerful front claws. They have worked out a way to survive, even though most of the time they live in complete darkness.

One feature of a mole's behaviour is that it is constantly active. Most of the time they will be busy digging away under the surface. They don't dig for nothing, though! They are almost always hunting for their favourite food – worms – although they do also live on different kinds of insects. If they stop eating, they soon run into problems. Scientists have found out something quite unusual: a mole will store worms that it has bitten but not killed, keeping them fresh until they need them! They've come up with an explanation for how they do this.

Apparently, moles' saliva contains a toxic substance that paralyses the worms so they cannot move. Evidence can back up these findings quite easily. For example, one mole was found to be storing about a thousand worms!

This may sound like a lot, but moles need to eat more or less continuously in order to survive. Unfortunately, we don't have time (or moles!) to carry out an experiment in class to test this, but scientists have found out that a mole can starve to death within only 24 hours of eating as much as it is able to. In other words, they cannot store their food like most other species – including humans – can. Getting enough food may be a problem, but moles do have a huge advantage when it comes to breathing underground. They are able to tolerate higher levels of carbon dioxide than most other mammals. They can actually re-use the air they have just breathed out – by breathing it in again. This means that they are perfectly adapted to underground living!

Of course, all of those tunnels they make and the large piles of soil they dig up do alter the nature of the soil and a lot of people see them as a nuisance. They often leave piles of earth on the surface, so you can imagine why many gardeners dislike them. Farmers too are concerned about damage to growing plants.

Although we're just going to study moles and their environment in this class, it's nice to remember some of the mole characters from children's literature. There's Kenneth Graham's classic story, *The Wind in the Willows*, with a mole as one of the main characters, which has such a wonderful description of Mole's underground home! *Duncton Wood* is another story featuring moles, as is *The Animals of Farthing Wood*. I'd say it's not hard to understand the appeal of these unusual creatures. They're small, they're cute and there's something very lovable about them, don't you think?

KEY

(Clues underlined in Audioscript.)
11 20/twenty **12** earth **13** longer **14** insects
15 toxic **16** starve (to death) **17** breathe
18 gardeners **19** C **20** C

DIFFERENTIATION

Strengthen: Pre-teach some of the key vocabulary from the Audioscript and write it on the board: *species* (a type of animal), *Russian desman* (a large mole), *in captivity* (living in cages or enclosures rather than in nature), *predator* (something that hunts and eats another creature), *survive* (stay alive), *toxic substance* (poison), *continuously* (all the time), *carbon dioxide* (a gas we breathe out when we breathe in oxygen), *saliva* (the liquid produced in your mouth to keep the mouth wet and to help to prepare food to be digested), *nuisance* (pest, causing harm).

Note there are various phrasal verbs in the text that are not included in this list as they are target words in later vocabulary activities.

Challenge: Conduct the activity entirely under exam conditions including setting a time limit. Put the students into pairs and then ask them to work in groups of four to correct and review the other pair's answers.

LISTENING PART 2   **UNIT 7: LISTENING PRACTICE**   141

TEACHING TIPS

- Some questions may seem to have more than one answer. For example, Q18 requires students to identify someone moles are *not very popular with*. Two options are mentioned in the passage, *farmers* and *gardeners*. However the information provided about gardeners, who are said to *dislike* moles is a closer match with the wording of the question than farmers who are said to be *concerned about damage to growing plants*. Although we can infer that farmers do not like moles either, the statement about gardeners is more directly relevant to the question, so *gardeners* is the correct answer.

- Similarly, Q19 refers to a description of a fictional mole's home and asks for the teacher's opinion of it. A good approach is to eliminate options that obviously don't match. Option B can be eliminated first – there is no suggestion that the home is not *pleasant*. Option D may be true, but there is no evidence in the passage to support it. Although the teacher mentions children's literature, she does not say anything directly about children *enjoying* the description (Option A). Option C is a closer match, as the teacher refers to the book containing *such a wonderful description* and the word *lovely* in option C is a synonym for *wonderful*.

PRACTICE TIME 2   PAGES 207–208

- Tell the class to review their results from the first Practice Time and the answers the Reflect questions. Ask them how they think they can improve their performance in the next Practice Time.
- Remind students to read the questions carefully and to note the advice in the Exam Hints before you play the recording twice for them to listen and answer the questions.
- You could give them the information that the word *deep* has two different meanings in this passage. It can relate to physical depth, i.e. how far below the surface something is buried and it can also be used to describe colour, i.e. the opposite of pale. Check that students are aware of both meanings.
- Check answers with the class. The key information is underlined in the Audioscript below.

REFLECT   PAGE 207

- Ask the class to work through the Reflect questions with a partner and discuss which of the things listed they did or did not manage to do.
- Tell students to help their partner evaluate his or her progress and set a target for the next Practice Time test.
- Encourage students to give each other positive support.

142 UNIT 7: LISTENING PRACTICE — LISTENING PART 2

Audioscript

Ian: Hello, my name is Ian Thomas and I'm going to talk to you today about gemstones and how they form. I always wanted to study geology as a child, because I loved the idea of finding things out about the Earth's secrets. I wanted to search for precious stones and dig them up.

I wanted to carry experiments out, to work out how different substances interact and form new substances. I was lucky enough to go to university in Edinburgh and now I work as a geologist.

My specialisation is in the different processes that make it possible for gemstones to form <u>many thousands of metres below the Earth's surface</u>. And that's what I'm going to talk to you about today!

First of all, let's think about how amazing these gemstones actually are. You've all seen pictures of diamonds, rubies, emeralds and so on – those incredible stones that are often used for jewellery. Humans have always been drawn to them, and as <u>they are so rare</u>, they are worth a lot.

Over the years, people have even committed serious crimes to acquire them! Even the tiniest gem can be worth millions and some of them have even become famous.

The Hope Diamond, for instance, is well known for its deep and rich blue colour. It is also known for the legend that says it is cursed and that anyone who owns it will run into serious problems.

Scientists are unlikely to come up with any basis for that particular belief, though! There really aren't any facts to back it up.

Of course, <u>some of the most highly-prized gemstones are also the largest</u>. A huge pearl which was unearthed in Mongolia weighed six tons and <u>measured 1.6 metres across</u>, for example. Imagine being the person to dig up that!

Another well-known gem is the biggest one ever discovered. It's a huge topaz <u>that was discovered in Brazil</u> and it weighs over 270 kg. That's pretty impressive! It's now kept in the American Museum of Natural History. Unfortunately, although it's large, it isn't a gem of particularly good quality. The largest high-quality gem (that is, good enough to be made into jewellery) was an aquamarine, also found in Brazil. <u>It was found in 1910</u> and weighs 103 kg, so that's still pretty big.

I've mentioned some of the most impressive gems we know about, but what do we know about how they've formed? There are two important factors to consider here: <u>time and pressure</u>.

I've already mentioned that precious stones tend to occur in rocks buried deep in the ground and also that it takes millions of years for them to form. But can we be more specific than that? Actually, we can.

Gems are mined in what we call the Earth's 'crust'. This is made up of different kinds of rock, and different kinds of gemstones are formed depending on the kind of rock, the location and the pressure exerted on the rock. For example, diamonds form in <u>the kind of rock we associate with volcanoes</u>. Perhaps that makes it less surprising that diamond is the hardest known natural substance. If you consider that it's been compressed under tonnes of rock for millions of years, you can see why it's so strong. In fact, this strength makes it very useful. Diamonds may look very attractive and it's true that they are highly prized as jewellery, but they're also extremely useful. You may be surprised to hear that we use diamonds as cutting tools and we also use them in computer processors and in microchips. We probably won't ever run out of uses for them!

Of course, as incredible as the gems I've been speaking about are, <u>the majority of them will never be found</u>. They'll just remain buried under masses of rock, forever. There may even be some many kilometres below the place you're standing now. It's quite strange to think about it! The Earth holds so many secrets like this and <u>that's what makes geology so challenging and fascinating</u>.

KEY

(Clues underlined in Audioscript.)
11 deep **12** (so) rare **13** highly prized **14** 1.6 metres (across) **15** Brazil **16** 1910 **17** time and pressure **18** volcanoes **19** B **20** B

DIFFERENTIATION

Strengthen: Revise or pre-teach some of the key vocabulary from the Audioscript and write it on the board: *interact* (act together/cause reactions between), *rubies* (precious stones which are red in colour), *emeralds* (precious stones which are green in colour), *legend* (well-known story) *aquamarines*, (semi-precious stones which are turquoise in colour).

Note that there are various phrasal verbs in the text that are not included in this list as they are target words in later vocabulary activities.

Challenge: Conduct the activity entirely under exam conditions including setting a time limit. Put the students into pairs and then ask them to work in groups of four to correct and review the other pair's answers.

EVALUATE YOUR EXAM PRACTICE
PAGE 208

- Tell the class to work through the Practice Time questions with a partner.
- Ask students to discuss and compare their results for the two practice tests and identify areas where they improved.
- Take feedback from the class regarding which of the question types students find more difficult and elicit ideas for strategies for overcoming those difficulties.

LISTENING PART 2 | **UNIT 7: LISTENING PRACTICE** | **143**

VOCABULARY AND GRAMMAR

VOCABULARY ACTIVITY 1 — PAGE 209

- This activity is designed to familiarise students with some more phrasal verbs.
- Ask students to work in pairs to combine verbs and prepositions to complete the sentences from audio they have just heard with appropriate phrasal verb.
- When they are ready, play the audio for them to check anything they are not sure about.
- Check answers with the class. Ask different students to read out their completed sentences.

KEY

1 finding ... out   2 dig ... up   3 carry ... out, to work out   4 run into   5 come up with   6 back ... up   7 dig up   8 run out

DIFFERENTIATION

Strengthen: Pause after each sentence for two or three seconds to give students a chance to fill in the gaps. Repeat as many times as needed.

Challenge: Ask students to predict which verbs and prepositions will go in each space before listening to the audio, and listen only to confirm.

VOCABULARY ACTIVITY 2 — PAGE 209

- Ask students to work individually to match the definitions with the phrasal verbs from Activity 1.
- Encourage students look carefully at the verbs as they are used in context in the sentences to help them deduce meaning.
- Ask students to compare their ideas with a partner before you check answers as a class.

KEY

to discover facts or information: find out
to support something with evidence: back up
to make a hole in the ground: dig up
to find the answer or solution: work out
to do something that you have planned to do: carry out
to no longer have something: run out
to encounter, perhaps unexpectedly: run into
to think of (an idea or solution): come up with

VOCABULARY ACTIVITY 3 — PAGE 210

- Ask students to read the sentences and circle the best option. Encourage them to try to complete the activity without looking back at the definitions in the previous activity.
- When they have completed the activity, encourage students to compare their ideas with a partner and to check against the definitions in Activity 2.
- Confirm answers with the class.

KEY

1 carry out   2 work out   3 dig up   4 back up
5 run out   6 came up with   7 found out   8 ran into

VOCABULARY ACTIVITY 4 — PAGE 210

- Tell students to work individually to read the sentences and to complete them with phrasal verbs they have studied in the previous two activities in the correct form.
- Encourage students to try to complete the activity without referring back to the previous two activities.
- Check answers with the class by asking different students to read the sentences and supply the phrasal verb in the correct form.

KEY

1 worked out   2 run out   3 dug up   4 carry out
5 ran into   6 back ... up   7 work out   8 find out

EXTENSION

- If students require further practice with these phrasal verbs, ask them to write five more sentences in the style of the previous activity, where the missing words are phrasal verbs. Make sure students also create an answer key.
- Students then exchange their sentences with a partner and try to complete them. When they have finished, they return the completed versions for their partner to correct.

UNIT 7: LISTENING PRACTICE — LISTENING PART 2

GRAMMAR ACTIVITY 5 — PAGE 211

- This activity is designed to help students know when to use the gerund (the *-ing* form of the verb, e.g. *doing*) and when to use the infinitive (the *to* form of the verb, e.g. *to do*).
- Refer the class to pages 259–260 of the Grammar Reference to revise this topic and remind themselves which verbs follow which structure.
- Ask students to complete the activity and place the verbs in the appropriate columns without referring back to the Grammar Reference.
- Confirm answers with the class.

KEY

verb + infinitive	verb + gerund
plan	enjoy
promise	avoid
hope	recommend
forget	suggest
help	forget
remember	remember
stop	stop

GRAMMAR GAME: VERB RELAY — PAGE 212

- Follow the instructions in the Student Book. Make sure all of the verbs the students write down on pieces of paper can be followed by another verb. The lists on Grammar Reference pages 259 and 260 are a good source of verbs for the students. Try to ensure that as many verbs as possible are used.
- The different teams should use different colour markers to write on the board to make scoring easier.
- At the end of the game, correct the words on the board with the class, asking them whether each word is in the correct section of the board. Give a point to a team for each correct answer that they have written.

SELF-EVALUATION — PAGE 212

Tell students to look at the Self-evaluation table and tick the boxes that are true for them. Ask them if there are any topics they don't feel confident about yet.

GRAMMAR ACTIVITY 6 — PAGE 211

- This activity allows students to put into practice what they have just learned in the previous activity about the use of gerunds and infinitives.
- Ask students to read the sentences and circle the best option, referring back to the table if necessary.
- Have students compare answers with their partner before correcting as a class.

KEY

1 to break down   2 finding out   3 to run out
4 to conduct   5 seeing   6 to buy   7 to rest
8 resting   9 making   10 to publish

GRAMMAR ACTIVITY 7 — PAGE 212

- This activity continues to help students practise using gerunds and infinitives, now with slightly less guidance.
- Encourage students to try to complete the activity without referring back to the previous two activities.
- Check answers with the class by asking different students to read the sentences and supply the verb in the correct form.

KEY

1 writing, to complete, to carry out   2 to discover
3 getting, to adapt   4 taking   5 performing, to be

EXTENSION

- Write the following additional 'tip for becoming a better scientist' on the board:

  6 Always remember _____ (tidy up) after your experiment!

- Ask students to discuss with a partner what they think the correct answer is, and then check as a class (*to tidy up*). Ask students to write three more tips for conducting a science experiment using the following verbs with the correct use of the gerund or infinitive after them: *avoid*, *help*, *stop*, e.g. *avoid making a mess*, *help to make everything safe*, *stop to make notes*

LISTENING PART 3

OVERVIEW

Topic: Language
Exam skills: Revise the requirements for Part 3 of the Listening exam, practise two Part 3 sample questions, evaluate your exam practice
Assessment Objectives: 3C, 3D
Vocabulary: Suffixes
Grammar: Use defining and non-defining relative clauses, use reported speech
Practice text type: Interview: talking with a linguist, Discussion: two English teachers talking about their jobs
Additional resources: audio player, dictionaries, recording devices (optional) (internet access)

PREPARING THE WAY   PAGE 214

- Tell students to read the chapter topic title and ask how many of them speak more than one language (insist on the idea that everyone in the class speaks English as well as their home language). Ask which other languages students would like to have the opportunity to learn and why.
- Focus students on the questions. If they are able to sustain a class or small group discussion, you can ask them to discuss each question in detail.
- If they need more support, put some key words and phrases on the board (see Key below). Ask students to produce brief written responses and compare their ideas with a partner or in groups.
- Take feedback from the class and find out how motivated they are by this topic. Ask students to explain why they think it is important to learn other languages and whether doing so is likely to become more or less important in the future.

KEY

Students' own answers.
Suggested sentence structures for discussion:
I think it is important to be able to speak more than one language because ...
I believe language is / is not unique to humans because ...
I think communication between people from different cultures is / is not easy because ...
I do / don't believe humans can communicate with other species. The reason for this is ...

Useful words and phrases: *monolingual, bilingual, multilingual, special ability, common ground, communication barriers, communication patterns, non-verbal communication, adaptable*

EXTENSION

Suggested activities:
- Some languages are in danger of dying out. Ask students to find out more about this topic and to find examples of languages that are in danger of extinction, and the reasons why. Elicit students' views about whether this matters; whether languages should be protected, and if so, why and how.
- Some scientists have claimed that chimpanzees can use language. Elicit responses to these claims before and after students have researched them.
- Ask students to write a story or article about a communication error that had serious consequences.
- Ask students to research polyglots (people who can speak multiple languages) from the past and present. What are the advantages of being a polyglot? Are there any disadvantages?
- Ask students to discuss this quotation from Ludwig Wittgenstein: *The limits of my language are the limits of my world.* As a follow-up, they could find other quotations on the topic of the langauge/communication and explain why they agree/disagree with them, in speech or in writing.

Background information

There are between 5,000 and 7,000 languages spoken in the world today. The precise number depends on how the difference between a language and a dialect or regional variation is defined. Languages can be spoken, written or transmitted through other media, such as signing or Braille. Language systems rely on the process of relating signs, sounds and patterns to particular meanings (semiosis). Humans acquire language through social interaction in early childhood, and children usually speak fluently by the time they are about three years old. A group of languages that descend from a common ancestor is known as a language family, and English language is part of the Indo-European family, which includes Romance, Germanic, Slavic and some Indian languages. The top five most widely spoken languages in the world today are Chinese, Spanish, English, Hindi and Arabic.

UNIT 7: LISTENING PRACTICE — LISTENING PART 3

ACTIVITY 1 PAGES 214–215

- Direct the class to the six photographs and explain that that they represent different forms of communication. Ask the class to work in pairs to match them with the words in the box.
- Confirm answers with the class and check pronunciation of any words that may be new to students such as *Braille* and *semaphore*. Make sure students are clear about what type of communication each photo illustrates, e.g. Braille is used by blind people because it's a way of reading using the sense of touch. You could mention that Chinese (picture e) is the most widely spoken language in the world, since this information will be of use to students in the next part of this activity.
- Explain that students are now going to hear four speakers talking about different communication systems. Four of the pictures are described, two are not.
- Remind students to listen out for lexical words which should give them helpful pointers.
- Play the recording twice for students to listen and choose the best option. Then check answers with the class. Ask students to tell you which language is being described in recording 2. Elicit how we know it is not Chinese (because Chinese is the number one mostly widely spoken language in the world and the one described here is only number four; also this language is spoken in the Middle East and North Africa). This latter information provides the clue to the identity of the language, which is Arabic.
- Ask students to discuss the questions in pairs before taking feedback from the class. Establish that all the communication systems, e.g. Braille, semaphore, computer code, have regional or country/language specific variants. Body language is the nearest to a universal medium of communication although there may be some gestures which are culture-specific (see answer Key).
- Find out which of the communication systems students would most like to learn.

Audioscript: Student Book page 290

1 This is a language which is used by the Navy. It's <u>a way of sending messages using flags</u>. Normally, a signalman holds two flags in different positions to show different letters.

2 This system was invented in 1824 by a 15-year-old boy. It is a <u>tactile alphabet which helps the visually impaired to read and write</u> and is now commonly used internationally.

3 This is the <u>fourth most widely spoken language in the world</u>. It is one of the six official languages of the United Nations. <u>Its many varieties are spoken by over 420 million people, mainly in the Middle East and North Africa.</u>

4 This is <u>a system of movements and gestures that people use in everyday life to show their feelings</u>. Sometimes these movements are conscious (we are aware of them), for example, gestures like bowing or waving, and some are sub-conscious (we are not aware of them), like when someone is shy and folds their arms.

KEY

(Clues underlined in Audioscript.)
1 a Braille b body language c semaphore
  d computer code e Chinese script f sign language
2 1 c 2 a 3 Not given (Arabic) 4 b
3 Students' own answers.

Background information

Braille: a system of raised dots on a page that make it possible for those who are blind or have visual impairments to 'read' it. It was invented by Louis Braille at the age of fifteen after he had lost his eyesight in an accident.

Body language: a person's non-verbal signs, shown through gestures and facial expressions; a way of communicating that does not use words. It is something people use instinctively, i.e. without conscious thought, and is a way of communicating feelings, responses and states of mind. It is important to note that body language varies between cultures, e.g. a thumbs-up sign is offensive in some countries and positive in others.

Semaphore: a way of communicating using hand-held items such as flags. Originally associated with communicating at sea in the nineteenth century, semaphore has since been developed in different ways and for different purposes throughout the world.

Computer code: extremely detailed step-by-step instructions written by computer programmers.

Chinese script: a system of writing that uses characters known as logograms to represent a word or phrase. It is extremely complex. Other systems using logograms are also used in other parts of the world, such as Japan and Korea.

Sign language: a system of communicating commonly associated with people with hearing impairment or loss. Words are represented by specific signals and hand gestures. Although sign language exists all over the world, it will vary from country to country, just as spoken language does.

EXTENSION

Ask students to research and discuss universal languages, e.g. body language, and to explore the cultural differences between them (where they exist).

EXAM REFRESHER — PAGE 215

- Ask students to read through the Exam Refresher box and remind themselves of what they have to do in Part 3 of the Listening exam.
- Give students half a minute to and read then ask them to tell you (without looking back at the text) what different activity types are mentioned. Also ask them how many marks they can score this part of the exam.
- Elicit that this part of the exam is worth 10 marks. The activity types mentioned are short answer, multiple-choice questions and table and diagram completion.

ACTIVITY 2 — PAGE 215

- Tell students they are now going to think about exam technique. Ask them to read the statements about the Listening Part 3 exam tasks and decide with a partner whether or not they think each one is correct.
- Give students a minute or so to go through the statements and compare their ideas about them with another pair. Then check answers with the class.

KEY

✓ Try to scan the questions before the recording starts so you know what sort of information to listen for.
Hint: This will help you focus on the most useful information.

✗ You should always answer in full sentences.
Hint: The instructions make it clear this is not expected.

✓ If your spelling is inaccurate, you may lose marks because the examiner may not understand your answer.
Hint: Try to spell as accurately as possible so the examiner can understand you, otherwise they cannot give you a mark.

✓ Never give more than one answer for a multiple-choice question.
Hint: If you cross more than one box, you will get no marks.

PRACTICE TIME 1 — PAGES 216–217

- Draw attention to the rubric for this part of the exam and to the information in the Exam Hint. Students do not need to write in full sentences, but there is no set word limit specified in this part of the exam (unlike in Listening Part 1).
- Explain that students should be guided by the space available and that it is general good practice to keep answers brief and to the point.
- Advise students that they will lose marks if they include extra information, as it will not be clear to the examiner that they have understood the question.
- Elicit or teach the meaning of *interviewer* (the person asking the questions) and *interviewee* (the person answering the questions). Then remind students that the exam questions might relate to the views of the interviewer (as here) and not just the interviewee.
- Play the recording twice for students to listen and do the tasks. Take feedback from the class. The key phrases have been underlined in the Audioscript.

UNIT 7: LISTENING PRACTICE — LISTENING PART 3

Audioscript

Nita: Hello, Jon! Thank you for coming to talk to me today.

Jon: Thank you, Nita. It's very nice to be here.

Nita: Now you're going to tell me about the subject of your area of research, neologisms. Can you begin by explaining exactly what 'neologisms' are?

Jon: Of course. Neologisms are simply new words that have entered a language. The term neologism comes from the Greek word 'neo', meaning 'new'.

Nita: Like the character, Neo, from the film *The Matrix*? Any film fans listening should be familiar with that!

Jon: Yes, and also from the Greek 'logos', meaning 'word'.

Nita: Aha, You've been doing this research for over ten years, right? You must really love your subject! So, if I understand correctly, you're saying that new words just arrive, sometimes? That's incredible! Where do these new words come from?

Jon: Well, that depends. There are many different reasons for new words appearing in our language. For example, if we think about the recent example of technology, there are lots of new developments and new gadgets appearing and a lot of new words have emerged as a result of that.

Nita: Oh, like the iPad, you mean? Or Wi-Fi?

Jon: Exactly. And sometimes words that were already present in a language are combined or used in a new way, like 'waterbed', for example.

Nita: I see.

Jon: But we've also started using old words in new ways in English.

Nita: Oh? Could you give me an example?

Jon: Take the word 'text', for example. A few decades ago, we used the word 'text' as a noun, often meaning a book or an article. Now, though, we often also use it as a verb to talk about sending a message on our mobiles, saying 'I'll text you later.' or 'I'll message you!'

Nita: Aha, that's true. And are all of these new words – or neologisms, I should say – linked to new technology?

Jon: Not at all. There are words such as 'Sellotape' or 'Kleenex' that were originally brand names but over time have come to be used more generally. Now these examples are widely used with a wider meaning: when we use the word 'Sellotape' to talk about any kind of sticky tape; when we talk about 'Kleenex', we often mean any kind of disposable tissue, not just the ones with that brand name.

Nita: Right. And how else do new words come into our language?

Jon: Well, words can get blended together.

Nita: Blended?

Jon: Yes, for example the word 'motel' is a blend (or a combination) of the words 'motorway' and 'hotel' and has a new meaning. I find these words quite fascinating!

Nita: Oh, I can think of another example: brunch! A blend of 'breakfast' and 'lunch'! One of my favourite meals.

Jon: Yes, I think you get the idea!

Nita: So, your job is to study all of this and write about it? I'm really envious!

Jon: I know. I'm really lucky to have work that I enjoy so much. It feels like there's always so much to learn.

Nita: I can see why! And do you think it's advantageous to have these new words appearing in our vocabulary all the time?

Jon: Yes, of course! I'm a linguist! Words represent meanings, objects or ideas. If something new appears, we need to have the language to talk about it.

Nita: I see. And are there any other ways that new words enter a language, apart from the ones you've mentioned so far?

Jon: Well, words travel. A lot of words that are now in the English language had their origin in other countries and vice versa. Words like 'café', for example, which comes from French. And 'algebra' was originally an Arabic word.

Nita: Fascinating. Is this a recent phenomenon?

Jon: Not at all. Even in very early times and throughout history, movements in population meant that language evolved. In recent years, though, the influence of media and especially social media, has made a tremendous impact. Young people often create words to use between themselves, or use old words in new ways. Do you realise that fifty years ago, 'cool' only referred to temperature, or to tone of voice? Then young people started using it to also mean something really great. This word is used everywhere now! With language, everything is shifting all the time, which is one of the reasons why studying it is so fascinating. It's full of uncertainty and creativity.

Nita: So, some words are new and some words are changing their meaning. How about words that disappear? Do some words also die out?

Jon: Indeed they do. There are words that have almost entirely died out, called obsolete words. One example in English is 'brabble', which means to argue loudly about something that isn't important. I don't think anyone uses this word any more! In old literature, it's possible to find examples of words that aren't used in conversation nowadays, for example words like 'thou' and 'thee' meaning 'you'. These are known as archaic words.

Nita: I suppose this concept of words changing is a bit like what happens with wildlife and nature. Some species are flourishing, some we have preserved in zoos and conservation areas, some are very vulnerable and others, like the dodo, have become extinct.

Jon: That's a very good analogy, Nita.

Nita: An interesting note to end on! Thank you for talking to me today, Jon. I've found it really fascinating.

Jon: Thank you, I've enjoyed it too.

KEY

(Clues underlined in Audioscript.)

21 new words **22** over ten years **23** new developments in technology **24** He finds them fascinating. **25** the influence of the media (especially social media) **26** A **27** A **28** C **29** D **30** B

DIFFERENTIATION

Strengthen: Pre-teach some of the key vocabulary from the Audioscript and write it on the board: *gadgets* (device, often electronic), *waterbed* (a bed filled with water), *brand name* (the name of a product made and marketed by a specific company), *phenomenon* (event, happening).

Note that there are various words with suffixes in the text that are not included in this list as they are target words in later vocabulary activities.

Challenge: Conduct the activity entirely under exam conditions including setting a time limit. Put the students into pairs and then ask them to work in groups of four to correct and review the other pair's answers.

TEACHING TIPS

The more challenging questions are often those where two answers seem valid.

Q30 may be challenging for students. In the listening, there is no mention of *environmental change* or *plants*, so options A and C can be eliminated. B and D may both seem valid, but *zoos* is used as a specific example and we need a more general term, which means the best answer is B *natural species*.

REFLECT — PAGE 217

- Ask the class to work through the Reflect questions with a partner and discuss which of the things listed they did or did not manage to do.
- Tell students to help their partner evaluate his or her progress and set a target for the next Practice Time test.
- Encourage students to give each other positive support.

PRACTICE TIME 2 — PAGES 217–218

- Tell students to think about their results from the first Practice Time in this part. Is there anything they have learned from doing the first practice sessions (in this section and in Unit 3) that could help them with the next one?
- Give the class the appropriate period of time, under exam conditions, to read the instructions carefully. This task gives students exposure to another variety of layout which might be used in the exam and it is useful for them to prepare them for a range of different possible formats.
- As this is the final practice for this part of the exam, students should ideally attempt it with a minimum of teacher support.
- Play the recording twice for students to listen and choose the correct answers. The key phrases have been underlined in the Audioscript.
- Check answers with the class. Note that the teachers are describing their personal experiences of teaching students in different countries, but both recognise that their experiences may not be typical.

UNIT 7: LISTENING PRACTICE — LISTENING PART 3

Audioscript

Camila: Well, that was a really interesting talk, wasn't it?

Gareth: Definitely! I'd wanted to learn more about common difficulties for English language learners, so I was pleased to see this talk advertised. And now I've got so many ideas for my lessons.

Camila: Me too, it's really helped me to think about my classes in a different way. And the speaker seemed very experienced. For example, when she talked about students in Asia generally being very polite. <u>Where I teach now in Japan</u>, the students are so <u>well-behaved</u>.

Gareth: You're so lucky! Getting to discover such different cultures and having polite students. I wouldn't say they're rude, but <u>some of my current students in Spain can be quite cheeky</u>!

Camila: Really? Well it doesn't depend on the country, I do get some naughty students from time to time too.

Gareth: You can never generalise, can you?

Camila: But you enjoy teaching most of the time, don't you?

Gareth: Yes, of course. Moving away from Wales, where I'm from, was a big commitment, but well worth it.

Camila: I know what you mean, it isn't easy to move, but the <u>big attraction for me was the possibility of travelling, seeing the world and meeting people from different countries</u>. There's nothing like it!

Gareth: You're right about that. For me, I <u>really want to study education and seeing other countries' systems is a great experience</u>. I think it'll be really interesting to study this at university.

Camila: Oh really? My brother is doing that now. He really likes it. Teaching may be a challenge, but it's never boring, is it?

Gareth: You can say that again! Sometimes I feel like I have so much work to do, but it's never dull. Helping students work through their different difficulties with English is really fascinating. You have to be quite adaptable, but when you help them find a solution, it's just brilliant!

Camila: It is amazing, isn't it? So what kind of difficulties do your students in Spain usually have?

Gareth: <u>Pronunciation is often a tricky thing for them to master</u>. They find vowel sounds in English particularly difficult because their vowel system in Spanish is very different. They find it hard to make a difference between words such as 'fit' and 'feet', for example.

Camila: Oh, I see. Yes, pronunciation is one of those things that doesn't always come naturally when you're learning a new language. <u>My students in Japan often struggle with English word order</u>, because this is very different in Japanese. It's not easy for them to think about the words in a different way.

Gareth: Yes, that's true. Often students find it hard to use a concept that doesn't exist in their native language. For example, in my previous job in Germany, I noticed that students had some problems with the two present tenses in English, because there is only one in German. But that's what I find so interesting about languages – the sheer variety. It would be so boring if they were all the same!

Camila: That's exactly what I think too! <u>Language learning, for me, is such an interesting process.</u> You really get inside a culture by learning its language. It's brilliant to be able to communicate with people in their first language and it just opens the culture up to you so much more than if you didn't speak the language.

Gareth: I totally agree with you there. So are you learning Japanese?

Camila: I'm trying …! It's always been my ambition to learn the language to a good conversational level. I've been learning it for two years now and I think I'm starting to feel more confident with using it in everyday life. But I still make a lot of mistakes!

Gareth: Well that's part of it, isn't it? <u>Immersing yourself in the language is key to enjoying the process</u>, I think. I had one student, Marco, who went for a week's holiday in Ireland and he told me that he could really see the improvement in his English after speaking to the local people. He really got into it! He tried the local food, went to a football match and made lots of new friends there. He was so happy because he gained confidence. Previously, he'd always been overly cautious whenever he used English.

Camila: That's brilliant that he could really see the benefit of travelling and spending time in an English-speaking country. It's not always possible for everyone to travel, but if they have the chance, I always encourage my students to have some time abroad if they can. <u>It's such a valuable experience.</u>

Gareth: It really is. Do you also find that students have lots of different learning styles?

Camila: Absolutely! Some students feel they really need to understand the grammar inside out, while others are happy to just have a go at speaking. Some people prefer using translation as a technique – to think of the word in their own language and then substitute it with English and others prefer to think in English. I think you just need to play to your strengths.

Gareth: No doubt about it. So, when's the next talk?

KEY

(Clues underlined in Audioscript.)

21 Japan **22** Spain **23** well-behaved **24** (quite) cheeky **25** travelling/seeing the world **26** to study education **27** (English) word order **28** pronunciation/vowel sounds **29** D **30** C

DIFFERENTIATION

Strengthen: Pre-teach some of the key vocabulary from the Audioscript and write it on the board: *good as gold* (very well behaved), *super keen* (very enthusiastic), *generalise* (make statements about a whole group based on an experience of a few members of it), *immersing yourself* (surrounding yourself by something), *got into it* (colloquial phrase meaning to enjoy something a lot).

LISTENING PART 3 — UNIT 7: LISTENING PRACTICE

Note there are various words with suffixes in the text that are not included in this list as they are target words in later vocabulary activities.

Challenge: Conduct the activity entirely under exam conditions including setting a time limit. Put the students into pairs and then ask them to work in groups of four to correct and review the other pair's answers.

TEACHING TIPS

- The headings show students which speaker to listen to for each piece of information. However, it is also important to listen for tenses, as some questions refer to their present experiences (key word – now), whereas the question about the teachers' reasons for teaching English relates to a past decision, at least for the female teacher.
- The multiple-choice questions, as usual, have several options that are clearly wrong and two that are right or nearly right.

EVALUATE YOUR EXAM PRACTICE — PAGE 218

- Tell the class to work through the Practice Time questions with a partner.
- Ask students to discuss and compare their results for the two practice tests and identify areas where they improved.
- Take feedback from the class regarding which of the question types students find more difficult and elicit ideas for strategies for overcoming those difficulties.

VOCABULARY AND GRAMMAR

VOCABULARY ACTIVITY 1 🔊 — PAGE 218

- Make sure students understand that a suffix is a letter or group of letters that is added at the end of words to make new words. Explain that the list given is of typical suffixes for English nouns and adjectives.
- Go through the list with the class and drill the pronunciation of the different suffixes. Try to elicit an example of an English word with each suffix from the students, e.g. *-ment*: moment, movement; *-tion*: attention, motivation.
- Tell students that they need to refer back to the interview with the linguist (Practice Time 1).
- Play the extracts from the recording, pausing as necessary at appropriate places for students to write the words they hear. There are four extracts and students will hear two or three of the target words in each.
- Check answers with the class. The key words have been underlined in the Audioscript.

Audioscript

1 Nita: Aha, OK! You've been doing this research for over ten years, right? You must really love your subject! So, if understand correctly, you're saying that new words just arrive sometimes? That's <u>incredible</u>! Where do these new words come from?

Jon: Well, that depends. There are many different reasons for new words appearing in our language. For example, if we think about the recent example of technology, there are lots of new <u>developments</u> and new gadgets appearing and a lot of new words have emerged as a result of that.

2 Nita: So, your job is to study all of this and write about it? I'm really <u>envious</u>!

Jon: I know. I'm really lucky to have work that I enjoy so much. It feels like there's always so much to learn.

Nita: I can see why! And do you think it's <u>advantageous</u> to have these new words appearing in our vocabulary all the time?

Jon: Yes, of course! I'm a linguist!

3 Jon: Even in very early times and throughout history, movements in <u>population</u> meant that language evolved. In recent years, though, the influence of media and especially social media, has made a <u>tremendous</u> impact. Young people often create words to use between themselves, or use old words in new ways. Do you realise that fifty years ago, 'cool' only referred to temperature, or to tone of voice. Then young people started using it to also mean something really great. This word is used everywhere now! With language, everything is shifting all the time, which is one of the reasons why studying it is so fascinating. It's full of uncertainty – and <u>creativity</u>.

4 Nita: I suppose this concept of words changing is a bit like what happens with wildlife and nature. Some species are flourishing, some we have preserved in zoos and <u>conservation</u> areas, some are very <u>vulnerable</u> and others, like the dodo, have become extinct.

Jon: That's a very good analogy, Nita.

KEY

Extract 1: incre<u>dible</u>, develop<u>ment</u>(s)
Extract 2: envi<u>ous</u>, advantage<u>ous</u>
Extract 3: popula<u>tion</u>, tremend<u>ous</u>, creat<u>ivity</u>
Extract 4: conser<u>vation</u>, vulner<u>able</u>

UNIT 7: LISTENING PRACTICE — LISTENING PART 3

VOCABULARY ACTIVITY 2 — PAGE 219

- Elicit from students what a noun is (a word for person, place, thing, animal or idea) and what an adjective is (a word that describes a noun). Explain that some suffixes are used for nouns only and some for adjectives.
- Give students some time to sort the words into the correct columns and check answers as a class. Explain that knowing these suffixes and how they are used will help students understand written and spoken English more easily because they will know whether a word is a noun or adjective.
- Ask students if they can think of any other suffixes which are used to make nouns and adjectives. For nouns: -ness (e.g. forgiveness, happiness); -ure (e.g. closure, failure); for adjectives: -ful (e.g. beautiful, peaceful), -ic (e.g. basic, scientific, fantastic).

KEY

Nouns	Adjectives
development(s)	envious
population	advantageous
creativity	tremendous
conservation	possible
	vulnerable

VOCABULARY ACTIVITY 3 — PAGES 219

- This article gets students to practise word-building by forming nouns and adjectives using the suffixes they have just been studying.
- Ask students to work individually to complete the article with suitable nouns or adjectives.
- Encourage them to use dictionaries to help them with forms they are not sure of.
- Students should compare their ideas with a partner before you check by asking different students around the class to read the article aloud, supplying the nouns and adjectives in the correct form.

KEY

1 admirable   2 courageous   3 ability
4 communication   5 development   6 nervous

VOCABULARY ACTIVITY 4 — PAGES 219

- This activity helps students recognise more suffixes used to create adjectives and nouns.
- Ask students to work in pairs to complete the word forms. Encourage them to use dictionaries to help them with forms they are not sure of.
- Check answers as a class. Ask students to say which forms are nouns and which are adjectives and explain how they know this.

KEY

1 eatable or edible (adjective)   2 disappointment (noun)   3 suspicious (adjective)   4 curious (adjective)   5 courteous (adjective)

GRAMMAR ACTIVITY 5 — PAGE 220

- This activity reviews and revises relative pronouns. Go through pronouns in the box with the class and elicit what they are used to refer to, e.g. *who* refers to a person. Direct the class to Grammar Reference page 279 to revise relative pronouns as necessary.
- Ask students to complete the activity by writing the appropriate pronouns in the middle column of the table.
- Encourage them to compare their ideas with a partner before you check the answers with the class.
- Ask students which of the relative pronouns can be replaced by 'that'. Explain that we can use *that* to talk about people, especially when speaking, but *who* is preferred in formal writing. Also explain that *that* and *which* are interchangeable in defining relative clauses.

KEY

That's the boy *who* helped me with my homework.
There's the beach *where* I lost my keys.
She's the doctor *who* wrote my prescription.
Those are the dogs *which* chased my cat.
That's the teacher *whose* daughter goes to this school.
These are the chairs *which* I made by hand.
They're the customers *who* left without paying.
That's the day *when* I met your mother.
He's the teacher *who* marks my work.

GRAMMAR ACTIVITY 6 — PAGE 220

- This activity is designed to give students further practice in using relative pronouns.
- Ask students to work individually to rewrite the sentences, using pronouns from the previous activity. Ask them to refer to Grammar Reference page 279 for extra help.
- Ask students to compare their answers with a partner before checking answers with the class.
- Ask students which of the relative pronouns can be replaced by 'that'.

KEY

(Answers may vary slightly.)

1 English is a language which many people learn for work.
2 This is the café where we meet once a month.
3 I need to find someone whose car is a red Porsche.
4 That's the computer which is broken.
5 This is the book which I lost last week.
6 The expert on languages who is giving a talk today has arrived.
7 I just got a new job which is much closer to where I live.
8 Olaf is a Swedish man whose flat I rent.

GRAMMAR ACTIVITY 7 — PAGE 221

- Revise the difference between defining and non-defining relative clauses with the class. You could refer to page 279 of the Grammar Reference for extra help with this.
- Establish that defining relative clauses may often omit the relative pronoun, but in non-defining relative clauses, which add extra information to the sentences, the relative pronoun must always be used.
- Ask students to work individually to complete the activity by deleting any unnecessary pronouns from the sentences.
- Encourage them to compare their answers with a partner before you check the answers with the class before moving to Q2.
- Give students a few minutes to write two sentences with defining and two with non-defining relative clauses. When they are ready, they should exchange their sentences with a partner to review and correct each other's work.

- Take feedback on this by nominating different students to dictate some of their partner's sentences for you to write on the board.

KEY

1 a This is the chocolate I told you about.
   b Saffron is the teacher who threw me out of class.
   c This is the school where I learn French.
   d The book they gave me was very helpful.
   e Mateo is the boy who helped me with my schoolwork.
   f Guillerme is the translator I met yesterday.
   g Gabe lives in the same house I live in.
   h That's Stephanie, whose husband works with me.
2 Students' own answers.

GRAMMAR ACTIVITY 8 — PAGE 221

- This activity reviews and revises reported speech. Go through Grammar Reference pages 275–277 to revise how to report speech in English and the rules for tense changes.
- Ask students to change the statements into reported speech.
- Students should compare answers with a partner before checking as a class.

KEY

1 *I like*
2 had written
3 was speaking
4 had thought
5 had listened
6 had been reading
7 she would explain
8 said, could translate
9 said, had to understand

UNIT 7: LISTENING PRACTICE — LISTENING PART 3

GRAMMAR ACTIVITY 9 — PAGES 221–222

- This activity provides students with further practice in reporting speech.
- Ask students to work in pairs to change the sentences into reported speech. Remind them not to forget to make any necessary pronoun changes, e.g. *he/she* instead of *I* and *his/her* instead of *my*.
- Check answers as a class.

KEY

1 Julie said she was learning to speak English.
2 Gabi said that they lived in Portugal.
3 Sandra said she would see me later.
4 Stefan said that Chen had forgotten her pen.
5 Tanja said that she had eaten at the restaurant already.
6 Mark said that he could fix the computer.
7 Silke said that she had to do her homework the next day or it would be late.
8 Yaz said that she had been going to the beach.

TEACHING TIPS

Hint Q7 and Q8: You may want to tell students that Silke and Yaz are female.

GRAMMAR GAME: AMONG THE STARS — PAGE 222

- Follow the instructions in the Student Book to play this Grammar Game. Give students a few minutes to choose which celebrity they want to be and to think of possible interview questions and answers.
- Tell students to prepare and write down their list of interview questions.
- Then ask students to work in pairs, with one student taking the role of the reporter and interviewing the celebrity using the list of questions s/he has prepared.
- Tell students to guess the answers to any questions their celebrity is asked if they don't know the answers.
- When they are ready, ask the reporters to work together and report back their interviews for each other to guess the identity of the celebrity. Monitor and make sure they are using reported speech throughout.
- The other two students (who were the celebrities) can also monitor for correct use of reported speech and for accurate reporting of the facts.
- When they have finished, the pairs should swap roles and start again, with the students who played the role of celebrities in the last round taking on the role of reporters and vice versa.

SELF-EVALUATION — PAGE 222

Tell students to look at the Self-evaluation table and tick the boxes that are true for them. Ask them if there are any topics they don't feel confident about yet.

LISTENING PART 4

OVERVIEW

Topic: The environment

Exam skills: Revise the requirements for Part 4 of the Listening exam, practise Part 4 sample questions, evaluate your exam practice

Assessment Objectives: 3B, 3D

Vocabulary: Prefixes

Grammar: Use *make* and *do*

Practice text type: Extract from a podcast: a researcher talking about the albatross, School talk: a marine biologist talking about the deep sea

Additional resources: audio player, map of local area (optional), dictionaries, recording devices (optional), coloured marker pens (internet access)

PREPARING THE WAY — PAGE 223

- Tell students to read the chapter topic title and ask them why they think the environment has become such an important topic of conversation all over the world.
- Elicit the names of any different types of natural environment or habitat that students can think of and write them on the board, e.g. *forests, woods, mountains, jungles, plains, river valleys, marshlands, beaches, seas, coral reefs, deserts, grasslands, volcanoes, lakes, islands, swamps*.
- Focus students on the questions. If they are able to sustain a class or small group discussion, you can ask them to discuss each question in detail.
- If they need more support, put some key words and phrases on the board (see Key below). Ask students to produce brief written responses and compare their ideas with a partner or in groups.
- Take feedback from the class and find out how motivated they are by this topic. Ask students to describe what kind of environmental issues they feel most strongly about and why.

KEY

Students' own answers.

Suggested sentence structures for discussion:

I would define the environment as …

A habitat is …

Habitats are places where …

…. and …. and … are different types of habitat.

Human beings take care of the environment by …

I believe the most serious environmental problems are … and humans could address these by …

I think the environment is important because …

Useful words and phrases: *global warming, wildlife, protection, to protect, endangered, species, disaster, ecosystem, mass destruction, rainforests, future generations, damage, responsibility, crisis, conservation area, sanctuary, renewable, recycle*

Background information

The following are generally recognised to be some of the most urgent environmental problems facing the world today: climate change, the search for renewable energy sources, growing population, water shortages, waste management, sustainable food production for the growing population, deforestation, habitat loss, endangered species.

UNIT 7: LISTENING PRACTICE — LISTENING PART 4

EXTENSION

Suggested activities:

- Research different aspects of the environment, positive or negative, e.g. global warming, destruction of the rain forest, renewable energy, carbon emissions. Which do students see as the most important issue? Why?
- Research an animal or bird that is now extinct, i.e. one that has died out. What did it look like? What did it eat? What caused its extinction? As a follow-up, they could research a species of animal alive now that is currently in danger of extinction. What could be done to protect it?
- Ask students to imagine they are the leader of their city for a day. What changes would they make to help the environment? They could write their ideas in the form of a list, or label a map of the area to show proposed changes.
- Research new technologies currently being developed to support the environment. For example, it might be useful to refer back to the text about driverless cars.
- Students write a letter to their headteacher explaining why the school needs an environmental committee. If the school already has one, they can explain why the committee needs more power.
- Ask students to discuss this quotation from Albert Einstein: *The environment is everything that isn't me.* As a follow-up, they could find other quotations on the topic of the environment and explain why they agree/disagree with them, in speech or in writing.

ACTIVITY 1 — PAGE 224

- Focus attention on the picture of the unusual creature. Ask students to try to work out what it is. Explain as necessary the meaning of *mammal* (warm-blooded creature that gives birth to its young, e.g. humans, dogs, cats, horses), *reptile* (cold-blooded creature, often lays eggs, e.g. crocodiles, snakes, lizards), *amphibian* (also cold-blooded but more likely to live in/near water, e.g. frogs, toads, newts) *habitat* (the place where an animal lives), *predator* (a creature that hunts/eats others), *nocturnal* (active only at night), *camouflage* (the ability to blend in with the surroundings).
- Give the pairs a few minutes to discuss the sentences. Tell students that some questions may have more than one correct answer.
- Take feedback from the class. Establish the correct answers (see Key) and, if possible, show pictures of the other animals in the creature category and tell the class something about them (see Background information).
- Tell students to think of a creature that not many people know. Ask them to research the creature and share their findings with the class.

KEY

1. bird
2. lives in (country and habitat) South America, jungle
   eats insects
   is a predator and prey
   protects itself by being nocturnal and using camouflage
   is a potoo
3. Students' own answers.

Background information

The creature in the photograph is a type of bird known as a potoo. There are several related species and they live in Central and South America, including near the Amazon River. They eat mainly insects, including moths and beetles. Potoos are famous for their odd appearance, and the fact that they are so well camouflaged, i.e. they blend into their surroundings. Often they resemble dead tree stumps, which is a good way to hide from predators. They also have a distinctive cry and large eyes, making them an interesting and unusual bird to study.

Other creatures:

Flamingos are long-legged water birds with distinctive pink feathers. They are found in the Americas and in parts of Africa and Southern Europe.

Capybaras are large rodents, a relative of the guinea pig, which are at home on land or in water. They are natives of South America.

Toucans are brightly coloured birds with large, often-colourful beaks. They live in the forests of Mexico and South America.

Garoupers (also spelt garoupa and grouper) are a type of fish with fat bodies and wide mouths in the same family as sea bass. They are an important food source and feature in Asian and Arab cuisine.

Salamanders are a type of amphibian, similar to a lizard but with moist soft skin. They live partly in water and are found mostly in the Northern hemisphere.

LISTENING PART 4 UNIT 7: LISTENING PRACTICE 157

EXAM REFRESHER — PAGE 225

- Ask students to read through the Exam Refresher box and remind themselves of what they have to do in Part 4 of the Listening exam.
- Give students half a minute to read and then ask them to tell you (without looking back at the text) what type of audio text they will hear and what kind of information they will have to listen for in this part of the exam.
- Elicit that the audio texts in Listening Part 4 are longer and usually cover more academic and complex subjects. Students have to understand the attitudes and viewpoints of the speaker(s) and listen for both essential and finer points of detail.

ACTIVITY 2 — PAGE 225

- Tell students they are now going to think about exam technique. Ask them to read the statements about the Listening Part 4 exam tasks and decide with a partner whether or not they think each one is correct.
- Take feedback from the class and elicit from the students the reasons why the incorrect statements are wrong and what the consequences would be if they did these things in the exam (see Key below).

PRACTICE TIME 1 — PAGES 225–226

- Remind students to spend time reading the question carefully and encourage them to underline key words in the rubric (or make a note of them if they are not allowed to write in their textbooks) since these will help them to sort the essential information from details as they listen. Remind the class to look at and follow the Exam Hints.
- Explain that the setting for the talk they are going to hear is a scientific conference. Explain what this is if necessary and elicit the reasons why scientists might be interested in studying different species of bird.
- Also make students aware that there is some specialist vocabulary related to birds which may be unfamiliar to them, but they should still be able to answer the questions.
- Play the recording twice for students to complete the tasks and check their answers. Remind them to follow the instructions in the rubric by not writing more than three words. Check answers with the class. The key information is underlined in the Audioscript below.

KEY

- ✓ The headings of the table (if included) are important.
  Hint: These supply important information.
- ✓ Don't miss out any questions, even if they are difficult.
  Hint: Questions missed out will definitely get zero. An attempt may earn a mark.
- ✓ You should not exceed the word limit if specified.
  Hint: The exam rubric cannot be ignored without losing marks. It is there to ensure the exam is fair to everyone.
- ✗ Grammar is the most important part of your answer when completing a table.
  Hint: It is not necessarily the most important, but it is very important.
- ✓ You should listen carefully to every word in the recording.
  Hint: This will improve your chance of answering the question correctly.

Audioscript

Dr Budiarto: Hello, my name is Dr Lini Budiarto and I'm here at the *Nature Today* conference to talk about a very special bird species, the wandering albatross, and why it is so urgent that action is taken to save these amazing creatures.

To begin with, allow me to paint you a picture of this magnificent bird. The wandering albatross has a wingspan of up to three and a half metres. Incredible! Just to give you a rough idea, if you are finding it impossible to visualise, three and a half metres is about the length of a large car. Albatrosses are so well adapted to the life they lead that they can go for hours without needing to flap their wings. They simply glide. Albatrosses weigh approximately 12 kilograms and on average they live for about 50 years. The word 'Wandering' in their name is based on the fact that they cover so much distance in search of food, sometimes travelling up to 10 000 kilometres in the course of their lifetime. The origin of the word 'albatross' is likely to have been derived from the Latin word 'albus', which means 'white', as these birds are largely white in colour and the small amount of darker plumage that younger birds have is not really visible from a distance.

I mentioned the albatross' capacity to travel long distances and this is one of the features that makes these birds so remarkable. They have to travel in order to feed, as mainly they eat schooling fish, squid and small crustaceans and will need to move to wherever these are most readily available. Overeating can, however, make it hard for them to take off.

Sometimes they float on the waves rather than gliding above them, but that does of course make them vulnerable to predators, so it can be problematic. Albatrosses also drink a great deal of salt water. To us, that sounds very unpleasant, but of course for them it's a way of life.

Albatrosses don't always have an easy life, though. Due to human activity, they are becoming endangered. Longline fishing poses a huge danger, for instance. This is a fishing method that uses long and short lines to catch fish.

Attracted by the bait, the albatross swoops down. Its strength means it can easily push other birds out of the way. Albatrosses can become entangled in the underwater lines and eventually drown. Because no single country has control of all the waters in which this fishing takes place, it's hard to find an antidote, or to put effective international measures in place to protect the albatrosses.

When there aren't these dangers posed by commercial fishing, when albatrosses do manage to catch fish, they have no problem digesting it easily and quickly. This is due to the high acidity in the digestive juices found in their stomachs.

In terms of where they live, these are birds that tend to be found in what's known as the sub-Antarctic region – in other words, the part of the southern hemisphere that is situated directly to the north of the Antarctic. Of course, within this geographical context, the albatross's preferred location and activities will be based partly on its age.

Younger birds, known as juveniles and non-breeding birds, will tend to stay in the slightly more southerly areas, but the breeding adult population will be extremely wide-ranging. We've managed to find out a lot of information about the species by tracking specific birds. To give you a specific example, one of these tracked birds travelled 6 000 kilometres in just 12 days. Really extraordinary, if you think about it, especially as the area is so inhospitable!

I mentioned before about the flight and breeding patterns of these birds and now I'd like to say a bit more about that. Breeding is the only time these birds gather in colonies. They mate for life and build their nests out of vegetation held together by mud – very enterprising of them to use the materials at hand so efficiently – on remote islands. Only one egg is laid in each breeding cycle and it takes 11 whole weeks before it hatches.

Once the young albatross emerges from the egg, the parents take it in turn to feed it and it will leave the nest at any time after the age of about three months. Breeding occurs every two years.

Of course, the fact that the breeding cycle is relatively extended does suggest that albatross numbers may be vulnerable and this is indeed the case. Of the 22 species of Wandering Albatross, 15 are now threatened with extinction and the threat shows no sign of decelerating. Tragically, for three of these species, the threat is so severe that they have been categorised as 'critically endangered'. A further seven species are in the 'near threatened' category, so the future's really looking very bleak for this magnificent bird and time is running out. Almost inevitably, the biggest threat of all comes from human beings and this is primarily connected with various fishing industries, legal and illegal, that operate in the areas the albatrosses frequent.

It's almost certain that they face extinction without this protection, though and that would be a real tragedy. That's why it's so important that we look after them.

LISTENING PART 4 — **UNIT 7: LISTENING PRACTICE** 159

KEY

(Clues underlined in the Audioscript.)
31 wingspan **32** (about) 50/fifty years **33** glide
34 overeating **35** salt water/seawater **36** underwater lines **37** digest **38** Age **39** life
40 extinction

DIFFERENTIATION

Strengthen: Pre-teach some of the key vocabulary from the Audioscript and write it on the board: *conference* (a gathering of people, often specialists, meeting to discuss a particular topic), *albatross* (the biggest bird in the world, at least in terms of wingspan), *to visualise* (to imagine; to picture), *plumage* (feathers), *crustaceans* (creatures with shells, like crabs), *digesting* (absorbing after eating).

Note that there are various words with prefixes in the text that are not included in this list as they are target words in later vocabulary activities.

Challenge: Conduct the activity entirely under exam conditions including setting a time limit. Put the students into pairs and then ask them to work in groups of four to correct and review the other pair's answers.

PRACTICE TIME 2 — PAGES 226–227

- Tell students to think about their results from the first Practice Time. Is there anything they have learned from doing the first practice sessions (in this section and in Unit 3) that could help them with the next one?
- Give the class the appropriate period of time, under exam conditions, to read the instructions carefully. As this is the final practice for this part of the exam, students should ideally attempt it with a minimum of teacher support.
- There is some specialist vocabulary because of the topic, but students would not be expected to know it. They will still be able to answer the questions.
- Play the recording twice for students to listen and choose the correct answers.
- Check answers with the class. The key phrases have been underlined in the Audioscript below.

REFLECT — PAGE 226

- Ask the class to work through the Reflect questions with a partner and discuss which of the things listed they did or did not manage to do.
- Tell students to help their partner evaluate his or her progress and set a target for the next Practice Time test.
- Encourage students to give each other positive support.

UNIT 7: LISTENING PRACTICE — LISTENING PART 4

Audioscript

Mr Boyal: OK everyone, so to help you think about different careers you could do in the future, we've invited some guests to come and talk to you all about their professions. The first guest I'd like you to meet is a respected scientist, Professor Sanjana Sharma. She's a marine biologist. Sanjana, thank you so much for coming to talk to us today.

Prof. Sharma: You're very welcome, Mr Boyal.

Mr Boyal: Please, Sanjana, in case some of the students are unsure about what the job involves, could you start by explaining what a marine biologist does?

Prof. Sharma: Well, marine biologists study the creatures and conditions under the sea, sometimes using specially-equipped submarines and cameras to explore. It's a fascinating career and one that allows you to travel all over the world. My specialisation is in the 'deep sea'. This is the very inhospitable environment far beneath the surface. I find it amazing that there are creatures that can survive such conditions. This environment is untouched by light and warmth and it has pressure levels of more than 1000 times the standard atmospheric pressure at sea level. To put that in perspective, it's the equivalent of one person trying to support 50 jumbo jets!

Mr Boyal: Wow! I'm amazed anything could survive there!

Prof. Sharma: Yes, it's easy to think that it would be impossible for anything to survive in such conditions, but this is far from the case. In fact, a number of ocean species are known to live in the deep-sea environment and they have developed interesting survival techniques as a result. They have adapted over time to have a chance of survival. The hatchetfish, for example, has an amazing skill. It has special organs that give off light. To use a technical term, we would say it has the capacity to manipulate bio-luminescent photophores in its body in order to avoid predators. Here's a photo of one of them, can you all see that?

The hatchetfish's skin can imitate the light from above. That, in turn, means that the fish beneath them don't notice that there are fish above blocking out the sunlight and so the prey is not as aware of the predator.

Mr Boyal: I see. So the hatchetfish has adapted really well to life at such a depth. What other types of adaptation do we see in these deep-sea creatures, Sanjana?

Prof. Sharma: Well, living at such depths can have other consequences. For example, the Colossal Squid is much larger than any squid in shallow water. Many deep-sea creatures have this tendency and we call it 'abyssal gigantism'. This particular squid can grow up to 14 metres long. That's the length of one and a half double decker buses. Even deeper, creatures called amphipods, which are a bit like crabs, can grow to lengths of up to 30 centimetres – whereas most of the commonly found surface amphipods are only about three cm. Again, that's quite a difference, nearly ten times bigger! But, of course, if you're expecting all deep-sea creatures to be enormous, then 30 centimetres might be a bit of an anti-climax. These amphipods are actually found in a place called the Mariana Trench. This is an amazing area. It's the deepest point of all the world's oceans and it's located in the western Pacific Ocean. It's remarkable for a number of reasons. For one thing, the trench has a maximum known depth of almost 11 kilometres. Mount Everest is only 8 848 metres high!

Mr Boyal: That's incredible. So you've said that the inhabitants of this underwater trench are quite different to those which are found on the ocean's surface. What other kinds of creatures live in the Mariana Trench?

Prof. Sharma: It's also home to sea cucumbers – creatures which feed on the ocean floor.

Mr Boyal: And do they look like the cucumbers we eat in salads, by any chance?

Prof. Sharma: Exactly! That's where they get their name from. There are also creatures with soft shells, known as forams. They hunt for food in the sand, but we know very little about them because they have a tendency to disintegrate whenever brought to the surface. To survive, they have to remain submerged at the depths their bodies have adapted to.

Mr Boyal: Oh dear. That must be frustrating for marine biologists like yourselves.

Prof. Sharma: Yes and that's one of the biggest problems with researching creatures of the Mariana Trench. This deep underwater world is so different to our own environment and so extreme. We simply can't replicate it to study these creatures, so we have to try to develop techniques that let us study them in their own environment. We're trying to develop new technology all the time to do that more effectively. But this is one of the things I love about my profession – there are always new developments needed. It's never boring!

Mr Boyal: I can see that! So you're saying that there's still a lot we don't know about the deep sea?

Prof. Sharma: Absolutely. The vast majority of the deep sea (and the Mariana Trench) remains unexplored, even compared to the moon and the surface of Mars! It's really mind-blowing for me to think that there are whole areas of our planet that no-one has ever seen or studied. This is what keeps me fascinated in my career. It's very difficult to predict what other species may be lurking in the depths. We're always curious to see what we will find next.

Mr Boyal: I expect you are! Thank you so much for coming in to speak with us today. Thank you very much, Sanjana, for sparing the time to be here.

Prof. Sharma: It's been a pleasure.

KEY

(Clues underlined in Audioscript.)
31 light and warmth **32** adapted **33** C **34** A
35 B **36** A **37** C **38** replicate **39** unexplored
40 species

DIFFERENTIATION

Strengthen: Pre-teach some of the key vocabulary from the Audioscript and write it on the board: *specialisation* (an area

LISTENING PART 4 **UNIT 7: LISTENING PRACTICE** 161

of expertise), *standard atmospheric pressure* (normal air pressure), *jumbo jet* (a type of plane).

Note there are various words with prefixes in the text that are not included in this list as they are target words in later vocabulary activities.

Challenge: Ask students to imagine Professor Sharma is offering an internship and write a letter applying for it, explaining why they would be a suitable candidate in terms of their enthusiasm, interest, experience, skills, etc. They could invent material if necessary.

EVALUATE YOUR EXAM PRACTICE
PAGE 228

- Tell the class to work through the Practice Time questions with a partner.
- Ask students to discuss and compare their results for the two Practice Time tests in this unit and identify areas where they improved.
- Take feedback from the class regarding which of the question types students find more difficult and elicit ideas for strategies for overcoming those difficulties.

VOCABULARY AND GRAMMAR

VOCABULARY ACTIVITY 1 PAGES 228–229

- Make sure students understand that a prefix is a morpheme (part of a word) that goes at the beginning of word. Explain that the list given is of typical prefixes for English nouns and adjectives and affects their meaning.
- Go through the list of prefixes with the class and ask if they can think of any English words beginning with any of the prefixes.
- Give the class some time to read through the sentences and encourage them complete any of the gaps with a prefix from the box.
- Play the extracts from the recording for students to listen, check and complete. Play the recording more than once if necessary.
- Check answers with the class. The prefixes have been underlined in the Audioscript.

Audioscript

1 ... in case some of the students are <u>un</u>sure about what the job involves, could you start by explaining what a marine biologist does?
2 Well, marine biologists study the creatures and conditions under the sea, sometimes using specially-equipped <u>sub</u>marines and cameras to explore.
3 This is the very <u>in</u>hospitable environment far beneath the surface.
4 it's easy to think that it would be <u>im</u>possible for anything to survive in such conditions, but this is far from the case.
5 But, of course, if you're expecting all deep-sea creatures to be enormous, then 30 centimetres might be a bit of an <u>anti</u>-climax.
6 ... you've said that the inhabitants of this <u>under</u>water trench are quite different to those which are found on the ocean's surface.
7 ... they have a tendency to <u>dis</u>integrate whenever brought to the surface.
8 The vast majority of the deep sea (and the Mariana Trench) remains <u>un</u>explored ...

KEY

(Prefixes underlined in Audioscript.)
1 un- 2 sub- 3 in- 4 im- 5 anti- 6 under-
7 dis- 8 un-

VOCABULARY ACTIVITY 2 PAGE 229

- Explain to students that the prefixes have a specific meaning which they might be able to guess by looking at the way they affect the meaning of the words in Activity 1.
- Give them a few minutes to work in pairs to match the prefixes to the correct meanings. Encourage students to use a dictionary to look up other words using the same prefix to help them.
- Check answers with the class.

KEY

anti-: against   dis-: opposite of   im-: not
in-: not   sub-: under   un-: not   under-: beneath

VOCABULARY ACTIVITY 3 PAGE 229

- The prefixes are shown here in a hyphenated form for purposes of the activity, but should not be hyphenated in normal usage.
- Ask students to work individually to circle the correct prefixes in the sentences.
- Check answers as a class.

KEY

1 under- 2 sub- 3 un- 4 anti- 5 dis- 6 in-
7 de- 8 im-

UNIT 7: LISTENING PRACTICE — LISTENING PART 4

VOCABULARY ACTIVITY 4 — PAGE 230

- Ask students to work with a partner to make a list of words beginning with the prefixes from Activity 2. Tell them they should try to find at least one more example for each prefix.
- Direct students to look at the Hint and point out that not all words beginning with the same letters contain prefixes, e.g. *im*agine, *dis*cuss, *un*iform, *im*ply.
- Compare answers as a class.

KEY

Students' own answers. Suggested answers:
under- *undergraduate, underpriced* **sub-** *sublet, subway* **un-** *unappreciated, unnecessary*
anti- *antisocial, antihero* **dis-** *disapprove, dislike*
in- *inaccurate, inefficient* **im-** *immaterial, immoral*

EXTENSION

- For some further practice with prefixes and suffixes, ask students to write five sentences. Each sentence should include one correct and one incorrect prefix in the style of Activity 3, e.g. *I was very happy to find some under- / over- priced clothes in a shop.*
- Students then exchange their sentences with a partner and try to complete them. When they have finished, they return the completed versions for their partner to correct.

GRAMMAR ACTIVITY 5 — PAGE 230

- This activity gives the students practice in choosing between *make* and *do,* two commonly confused verbs with a similar meaning.
- Explain to students that we generally use *do* in the sense of completing a task, e.g. *do a job, do the washing up.* We generally use *make* to talk about creating something new, e.g. *make a cake, make a request.* These rules do not always apply but are useful guidelines.
- Point out that some of the items in the box such as *lunch* and *crossword* are concrete items whereas others such as *mistake* and *choice* are concepts.
- Ask students to work in pairs to sort the words into the correct columns.
- Check answers with the class.

KEY

do	make
homework	a suggestion
a crossword	a choice
your hair	a noise
a favour	lunch
an exam	a change
a course	a cup of coffee
a job	a demand
laundry	a mistake
an assignment	a comment

TEACHING TIPS

Note that we have to say *(the) laundry.* We cannot say *a laundry*, because *laundry* is an uncountable noun meaning dirty sheets, dirty clothes, etc.

GRAMMAR ACTIVITY 6 — PAGES 230–231

- This activity provides further practice for students using *do* and *make*.
- Ask students to work in pairs to circle the correct verb in each sentence. Encourage them to use dictionaries, where possible, to check any collocations they are not sure about. This is good practice in looking up collocations. Note it may be best to use an online dictionary for this exercise as not all print dictionaries include collocations.
- Encourage pairs to check their ideas with another pair before you check answers with the class.

KEY

1 Do 2 make 3 do 4 Do 5 make 6 do 7 do
8 Make 9 make 10 make 11 do

GRAMMAR ACTIVITY 7 — PAGE 231

- Ask students to complete the email with the appropriate forms of *make* and *do*. Again, encourage them to use dictionaries to help them with forms they are not sure of.
- Check answers with the class by asking different students to read the email aloud and supply the appropriate verb.

KEY

1 do 2 did 3 made 4 did 5 made 6 make
7 do 8 making 9 do 10 make

GRAMMAR ACTIVITY 8 — PAGE 232

- Elicit or explain what a fact file is (an informational text, divided into sections) and explain that students are going to write one about an imaginary sea creature.
- Go through the prompts a–e in Q1 with the class and elicit the correct verb forms.
- Direct students to Q2 and give them some time to prepare and write the fact file. They could also illustrate it, if they would like to do this for fun, and they could label their illustration.
- You could make the Audioscript for Practice Time 2 about undersea life available to students because this contains useful vocabulary for this topic.
- You could also write the following vocabulary on the board: *silent, noisy, loud, vicious, ink, poison, defend, spines, dangerous, bury, sand, shells, coral, luminous, shining, technique, special ability, micro-organisms, shellfish, jellyfish, prey, predator, attack, toxic, harmless*.
- Additional details could refer to appearance, size, depth at which the creature lives, special behaviours, why it has remained undiscovered for so long.
- When students have finished their fact files, they should swap them with a partner and read each other's work.
- Take feedback from the class by asking different students to tell the group the most interesting thing about their partner's sea creature.

KEY

1 a make b do c make d make e do
2 and 3 Students' own answers.

EXTENSION

- Ask students to research a real-life underwater creature and/or treasure of their own choosing.
- They could present their findings in speech or writing, or they could be used as the basis for a classroom display.

- Ask students to work in pairs or groups to role-play marine scientists competing for research 'funding' to study the topic they selected in more detail. Each group could prepare a 'bid' explaining their reasoning. The bid could include what they wish to research; why it is important that the research is done; how it might benefit environmental/medical knowledge; what is known about the topic already; what other information they would hope to learn.

GRAMMAR GAME: *MAKE* OR *DO* RACE — PAGE 232

- Follow the instructions in the Student Book. Either ask the students to write down words that go with *make* and *do* on separate pieces of paper, or write them yourself using the list below.

  make: an appointment, arrangements, an attempt, the bed, breakfast, a change, a choice, a decision, dinner, a comment, a complaint, a declaration, a deal, a discovery, a difference, an effort, an enquiry, an exception, an excuse, friends, fun of somebody, an impression, lunch, a meal, a mistake, money, a noise, an offer, a phone call, a plan, a point, a presentation, progress, a reservation, a speech, a statement, a suggestion, sure (of something), a threat, a wish

  do: an assignment, badly, business, your best, a course, a crossword, damage, a degree, the dishes, a drawing, an exam, exercises, a favour (for someone), the gardening, good, a good job, your hair, harm, (the) homework, the housework, the ironing, a job, the laundry, a lesson, your make-up a project, research, the shopping, a survey, a test, a translation, the washing up, well, work, without something

- The different teams should use different colour markers to write on the board to make scoring easier.
- At the end of the game, correct the words on the board with the class, asking them whether each phrase is in the correct section of the board. Give a point to a team for each correct answer that they have written.

SELF-EVALUATION — PAGE 233

Tell students to look at the Self-evaluation table and tick the boxes that are true for them. Ask them if there are any topics they don't feel confident about yet.

UNIT 8: SPEAKING PRACTICE

SPEAKING

OVERVIEW

Topic: The home
Exam skills: Revise the requirements for the Speaking exam, practise Speaking sample questions, evaluate your exam practice
Assessment Objectives: 4A, 4B, 4C
Vocabulary: Adjectives: the home
Grammar: Revise verb tenses
Practice text type: Answering questions about yourself, talking about the role of 'home' in your life
Additional resources: audio player, dictionaries, recording devices (optional) (internet access)

PREPARING THE WAY   PAGE 236

- Tell students to read the chapter topic and ask them what the difference is between a house and a home. Elicit that a *house* is a specific type of building, but the word *home* refers to the place where people live and could mean many different types of living places.
- Elicit words for different types of living places and write them on the board, e.g. *studio, flat/apartment, terraced house, detached, semi-detached house, bungalow, cottage, townhouse, mansion* (big, grand house), *castle*. Also think about words for different living environments, e.g. *city centre, suburb, village, a housing estate, street of houses, countryside, seaside.*
- Focus students on the questions. If they are able to sustain a class or small group discussion, you can ask them to discuss each question in detail.
- If they need more support, put some key words and phrases on the board (see Key below). Ask students to produce brief written responses and compare their ideas with a partner or in groups.

KEY

Students' own answers.
Suggested sentence structures for discussion:
One thing I like/dislike about my home is …
One thing about my home that really appeals/does not appeal to me is … because …
I think the home where you grew up is important because …
Once you have lived somewhere for … it starts to …
For me, it matters that my home reflects my personality because …
Some homes reflect personality more than others. My view is that …
Useful words and phrases: *cosy, comfortable, safe, stylish, modern, minimalist, tidy/messy, to feel at home*

EXTENSION

- Ask students to design their ideal home. They could do this in writing or as a speech.
- Elicit some ways in which a home could be adapted or changed. They may be able to draw on their experience. Examples of reasons to adapt houses could be: for people with mobility problems; for different aged children; for different types of pets; for people who love plants.
  Examples of changes would be: window boxes (containers placed outside, just below windows, to grow flowers or plants); stair lifts (lifts that help people with mobility problems get upstairs); cat flaps (a small hole made in a door that allows pet cats to enter and leave the house; satellite dish (a receiver for extra television channels); stairgates (barriers to stop children or pets from accessing stairs); barbecues (special grills for cooking food outside); a greenhouse (a building made of glass specially for growing or protecting plants); swimming pools (large structures filled with water and used for swimming in); hammocks (hanging beds made from netting or canvas and tied between two trees or poles); garden sheds (small wooden buildings used for storing garden tools). Then ask them when and for whom each of these items would be useful.
- Ask students to think of how they would transform a room they know well for: a surprise birthday party, a visit by a large and lively dog, a visit by a toddler, a festival special to their country.
- Ask students to research the following appliances and their purpose: air-conditioner, dishwasher, heating, microwave oven, digital radio, flat-screen TV, smoke detector, vacuum cleaner, washing machine. They should then write a sentence or two for each item on the list, explaining what they do and why they are useful. Finally, they could rank order the usefulness of the appliances and compare their rank-ordered list with their partner's.

SPEAKING **UNIT 8: SPEAKING PRACTICE** 165

- Ask students to discuss this quotation from Henning Mankell: *You can have more than one home. You can carry your roots with you, and decide where they grow.* As a follow-up, they could find other quotations on the topic of home and explain why they agree/disagree with them, in speech or in writing.

ACTIVITY 1   PAGES 236–237

- Ask students to look at the six photographs and elicit descriptions of them. They will probably need some of the following vocabulary, e.g. *roof, walls, staircase, balcony, covered with, palm tree, upside-down.* Also teach the word *setting* to talk about where a house is.
- Ask students to work in pairs to discuss which house they like most and least and why.
- For their discussions, the following structures might be useful:

  The house that appeals to me most / least is … because …

  I would love / hate to live in a house that …

  One thing I like / dislike about the … house is …

  One aspect of the … house that does / doesn't appeal to me is …

- For Q2, elicit or teach the word *estate agent*. Explain that this is someone who sells houses and tries to describe them persuasively in order to make them sound attractive to buyers.
- Explain to students that they are going to hear a recording of some descriptions of the houses in the photos from an estate agent, and that their task is to match the photos with the six extracts they are going to hear and write the description given in the box under each photo. Elicit or explain the words: *peaceful retreat* (calm sanctuary/restful place of safety), *organic* (coming from plants or animals; not artificial), *nature lover* (someone who likes the natural environment), *secluded* (hidden, secret), *heart of* (centre of/ deep within), *fairy tales* (traditional stories told to children), *enchanted* (magical), *tropical setting* (very warm, perhaps like a jungle), *intriguing* (mysterious), *bamboo* (a type of tall tropical grass with hard, hollow stems), *palm-covered* (a sort of tree or shrub associated with warm climates), *picturesque* (attractive in appearance), *quirky* (unusual in an attractive and interesting way).
- Play the recording twice for students to number the photos in the order they hear them. Explain that students don't need to understand every word of each description, just enough key words so that they can match with the photo.

Some key expressions are underlined in the Audioscript below.

- Give students some time to match the words in the box with the pictures that illustrate them. Encourage them to use dictionaries to help.
- Play the recording again for students to check their answers before confirming with the class.
- Give students a few minutes to imagine they live in one of the houses and write the sentences. Then ask them to work in pairs to take turns to read their sentences aloud for their partner to guess which house they refer to.
- Take feedback from the class by asking for volunteers to read their sentences aloud for the whole class to guess.

Audioscript: Student Book page 290

1 The first house I'd like to show you is a peaceful retreat on a mountainside. <u>The roof is obviously organic</u>, so this is definitely the perfect choice for a nature lover.

2 Next is another house that's pleasantly secluded, but this one is set <u>deep in the heart of the forest</u>. Lovers of fairy tales will be enchanted by it!

3 If you prefer a more <u>tropical setting</u>, how about this intriguing home built out of bamboo? The views of the <u>palm-covered island</u> are spectacular.

4 If you want to get <u>really close to the water</u>, how about this house? It's actually <u>standing in the sea</u> – property doesn't get much more picturesque than that!

5 Of course, if you're looking for picturesque, this <u>flower-covered gem</u> might be for you. It's a real feast for the eyes and smells delectable too.

6 Finally, for those of you who enjoy something quirky, how about this <u>upside-down cottage</u>, whose foundations point to the skies?

KEY

1 Students' own answers.

2 (Clues underlined in Audioscript.)

a forest retreat **b** house on stilts **c** upside-down house **d** island home **e** remote cottage **f** floral mansion

(Order mentioned in Audioscript: **1** e **2** a **3** d **4** b **5** f **6** c

3 Students' own answers.

UNIT 8: SPEAKING PRACTICE

SPEAKING

EXAM REFRESHER — PAGE 237

- Ask students to read through the Exam Refresher box and remind themselves of what they have to do in the Speaking exam.
- Give students a minute to read then ask them to tell you (without looking back at the text) what the three parts of the Speaking exam are and the three different sorts of activities mentioned.
- Elicit the three parts of the Speaking exam. Part 1 is an introductory interview talking about a specific topic in response to questions. Part 2 is giving a talk (with the option of making notes for a minute beforehand). Part 3 involves participating in an extended discussion.

ACTIVITY 2 — PAGE 237

- Tell students they are now going to think about exam technique. Ask them to read the statements about the Speaking exam tasks and decide with a partner whether or not they think each one is correct.
- Give students a minute or so to go through the statements and compare their ideas about them with another pair. Then check answers with the class.

KEY

✓ Listen for and pay attention to the key words.
Hint: It is important for students to understand what information the examiner is looking for.

✓ Listen to everything the examiner says.
Hint: Sometimes there will be extra details or reasons requested. Or the information could be framed positively or negatively, e.g. *Tell me what you do not like about …*

✗ You should try to speak for longer than the set times to get a higher mark.
Hint: The interviewer will not allow students to speak for longer than the set times. The exam rubric has to be followed here as in other parts of the exam. The maximum timings allowed for each part are as follows: Part 1 – three minutes; Part 2 – one minute of preparation and one to two minutes of speaking; Part 3 – five minutes.

✗ Prepare and take notes into the exam with you to remind you what to say.
Hint: Taking notes in with you is not allowed.

✗ Take notes on the examiner's questions.
Hint: This is not a possibility suggested within the rubric. The interviewer may repeat questions if necessary.

✓ You should plan your talk in Part 2 by using brief notes.
Hint: Students are encouraged to do this. They can note down key vocabulary, for example. However, they should not over-plan, as this is a test of speaking, not of reading aloud, and over-reliance on notes will make them sound stilted and unnatural.

PRACTICE TIME — PAGE 238

- Students now have another opportunity to practise some exam tasks. As with Unit 4, they will need individual time slots for this which may be challenging to organise. However, practising in pairs, recording answers and getting feedback will all be helpful, even if it is not possible to create exam conditions.
- Remind students that Part 1 is an individual interview with the examiner. As this is the final practice opportunity, it may be best if they can approach it as they would in the exam, i.e. without knowing the questions beforehand. They will have done some work on the topic of home so will have had some preparation, though.
- Remind students of the need for variety and interest. As advised in Unit 4, students must avoid giving one-word answers but should aim to provide relevant detailed responses using a range of vocabulary and grammatical structures.
- If possible, you should interview all students in the class individually, rather than relying on pair work, to make this a more authentic practice. If there are other teachers available to conduct the interviews, that may be helpful, especially where the interviewer for the exam will not be known to students.
- It would be very helpful to record the dialogues. You could listen to these after the class and provide feedback in the next lesson.

KEY

Students' own answers.

PRACTICE TIME — PAGE 238

- Students should be reminded that in Part 2 they must give an extended talk about a given topic. As before, it is important for students to practise preparing, making notes effectively and structuring their answers, as they will be given only a short time for this in the exam. The notes should be key words and phrases rather than sentences.
- Direct students to the guidance given in Unit 4 if necessary. Remind them to support their answers with details and examples. They should select details that are relevant to their answer.
- It is possible to support students through the different stages of this task, as in Unit 4, but as with Part 1, it might be better to encourage a more independent approach to give them an experience that is closer to the exam.
- Again, in an ideal situation they will work one-to-one with their interviewer rather than relying on pairs or groups.

KEY

Students' own answers.

TEACHING TIPS

Although students cannot know the topic beforehand, they do know that they will have the opportunity to take notes for Part 2 (for one minute) before giving their talk. It would be useful, therefore, for them to practise the note-taking process on a range of topics, perhaps starting off in their first language and then practising with several different topics or question prompts in English.

PRACTICE TIME — PAGES 238–239

- Remind students that Part 3 of the exam involves discussion and exchange so is arguably the most challenging task. However, they can be reassured that they have had much more practice at these activities now than when they attempted the same task before in Unit 4.
- As for Parts 1 and 2 in this unit, preparation beforehand is possible, but not desirable, if it can be avoided.
- Remind students to try to support their opinions and develop them in a coherent way, with reasons and arguments.

- Individual dialogues are preferable if possible. Ideally these should be recorded so that feedback can be given.
- As before, give students feedback on their performance for all three parts of the exam. Indicate any areas of weakness you have identified and direct students to available resources to work on improving these areas, for example, pronunciation activities for particular pronunciation issues or extra grammar practice.
- An additional benefit of recording the exam practice is that it provides better preparation for the actual exam, in which candidates will be recorded. It will help students to be familiar with the formality of the situation beforehand, including the recording procedure and the scripted input from the examiner.

KEY

Students' own answers.

EVALUATE YOUR EXAM PRACTICE — PAGE 239

- Tell the class to work through the exam evaluation questions with a partner.
- Ask students to help their partner evaluate his or her progress and set targets for areas to work on and for the forthcoming exam.
- Encourage students to distinguish between different types of errors they may have made, e.g. not following the exam rubric, not knowing specific vocabulary, getting confused about the questions, and so on. Do any patterns emerge?
- Encourage students to give each other positive support.

UNIT 8: SPEAKING PRACTICE — SPEAKING

VOCABULARY AND GRAMMAR

VOCABULARY ACTIVITY 1 — PAGE 239

- Read the rubric with the class and elicit or explain *interior designer* (someone who specialises in advising people how to decorate/present the inside of their homes).

- Give students some time to read through the questions and underline key words. Check the meaning of *kitchen appliance* (machines that we use for the different sorts of jobs that we need to do in the kitchen, e.g. preparing food, cooking, washing, cleaning). Ask students to give you the names of all the different sorts of kitchen appliances they can think of and write them on the board.

- Also check the meaning of *convenience* (helping you and being suitable for what you want to do), *colour scheme* (the different colours chosen for a particular room), *hygiene* (keeping things clean, especially to prevent disease). Even though they are covered in the following activity, you could also consider teaching *minimalist* (using or having the smallest amount possible) and *cluttered* (covered with lots of different objects in a badly organised way).

- Before you play the recording, focus students on the photo of the kitchen and ask what they like and don't like about it. Do they think the design of the room would make it easy for a people to store and prepare food there? Why/Why not?

- Play the recording twice for students to listen and answer the questions.

- Ask students if the recording is about someone expressing opinions or preferences, or simply giving facts.

Audioscript: Student Book page 290

Jane: Well, for me the perfect kitchen <u>is all about convenience</u>. The design doesn't have to be completely empty and minimalist, but it shouldn't be over-full or cluttered. It should be clear where everything is and only gadgets and appliances that have real value deserve a place in it. For example, if your kitchen is nice and spacious, you'll have lots of room for items such as a dishwasher. If the room is a bit on the small side, though, adding a dishwasher may make it feel cramped, so you need to think carefully about whether it's really necessary.

Of course, <u>the problem with some appliances is that they have very specific uses so they're highly functional</u> but not designed to be decorative. Washing machines are a great example of this.

They're essentially just large metal cubes, so they don't really look that attractive – although they can transform our dirty washing back into gleaming clean clothes again, all in less than an hour, so we definitely wouldn't want to be without them!

Given that a lot of the appliances you want in your kitchen, like washing machines and fridges, are often white, black and silver, they do lend themselves to a look that's quite striking, especially if you add a feature wall in a bright, bold colour like red, rather than a colour scheme that's more understated. Of course, the problem with kitchens is that they tend to look rather characterless. They're not really the place to hang pictures, or have candles, or photos, or vases, or anything else that may make a room look interesting and atmospheric.

<u>The emphasis has to be on hygiene</u> and shining, empty surfaces are best for that. It's quite a challenge to balance that with making the kitchen warm and welcoming, though!

KEY

(Clues underlined in Audioscript.)
1 convenience **2** They have very specific uses so they are functional but not decorative.
3 hygiene

VOCABULARY ACTIVITY 2 — PAGE 240

- Focus students on the adjectives in the box. Explain that these are all adjectives used by the kitchen designer in the recording they have just heard. Read them aloud with the class to teach/review the pronunciation. You could ask students to repeat each one after you to consolidate this.

- Ask students to work in pairs to match any words that they can at this stage with their definitions. The words are highlighted in the Audioscript above.

- Play the recording again for students to listen and check anything they are not sure of. Alternatively, or in addition, you could make copies of the Audioscript available for students to read so that they can review the words as they are used in context at their leisure.

- Check answers with the class. Introduce the word *subdued* as the opposite of *bold* (in the context of talking about design), as this appears in the next activity.

SPEAKING — UNIT 8: SPEAKING PRACTICE

KEY

(Adjectives highlighted in Audioscript.)
1 cramped 2 functional 3 spacious
4 characterless 5 cluttered 6 decorative
7 understated 8 bold 9 atmospheric
10 minimalist

TEACHING TIPS

If students find some of the adjectives particularly difficult to identify as they listen, you could stop the recording in places where the word is mentioned. Repeat the sentence containing the word slowly so that students can hear it and try to understand the meaning from the context.

DIFFERENTIATION

Strengthen: Remind students that even where vocabulary is new to them, a clue can sometimes be found in similarities to words they know, e.g. *decorative > decorate* (to change the appearance of something to make it more pleasing), *minimalist > minimum* (the smallest amount possible). They might also be able to recognise words they know in other contexts, e.g. *bold*, (emotionally daring, but here it means daring in design choice).

Challenge: Ask students to write a short description of another room in a house, e.g. living room, bathroom, bedroom, and what the ideal design should or should not be like.

VOCABULARY ACTIVITY 3   PAGE 240

- Tell students that they are going to read a diary entry from the singer Rachel Ritz, a character they have already met in earlier units. Elicit from the class anything they remember about her (see pages 16, 17, 21, 23 and 118).
- Ask the class to read the diary entry and circle the best adjective in each case. Reading the diary entry aloud will help students if they find the passage challenging.
- Encourage students to use dictionaries to help them and to compare their answers with a partner before you check answers with the class.

KEY

1 bold 2 minimalist 3 cramped 4 cluttered
5 spacious 6 characterless 7 decorative
8 functional 9 atmospheric 10 subdued

EXTENSION

- Ask students to imagine they are the interior designer hired by Rachel and to write an email to a friend describing their experience of working with her.
- Elicit the differences between Rachel's view of her apartment (*has atmosphere, full of treasured possessions*) and the interior designer's view of it (*small, crowded, full of clutter*).
- Ask students to underline or highlight any other specific details in the passage that might be helpful, e.g. *my new interior designer turned up unexpectedly, he came up with the oddest ideas for my apartment.* Tell them that the word *he* (referring to the designer) will give clues to the relevant sentences.

VOCABULARY ACTIVITY 4   PAGE 241

- Elicit and revise the meanings of the pairs of adjectives and ask students to decide which one in each pair best describes their bedroom.
- Give students a few minutes to write sentences about their bedroom. Then put them into pairs and ask them to take turns to read and explain their sentences to their partner, giving as much detail as possible.
- As a follow-up, ask students to write an extended description of their bedroom, using the adjectives given, while also writing about changes they would like to make in future.

KEY

Students' own answers.

GRAMMAR ACTIVITY 5   PAGE 214

- This activity gives students an overview of all the tenses. Ask them to try to complete the table individually without using any other sources to help. Explain to students that they can use contractions if they wish.
- When they have done as much as they can, ask students to compare their ideas with a partner. They can also refer to Grammar Reference pages 260–267 to help fill in any gaps.
- Check answers with the class.

UNIT 8: SPEAKING PRACTICE — SPEAKING

KEY

Positive sentences

Present: *I walk, I am walking/I'm walking, I have walked/I've walked, I have been walking/I've been walking*

Past: *I walked, I was walking, I had walked/I'd walked, I had been walking/I'd been walking*

Future: *I will walk/I'll walk, I will be walking/I'll be walking, I will have walked/I'll have walked, I will have been walking/I'll have been walking*

Negative Sentences

Present: *I do not walk/I don't walk, I am not walking/I'm not walking, I have not walked/I haven't walked, I have not been walking/I haven't been walking*

Past: *I did not walk/I didn't walk, I was not walking/I wasn't walking, I had not walked/I hadn't walked, I had not been walking/I hadn't been walking*

Future: *I will not walk/I won't walk, I will not be walking/I won't be walking, I will not have walked/I won't have walked, I will not have been walking/I won't have been walking*

Questions

Present: *Do you walk?, Are you walking?, Have you walked?, Have you been walking?*

Past: *Did you walk?, Were you walking?, Had you walked?, Had you been walking?*

Future: *Will you walk?, Will you be walking?, Will you have walked?, Will you have been walking?*

GRAMMAR ACTIVITY 6 — PAGE 242

- This activity encourages students to think about patterns within the tenses.
- Ask students to complete Q1 and Q2 and check answers with the class.
- Ask students why the perfect continuous is named the perfect continuous and elicit that this is because it contains all the ingredients of both perfect and continuous tenses: *to have*, the participle form of *to be* and the *-ing* form of the verb.
- Ask students to complete the remaining questions and confirm answers with the class.

KEY

1 continuous tenses **2** perfect tenses **3** simple tenses (except in future) **4** the verb form

GRAMMAR ACTIVITY 7 — PAGE 242

- This activity is designed to practise a range of tenses.
- Ask students to work in pairs to circle the correct option.
- Check answers with the class by reading the dialogue aloud. Discuss the reasons why the wrong options are incorrect.

KEY

1 are you **2** are you doing **3** Will you be
4 wanted **5** Weren't you going **6** I've been waiting
7 must have been showering **8** you've been
9 we'll be eating **10** had hoped **11** will have cleaned **12** I'll have been eating

TEACHING TIPS

Hint Q1: The mother is questioning George about the current moment. We would usually use the present continuous in this case, but *be* is a stative verb, so we use the present simple: *Where are you?*

Hint Q2: *What are you doing* refers to the current moment, using the present continuous. The present simple would refer to what George does generally.

Hint Q3: We use the future simple to make a prediction, which the mother is asking George to do. We would not say *Will you be being* because *be* is a stative verb.

Hint Q4: *I wanted* refers to a past wish, while *I will want* would refer to a future plan. The wish became impossible to fulfil when George left, so we use *I wanted*.

Hint Q5: *Weren't you going to* refers to a past plan, whereas *will you be going to* would be redundant (*will* and *going to* together).

Hint Q6: *I've been waiting ... for nearly a week* refers to a continuing action over a point prior to the present, so we use the present perfect continuous. *I am waiting* would refer only to the current moment, not the previous week.

Hint Q7: *must* is used rather than *will* as a modal auxiliary of speculation. We use the present perfect continuous because we are talking about a recently completed action in the past, the consequence of which is still visible (the water).

Hint Q8: *You've been* refers to a continuous action during the time prior to now, so we use a present perfect tense. We use the present perfect simple because *be* is a stative verb. *You are being* is incorrect because *be* is a stative verb, and it would be used only to talk about the present moment, not about the entire day.

Hint Q9: *We'll be eating* is a continuous action that is planned to be taking place at a point of time in the future (*in less than an hour*) so we use the future continuous. *We had eaten* would be used to talk about an action prior to a point in the past (past perfect simple).

Hint Q10: *I had hoped* is used because we are talking about a finished action prior to a point of time in the past (George leaving), so we use the past perfect. We use the simple not the continuous because *hope* is a stative verb. *I will hope* would be used when talking about the future.

Hint Q11: *I will have cleaned it all up by the time you get here* refers to a finished action during the time prior to George arriving home, so we use the future perfect simple. *I am cleaning* would be acceptable if we were speaking about now, not a point in the future.

Hint Q12: *I'll have been eating for half an hour* refers to a continuous action during the time prior to George arriving home, so we use the future perfect continuous. *I will be eating when you get home* would be acceptable if we did not mention the time period.

GRAMMAR ACTIVITY 8   PAGES 242–243

- Ask students to complete the sentences individually, referring to pages 260–267 of the Grammar Reference if necessary.
- Allow students to check answers with a partner before discussing as a class.

KEY

1 are you doing **2** I didn't go, I had **3** has Fred had **4** we will be eating **5** I was walking, I bumped into **6** Lucia hadn't tried **7** Aisha has known **8** It has been raining **9** Sam doesn't read **10** do you do

TEACHING TIPS

Hint Q1: This refers to a continuing action in the current moment, so we use the present continuous.

Hint Q2: This refers to finished actions in the past, so we use the past simple.

Hint Q3: This refers to a continuing action in the past and the present, so we use a present perfect tense. *Have* is a stative verb, so we use the present perfect simple.

Hint Q4: This refers to a continuing action at a point in the future, so we use the future continuous.

Hint Q5: This refers to an interrupted action in the past, so we use the past continuous for the longer action and the past simple for the shorter, interrupting action.

Hint Q6: This refers to an action prior to a point in the past (yesterday), so we use the past perfect simple.

Hint Q7: This refers to a continuing action in the past and the present, so we use a present perfect tense. *Know* is a stative verb, so we use the present perfect simple.

Hint Q8: This refers to a continuing action in the past and the present, so we use the present perfect continuous.

Hint Q9: This refers to a habitual action in the present, so we use the present simple.

Hint Q10: This refers to a habitual action in the present, so we use the present simple.

GRAMMAR GAME: VERB TENSE BASKETBALL   PAGE 243

- Choose the tenses you would like to focus on for further practice and prepare slips of paper with tense functions from pages 260–267 of the Grammar Reference written on them, e.g. for the present simple, *facts which are always true*.
- Divide the board into twelve squares, one for each of the tenses in Activity 5. Put the students into two teams and line them up facing the board.
- Demonstrate the activity by giving a student one of the tense functions and elicit which one it is. The student then rolls the piece of paper into a ball and throws it at the board to try to hit the correct square (the one with the tense function written in it).
- When you are confident students understand what they need to do, let them continue the game. You could offer bonus points for them being able to say a correct example sentence with the right tense in it.

EXTENSION

- For further practice with tenses, give students a written composition task to describe any of the following:

  Their last holiday or weekend (past simple)

  A moment in the past (past continuous)

  Their life before starting school (past perfect simple and past perfect continuous)

  Their normal routine (present simple)

  Their life up until this point (present perfect simple)

  Their plans for the day (present continuous and future simple)

  A moment in the future (future continuous)

  Their goals by the time they are 30 (future perfect simple)

- If necessary, let students know which tense to focus on.

EXTENSION

Ask students to write a story that is exactly 200 words long on a topic of their choice. They should include at least two examples of each of the six verb tenses you have studied.

SELF-EVALUATION — PAGE 243

Tell students to look at the Self-evaluation table and tick the boxes that are true for them. Ask them if there are any topics they don't feel confident about yet.

GLOSSARY

antonym a word that means the opposite of another word

audience people who read someone's writing or listen to someone's speech

context the situation, events or information that are related to something and that help you to understand it; the words that come just before and after a word or sentence and that help you understand it

contractions shorter forms of a word or words

explicit expressed in a way that is very clear and direct

formal register formal language used in official or serious situations

genre a particular type of art, writing, music, etc., which has certain features that all examples of this type share

implicit suggested or understood without being stated directly

implied not stated openly, but understood to exist or to be true

inference something that you think is true, based on information that you have

informal register an informal style of writing or speaking suitable for ordinary conversations or letters to friends

informal writing an informal style of writing suitable for letters to friends

intonation the way in which the level of your voice changes in order to add meaning to what you are saying, e.g. by going up at the end of a question

inversion the act of changing something so that it is the opposite of what it was before, or of turning something upside down

layout the way in which writing and pictures are arranged on a page

lexical words dealing with words, or related to words

metaphor a way of describing something by referring to it as something different and suggesting that it has similar qualities to that thing

paraphrase to express in a shorter, clearer or different way what someone has said or written

prediction a statement about what you think is going to happen, or the act of making this statement

purpose what something is intended to achieve

register the words, style and grammar used by speakers and writers in a particular situation or in a particular type of writing

scan to read something quickly

simile an expression that describes something by comparing it with something else, using the words 'as' or 'like', for example 'as white as snow'

skim to read something quickly to find the main facts or ideas in it

state to formally say or write a piece of information or your opinion

summarise to make a short statement giving only the main information and not the details of a plan, event or report

synonym a word with the same meaning as another word

viewpoint a particular way of thinking about a problem or subject

NOTES

NOTES

NOTES

NOTES

NOTES